STUDY NOTES

UGC

PHILOSOPHY
(PAPER - II)

VOLUME -4

Content Table

Unit No	Unit	Page No
10.	Applied Philosophy	2–139

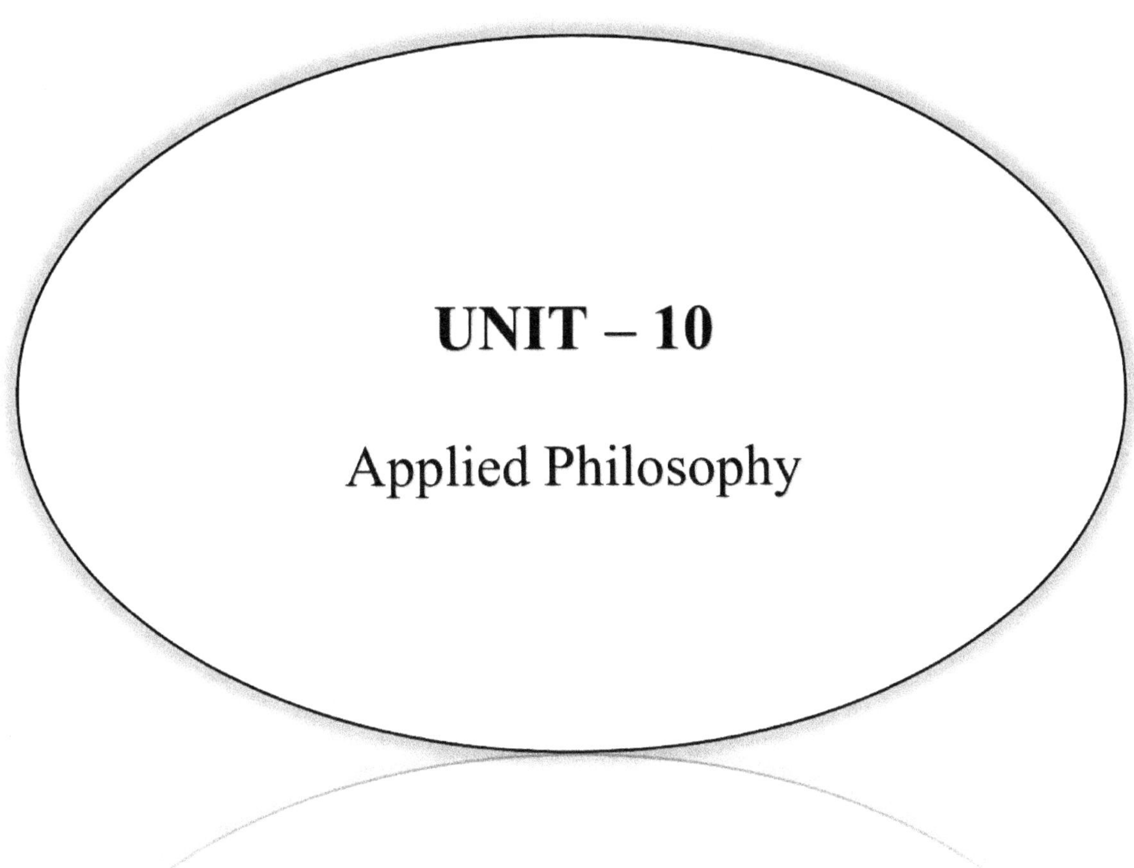

UNIT – 10

Applied Philosophy

Applied Philosophy

Applied philosophy is marked out from philosophy in general by its focus on matters of practical concern. It is often identified with applied ethics, but although this forms a large part of the area of applied philosophy, the broader term includes discussion of philosophical problems, some metaphysical, some epistemological, in fields such as law, education or art, that are not strictly or uniquely ethical. Applied ethics also includes the area of professional ethics; it examines the ethical dilemmas and challenges met with by workers in health- care, business and other areas where specific ethical issues such as confidentiality and truth-telling may arise.

The Proper Preoccupations of Philosophy

Philosophy is often regarded as the most abstract of studies, so the term 'applied philosophy' needs some explanation. It represents the claim that it is possible to build bridges between theory and practice and, in particular, that philosophy is not only an internal movement in philosophy but that it can and should play a rolein public debate. This should not be seen, though, as a bid to claim expertise on the part of philosophers but rather as a reassertion of the traditional conception of the philosopher, not as an expert, but as an honest and open seeker after truth. This search involves accepting the possibility of rational argument about normative directions. It does not mean, though, maintaining a posture of uninvolved neutrality As philosophy, indeed, it involves a prior commitment to the values of rationality, impartiality and equality of respect for individuals, and these provide the foundation for the moral values and range of rights that are fundamental to applied ethics. Applied philosophy, then, is part of a whole view of the human condition and takes a broad view of ethical decision-making. It can therefore accept as part of its task the identification and discussion of values capable of securing widespread acceptance in the contemporary world. For philosophy has traditionally been concerned, not only with abstract reflection but also with questions about how we should live and how we should conduct our social life and political affairs.

Today's applied philosophy, then, marks a return to what have always been proper preoccupations of philosophers. Some of these preoccupations are old andcould be said to have a perennial interest - intimate relationships and family life, for example, or global issues of peace and war. Others are the product of new technologies, revolutions in communication, new weapons of indiscriminate destruction, and an unprecedented increase in the impact of humans on their environment and support systems. Applied philosophy and especially applied ethics yields scope and space for discussion of these issues of public policy. To all these debates, it can bring clarity, openness, critical analysis, and respect for careful evaluation of arguments.At the same time, it represents a shift from the view that philosophy can only analyse and clarify problems but is not able to take on the task of seeking answers to them.

Applied philosophy differs in style and approach from some mainstream philosophy in other ways, too. It gives greater attention to context and to the detailed texture of complex situations and it is also more holistic in approach - that is to say, it is much more ready to include the insights of psychology, sociology and other relevant areas of knowledge in its deliberations, and to allow the facts it finds there to influence its conclusions. Its method of reasoning could be compared to that of a designer who starts with a blueprint, but has to adapt it to the materials to hand and to the situations in which it is required. The origins and background of applied philosophy can be traced back to the first of the early Greek philosophers, Thales (c.585 BCE), who could well qualify as the first applied philosopher. Having been scorned for his speculative and impractical interests - he was so preoccupied with studying the stars that he fell down a well! - he decided, very successfully, to go into business and use those observations to make a fortune, thus demonstrating that philosophical abstraction had its uses, and even a potential cash-value. Later schools of philosophy in ancient times - Pythagoreans, Epicureans, Stoics - offered their followers principles for living and guidance on life-style. Socrates (469-399 BCE.), too, while he avoided preaching any dogma, did offer in his own approach to life and also to death an example of a way of living appropriate to thepursuit of philosophy.

Plato (c.430-347 BCE), the chronicler of Socrates' discussions, described his own blueprint for the good society in his dialogue the Republic, which covered not only political arrangements, but also the way social life should be organised. He set out there his ideals for education, for sexual relations and reproduction, for art, literature and censorship.

In the modern period, too, many philosophers have applied their philosophical insights to practical issues. St. Thomas Aquinas (1225-74) treated such topics as marriage and the family in his Summa Theologiae. John Locke (1632-1704) wrote on toleration, and also on education; his political theory also provided the philosophical underpinning of the American Declaration of Independence. The principle of human dignity formulated by Immanuel Kant (1724-1804) is central tomost modern conventions of human rights, and Kant also treated the subject of suicide, and the question of whether it is ever right to tell a lie from benevolent motives - questions which continue to be important for medical ethics. Utilitarians like Jeremy Bentham (1748-1832) and John Stuart Mill (1806-73) have a continued if not always acknowledged influence on public policy, while Karl Marx's (1818-83) political philosophy has played a dramatic role in the shaping of the modern world. Applied philosophy, then, is not a new subject. Nevertheless, it suffered a period of neglect as the pendulum in philosophy swung from the speculative metaphysics of the nineteenth century to the materialistic scientism of the twentieth.

A number of factors contributed to the return to applied ethics, dating fromapproximately the mid-twentieth century. Perhaps the most important of these was the development of new kinds of medical technology, particularly thoseinvolving new methods of reproduction, and those affecting the end of life; another has been controversy about war and international relations. The publication of Peter Singer's Animal Liberation (1975) prompted increased academic debate about the relationship between humans and the animal world, and at the same time, there was a dawning public awareness of environmental threats on a global scale. Finally, interest in business and corporate ethics has grown, in reaction to scandals of public and business life.

For all these reasons, then, and many others, applied philosophy has today entered a new, more self- conscious and better-defined phase of development.

PHILOSOPHY OF TECHNOLOGY

The philosophy of technology brings logical, metaphysical, epistemological, ethical, and political philosophical questions to bear on the making and using of artifacts. The particular balance among these questions will differ within related regionalizations of philosophy, such as the philosophy of science or the philosophy of art. In the philosophy of technology, for instance, epistemology typically plays a lesser role than in the philosophy of science but a greater role than in the philosophy of art. Any philosophical assessment of technology is thus partially defined by its own inner balance in relation to philosophy as a whole.

Historical Emergence

Although limited discussions of techne and associated or derivative phenomena can be found in ancient, medieval, and early modern philosophy, it was not until the late nineteenth and early twentieth centuries that technology, as something distinct from technics or technique, became a subject for theoretical examination. Among the earliest contributing texts, the mechanical engineer Franz Reuleaux's Theoretische Kinematik (1875) developed an extended conceptual analysis of different types of tools and machines. More generally, Ernst Kapp's Grundlinien einer Philosophie der Technik (1877), in the first book to use "philosophy of technology" in its title, outlined a theory of culture grounded in technics understood as the extension and differentiation of human anatomy and physiology. The hammer, for instance, functions as an extension of the fist, the camera as an extension of the eye, and the railroad as an extension of the circulatory system; and vice versa, the fist can be said to be like a hammer, the eye like a camera, and rail lines like blood vessels. Elaborations of this view of technology as organ projection are representative of a school of what Carl Mitcham (1994) calls engineering philosophy of technology, an approach that was further developed in the work of thinkers as diverse as the Russian Peter Englemeier, the German Friedrich Dessauer, the Frenchman Gilbert Simondon, and the Spaniard Juan David García Bacca (all of whom have been largely ignored in Anglo American philosophy).

The research engineer Dessauer, for instance, developed a neo-Kantian critique of the transcendental possibility of technological invention that sees technology as bringing noumenal power into the world. Dessauer was also instrumental in promoting philosophical discussion within the Verein Deutscher Ingenieure (VDI; Society of German Engineers). The psychologist Simondon explored relations among parts, artifacts, and technical systems and the evolutionary manifestation of what he called technicity. The engineer Englemeier and the philosopher García Bacca both saw technological change engendering world-historical transformations that were at once humanizing and transcending of the merely organically human. Additional contributions to this school can be found in theoretical discussions about cybernetics and artificial intelligence. Also illustrative of achievements in engineering-oriented philosophy of technology are the scientific philosopher Mario Bunge's (1985) systematic metaphysics, epistemology, and ethics of technology and the engineer Billy Vaughn Koen's (2003) brief for engineering as the one right method for problem solving.

In its emergence, however, philosophy of technology was more commonly associated with what might be called a counter-philosophy that interprets technology not as extending but as encroaching on or narrowing the dimensions of human experience. Following Immanuel Kant's attempt "to deny [scientific] knowledge, in order to make room for faith," this humanities philosophy of technology has sought to limit technological thought and practice to make room for human culture in all its rich diversity. A case in point is the public intellectual Lewis Mumford's (1967) criticism of what he calls monotechnics, the technics of power, in contrast to poly- or biotechnics. The problem with monotechnics is that it promotes the pursuit of physical power and control at the expense of other aspects of human flourishing such as friendship and art. For Mumford the "myth of the machine" is to think that power is the source of all human benefit. In fact, it constitutes an unrealistic narrowing of human activity. Some version of this argument has been promoted especially by the continental European philosophical tradition in the works of José Ortega y Gasset (1939), Martin Heidegger (1954), and Jacques Ellul (1954). Indeed, even more broadly, the relation between technology and life—whether in the sense of zoe (organic existence) or bios (human flourishing)—has become one of the most crucial issues in both the metaphysics and ethics of technology. Until the latter half of the twentieth century, the argument for delimitation had the unintended side effect of relegating technology to marginal status in professional philosophy. Only as technology became more than an engineering interest or a social problem has it begun to be a mainstream topic in philosophy. One of the challenges in the twenty-first century will be to pursue the professional development of philosophical reflection on technology in ways that bridge the oppositions inherent in its bimodal historical origins without compromising their basic if divergent concerns.

Ethical and Political Issues

Because of their prominence in public affairs, the philosophy of technology properly highlights ethical and political issues. Indeed, contemporary work in practical or applied ethics—as in nuclear, environmental, biomedical, and computer ethics—emphasizes the moral challenges of technology, although in ways that sometimes reduce the field to an aggregate of different ethics for different technologies. Such subspeciation can deprive ethics of possible synergistic strengths. Access equity issues, for instance, occur in both biomedicine and computers, and the concepts and principles for dealing with one might well inform or enhance the other. Speaking generally, then, one can identify at least six competing and overlapping interpretations of technology as an ethical or political problem. Three of these arose initially before World War II, although they have continued to cast a shadow of concern, often in new and distinctive forms.

First, there is a problem of the just distribution of technological products and powers—that is, technology as a political issue. Since the Industrial Revolution the social-justice question has found numerous expressions in authoritarian and democratic regimes, in developing and developed countries. Authoritarian regimes have often justified themselves as acting to promote access to technological benefits against entrenched special scientific, technical, or corporate interests or against those whose commitment to equality undermines the invention and production of goods and services. Democratic regimes have placed more emphasis on promoting equality by means of due process and regulatory agencies. One aspect of due process that has been given special philosophical attention concerns the legal protocols to promote free and informed consent, extending the concept from human experimentation to engineering at large (Martin and Schinzinger 2005). With the engineered design of new products and processes social justice issues have often taken special form in association with some otherwise morally neutral concepts. The advent of electronic computer and Internet communications, for instance, has helped impart ethical significance to questions of privacy and the so-called "digital divide." Additionally, according to Ulrich Beck (1992), concerns for the fair distribution of goods and services were, during the late twentieth century, superseded by those dealing with the fair distribution of dangers and risks, thus giving social justice debates a special twist. One of the strongest criticisms of some of the resulting twists and turns has been Kristin S. Shrader-Frechette's (1991) careful dissecting of the antidemocratic assumptions of much risk-cost- benefit analysis.

Second is the problem of the alienation of workers from their labor in the industrial means of production, which has been presented especially by Marxists as an economic and by some non-Marxist social scientists as a psychological issue. Langdon Winner's (1977) analysis of the theory of autonomous technology or the idea that technology as resistant to human control is a more general statement of the issue. Critical theory work by Herbert Marcuse (1964) and Andrew Feenberg (1991, 1999) extended the classic Marxist discussion into situations reconfigured by consumerist culture and globalization. Opposing Marcuse's pessimism about transformation, Feenberg (especially 1995) has been more optimistic about alternative possibilities. Environmentalists, however, have further argued that technology in general alienates human beings from nature.

Don Ihde's (1990) phenomenology of the techno-lifeworld offers another take on this issue through an analysis of human—technology—world relations. Two fundamental types of such engagements are instrumental relations, in which the technology is integrated into the human sensorium as its extension (the blind man's cane), and hermeneutic relations, in which the technology becomes part of the world to be interpreted (a thermometer). Both engagements manifest an invariant structure that amplifies some aspect of the world (exact metric of temperature) while simultaneously reducing others (general sense of climate). The former tends to bring humans closer to the world, the latter to distance (or alienate) them from it.

Third is the problem of the destruction or transformation of culture by modern science and technology—either directly through new weapons and forms of military conflict or indirectly through the impact of new means of transportation, communication, and media. The destruction of World War I, the most violent in human history, was a manifestation of technology that only became worse during World War II with the development of nuclear weapons. The long cold war practice of nuclear deterrence and the early twenty-first-century challenges of terrorism present special problems for learning to manage the destructive potential in technology.

Between the two world wars concern for the more indirect technological transformation of culture took on special salience, as variously illustrated by the cultural lag theory of the American sociologist William Fielding Ogburn, the elegiac ruminations of the Catholic theologian Romano Guardini, or the active nihilistic enthusiasms of Ernst Jünger. In the latter half of the twentieth century the issue found small-scale manifestation in personal efforts to come to terms with new choices (e.g., in diet, drugs, and consumer lifestyle options) and large- scale manifestation in debates about the dynamics of sociotechnical change (e.g., the role of technology in economic development and technological determinism versus social constructionism). Questions can also arise about the transformed character of cultural life under the influence of information and image technologies, from television to the Internet and virtual reality machines.

Since World War II three more issues have emerged to ethical and political prominence. One is that of democratic participation. An anticipatory version of this issue emerged in interwar proposals for technocracy. For some theorists (such as Thorstein Veblen) rule by technical elites offered a better alternative than rule by economic or political elites. However, in the postwar revival of democratic theory, and with recognition that technology (like law) is a creation that also influences the creators, it was argued that the principle of "no taxation without representation" should be extended to "no innovation without representation" (Goldman 1992). Winner, for instance, describes "technologies as forms of life" and calls for the abandonment of "technological somnambulism" (1986, p. 10) in favor of public debate about the design of technological projects as diverse as highway bridges, tomato harvesters, and nuclear power plants. Efforts to determine how such democratic participation should be structured both within communities of technical expertise and in the negotiations between technical experts and the nontechnical public have been the subject of ongoing debates.

Fifth is the industrial pollution of the natural environment, which has contributed to attempts to develop an appropriate environmental or ecological ethics. What is the difference between artifice and nature—and the moral status of wilderness or the nonhuman environment? As nature is humanly transformed, to what extent should contemporary technological action take into account the welfare of future generations, whether human or nonhuman? What is the relation between values that are divided between the anthropocentric and ecocentric, extrinsic or instrumental and intrinsic? Another morally relevant concept, closely related to issues of both participation and environmentalism, is that of unintended consequences. To what extent are scientists and engineers responsible for the unexpected and perhaps even unforeseeable results of their technological actions? Two attempts to deal with the plethora of environmental issues, especially in relation to the challenge of unintended consequences, are those associated with sustainable development and the precautionary principle—with competing interpretations of both becoming major themes of moral and political deliberations.

Finally, there is the issue of responsibility: How are humans to respond ethicallyto the power placed in their hands by modern technology? Such a question has personal, professional, and policy dimensions. At the personal level, quantitativelyand qualitatively enhanced choices, with expanding knowledge production relevant to such choices (scientific research and consumer reports), place existential pressures on individuals to increase conscious reflection. The principle of free and informed consent appears to require not only that medical professionals inform the subjects of human experimentation about the risks and benefits of their participation but also that medical patients of all sorts become reflective participants in their own treatment—and that consumers of any technological goods or services weigh multiple costs and benefits as if they were engineers designing their lives. Are such demands both reasonable and possible?

At the professional level, scientists and engineers, falling under similar existential pressures to expand the conscious exercise of responsibility, have formulated codes of conduct for technical practices related to both research and design. In engineering ethics, for instance, the primacy of protecting public safety, health, and welfare is now a well-established general principle. In what sense, however, are engineers qualified to make such judgments? Does technical expertise provideany basis for determining appropriate levels of public safety, health, or welfare?

Finally, at the level of public policy, responsibility takes two closely related forms. Policy for science and technology seeks out the best ways to fund or regulate developments in science and technology. Science and technology for policy searches for the best ways to bring scientific knowledge to bear on politicaldecision making while making technological power most effectively available for political action. Responding to and exemplifying these dual drives scientific and technological research agencies such as the U.S. National Science Foundation, the Human Genome Project, and the National Nanotechnology Initiative have created specific programs to promote ethical reflection on the creation and use ofnew scientific knowledge and technological products, processes, and systems.

Again speaking broadly, it is possible to identify two fundamental attitudes toward this spectrum of ethical and political issues. One attempts to explainmodern technology as rooted in human nature and culture (engineering philosophy of technology), the other interprets modern technical methods and effects as deformations of human action, however preferable in particular instances to those of nature (humanities philosophy of technology). Theengineering approach in its expansive confidence calls in one way or another for more and better technology, the humanities approach in its restrictive questioning for some relinquishment or delimitation of technology. The tensions between such alternative attitudes repeatedly come to the fore in analysis of suchkey concepts as privacy, risk, participation, and the environment, and in assessments of new opportunities in virtual reality construction, biotechnological design, and nanotechnological research and development.

There is also a tendency for the engineering school to make alliances with the Anglo American analytic tradition in philosophy, and for the humanities school to find a convenient partner in the European phenomenological tradition. The former, viewing technology as a complex amalgam of artifacts, knowledge, activities, and volitions, each with diverse structural features scattered across historical epochs and societal contexts, prefers to deal on a case-by-case basis with one technology after another. The latter strives for bolder generalizations about technology as a whole, at least across each historical or societal context. From the phenomenological perspective, too great an emphasis on individual technological rocks can obscure the extent to which such geological specimens are constituents of mountains extended in both space and time.

Metaphysical Issues
The attempt to speak of technology rather than technologies rests on an attempt to identify some inner or essential feature of diverse technologies. This hypothetical essential feature may be termed technicity. One can then immediately note that, before the modern period, technicity was at a minimum scattered throughout and heavily embedded within a diversity of human engagements, and indeed that philosophy took a stand against any separating of technicity from its embedding context. Plato's argument in the Gorgias is preciselyan argument against disembedding techne from social or cultural contexts and traditions, not to mention ideas of the good. For Aristotle, techne is an intellectual virtue, and thus properly subordinate to the flourishing of human nature. What is distinctive about modern philosophy, by contrast, is the attempt, beginning with Galileo Galilei, Francis Bacon, and René Descartes to disembed technics from particular human activities, to study them in systematic ways, and thus to create technology.

John Stuart Mill in his Logic (1843) already assumes the success of this disembedding project when he explains the practical value of science. For Mill therationality of any art is grounded in a corresponding science. The art proposes to itself an end to be attained, defines the end, and handsit over to the science. The science receives it, considers it as a phenomenonor effect to be studied, and, having investigated its causes and conditions, sends it back to art with a theorem of the combinations of circumstances by which it could be produced. Art then examines these combinations or circumstances, and according as any of them are or are not in humanpower, pronounces the end attainable or not.(logic, book 6, ch. 12, section 2)

Remarkably, Mill's analysis does not recognize art (or traditional technics) asincluding any knowledge of means. Art is concerned solely with determining an end, to achieve which it deploys appropriate means as determined by science. It isthe scientific study of means that constitutes what even during Mill's lifetime was coming to be called technology. Modern technicity may thus be defined as a systematic or scientific study of means that suspends examination of ends. Does such an approach have distinctive social and cultural implications, independent ofany particular technologies and contexts?

Among the first philosophers to analyze such a disembedding of means from endswas Ortega. In the English translation of his La rebelión de las masas (1929),Ortega writes that "[t]hree principles have made possible [the] new world: liberal democracy, scientific experiment, and industrialism. The two latter may be summed up in one word: technicism" (1939, p. 56). Ortega himself actually uses the word técnica, but the term technicism is significant, and this in fact constitutes one of its first English occurrences with this sense. (Before the 1930s, technicism simply meant excessive reliance on technical terminology. The previous decade Max Scheler used the cognate Technizismus to name the industrial ethos.)

As part of a further "Meditación de la técnica" (1939), Ortega outlined a historical movement from the chance inventions that characterize archaic societies, through the trial-and-error techniques of the artisan, to the scientific technologies of the engineer. According to Ortega, the difference between these three forms of making lies in the way they create the means to realize a human project—that is, in the kind of technicity involved. In the first epoch, technical discoveries are accidental; in the second, techniques emerge from intuitive skill. In both instances they are preserved and elaborated within the confines of myth and craft traditions. In the third, however, the engineer undertakes scientific studies of technics and, as a result, "prior to the possession of any [particular] technics, already possesses technics [itself]" (Obras, 5:369). It is this third type of technicity that constitutes modern technicism (and here Ortega himself uses the term tecnicismo).

But technicism, understood here as the science of how to generate all possible technical means, disembedded from any lived making and using, creates a unique challenge. Before the modern period human beings were commonly limited by circumstances, within which they inherited a way of life and the technical means to achieve it. Now, however, they are given in advance many possible ways to live and a plethora of technical means but little in the way of a substantive vision of human flourishing. "To be an engineer and only an engineer is to be everything possibly and nothing actually," all form and no content (Obras, 5:366). There is in the midst of modern technicism what Ortega describes as a hidden ethical challenge to imagination and choice. Insofar as people can be anything they want, why should they take the trouble to be any one thing at all? Will not some extranatural motivation (not to say fanaticism) not be needed to help Buridan's cyborgs select among (rejecting some) the equally liberal options that surround them?

According to Heidegger modern technology is a challenge not just to ethics but to ontology. For Heidegger (1954) scientific technics constitutes a new kind of truth: truth not as correspondence, not as coherence, and not as functional knowledge, but as disclosure or revelation. Technology discloses Being in a historically unique way: as Bestand or resource. A castle constructed with traditional technics on a cliff overlooking the Rhine makes more fully present than before the stone that invests the landscape with its particular contours, while it sets off the curve of the river against the backdrop of its walls and towers. It invites people to settle near and experience the particularities of this place. By contrast, a poured concrete, hydroelectric power station compels the river to become an energy resource and converts the landscape into, not a place of human habitation, but a machine for the generation of electricity. It encourages people to draw on its energy for multitasking business in production and travel. The distinctly modern technicity that manifests itself in the disclosure of nature as resource Heidegger names Gestell (enframing).

Gestell at first sight appears to be a human work, something human beings in the course of history have chosen to practice for their own benefit. It gives them power over nature. However, as it digitalizes nature physically (dimensioned vectors), geographically (longitude and latitude), chemically (molecules, atoms, and subatomic particles), and biologically (genetic mapping), it also transforms language (computer signal processing) and art (pixel imaging) so that impact outstrips original intentions. Hidden in the midst of Gestell is Being as event, that which lets this dominating transformation come to pass. Gestell is at once destiny and, precisely because it appears so clearly to be the result of a human activity, an obscuring of the transhuman imparting of a destiny that is its ground.

In the same year that Heidegger's Die Frage nach der Technik appeared, Jacques Ellul published La Technique, later translated into English as The Technological Society (1954). For Ellul, too, what is happening is something transhuman, or at least transindividual, the emergence of a new social order in which people give themselves up to the systematic analysis of actions into constituent means that are then evaluated in terms of output/input metrics. The scientific analysis of techniques extends technoscientific methods into economics, politics, education, leisure, and elsewhere creating what he calls the technical milieu. After the milieux of nature and of society, technology is the third great epoch of human history. Ellul's characterology of this new reality—describing its rationality, artificiality, self-directedness, self-augmentation, indivisibility, universality, and autonomy—reveals the technical milieu as something more than simply human. Although more hospitable to human biological existence, it nevertheless also manifests certain inexorable laws of artifice (such as those of economics). Just as the natural milieu once provided a framework for human life, a differentiated but overriding order to which human beings adapted in a variety of ways, so now a much more homogeneous technical milieu presents itself, not simply as a realm of freedom that human beings have constructed, but as that which also constructs and constrains them even when they fail to recognize it.

From Metaphysics to Ethics

Efforts to make phenomenological metaphysics fruitful for ethics can be found in the work of two German American philosophers, Hans Jonas and Albert Borgmann. Jonas's (1966) work begins with a fundamental inquiry into the phenomenon of life, arguing that in the organic world there emerges a new kind of being. For Jonas the key features of human inner life (introspection and subjectivity) are present in embryo in the most primitive organisms, and in metabolism there emerges the primordial form of freedom. In metabolism a detachment enters the world insofar as being becomes distinguished from physical identity. However, in the materialism of modern science this unique reality is easily overlooked. Adopting a teleological approach to ontology, Jonas argues that only from the perspective of the more fully realized freedom manifest in humans can the reality of the organic as a whole be recognized for what it is. On this ontological basis Jonas (1984) undertakes an extended philosophical scrutiny of the technological projects of nuclear weapons and biomedical health care. In the presence of technical powers to end or alter human life Jonas reformulates the Kantian categorical imperative as: "Act so that the effects of your action are compatible with the permanence of genuine human life" (p. 11). Such a reformulation of the fundamental deontological principle constitutes an attempt at the re-embedding of technology in moral philosophy.

More broadly and in sustained dialogue with a range of discussions about the place of technology in human affairs, Borgmann's (1984) work draws a fundamental distinction between two kinds of artifice and action. On the one side are technological devices that obscure their inner functions to deliver without engagement commodities for easy and effortless consumption. This constitutes what Borgmann calls the device paradigm, an ideal type at which the products and processes of modern technology aim. On the other are focal things and practices whose workings are more transparent and that demand of their users some reordering of interests if they are to be used. The model for the first is the central heating system that only needs its thermostat set, for the second the wood-fired hearth.

In a series of studies arguing the nondeterminist importance of material culture to ethics and politics, Borgmann (1992, 1999) calls on citizens in the high-tech world to reconsider their ways of life to develop a deeper sense for the possibilities of human flourishing in the midst of liberal options for self-determined self- fulfillment. For Borgmann the ideal is not a forced return to the past but a voluntary recovery of the commanding presence of things in the technological present. As he concludes in a volume devoted to the critical assessment of his thought:

Science makes reality ever more transparent, and technology makes it more and more controllable. But at the end of our inquiries and manipulations there is always something that reflects rather than yields to our searchlight and presents itself as given to us rather than constructed by us. It is intelligible not because we have seen through it or designed it but because it speaks to us [in the form of] an unforethinkable and uncontrollable reality. (Higgs, Lights, and Strong 2000, pp. 368–369).
It is such a reality to which human flourishing is ultimately in thrall even in the midst of its highest exercises of insight and mastery.

Epistemological Issues
Epistemology has often been treated as a stepchild in the philosophy of technology family of philosophical interests. Technological forms of knowledge are commonly thought to be derivative of scientific knowledge, so that any attempt to bring the theory of knowledge to bear in the examination of technology has regularly been part of a discussion of the relation between technology and science. At the same time this common privileging of science has been philosophically criticized, although the criticism has taken different forms in the European phenomenological and in the Anglo American analytic philosophical traditions.

From a phenomenological perspective the argument has been that technology is not so much applied science as science is theoretical technology. In his historico- philosophical studies of the scientific and technological revolutions of the seventeenth century and after, for instance, Jonas (1974) argues that from its origins modern science was animated by a technological interest that gives it an inherently applicable or technological character. Related studies of the dependency of science on technological instrumentation, from Galileo's telescopes to particle accelerators and PCR (polymerase chain reaction) machines suggest that science might even be described as applied technology. This approach to the epistemology of technology has parallels with the pragmatic tradition of conceiving scientific knowledge in fundamentally instrumentist terms. The Venezuelan phenomenologist Ernesto Mayz Vallenilla (2004) likewise offers a more Husserlian-based but complementary effort to describe the unique epistemological features of what he calls meta-technical instruments.

From the analytic perspective there has been more of an effort to identify distinctive types of knowledge operative in technology. Summarizing the results from such an approach, Mitcham (1994) draws attention to at least four types of distinctly technological knowledge: sensorimotor skills, technical maxims (including rules of thumb and recipes), descriptive laws or technological rules (which take an "if A then B" form), and technological theories (either grounded in scientific theory or bringing scientific method to bear on human-technology interactions). German philosophers of technology such as Hans Lenk, Gunter Ropohl, and Bernhard Irrgang, all associated with the VDI promotion of philosophical reflection on technology, are pursuing efforts to develop epistemological analyses of the engineering sciences. And Joseph C. Pitt (2000) makes a determined effort to identify the distinctive forms of technological and engineering knowledge, drawing especially on the careful analyses of aeronautical engineering history by Walter G. Vincenti (1990) to argue that engineering design possesses its own cognitive features.

Important issues for any theory of technological knowledge remain the characterization of whatever basic epistemic criteria might be analogous to those operative in science such as truth, simplicity, coherence, and explanation. There may be distinctive technological forms of such criteria. But two major candidates for uniquely technological criteria are effectiveness and efficiency. Certainly, many propositions of engineering knowledge are assessed in terms of effectiveness and efficiency more than truth or explanation. A further epistemological challenge is to explicate the distinctive character of models and modeling in the technological and engineering contexts. The relevance of such epistemological analyses nevertheless remains of problematic relevance to ethics and politics.

Empirical, Anthropological, and Policy Turns
Concern for the adequacy of metaphysical definitions of technology—and perhaps exhaustion with endless ethical and political difficulties (with hopes that new approaches might prove more fruitful)—has given rise to what has been called an empirical turn in the philosophy of technology. As advocated by the Dutch philosophers Peter Kroes and Anthonie Meijers, this program argues that "philosophical reflection should be based on empirically adequate descriptions reflecting the richness and

complexity of modern technology" (2000, p. xix) and promotes a greater analysis of what technologists and engineers actually do over any extended exegesis of texts, whether those of other philosophers of technology or even engineers and technicians. As such, a natural alliance has developed with social constructivist approaches to science, technology, and society studies in the pursuit of richer metaphysical or ontological understandings of artifacts, epistemological analyses of technical practice, and even ethical decision making among professional engineers. From the perspective of Jozef Keulartz et al. (2002), this also provides a solid opportunity for advancing a pragmatist ethics for technological culture.

Two topics of prominence in the empirical turn from the interpretation of texts to the interpretation of technical artifacts have been those of design and function. Design is often identified as the essence of engineering, and there have been numerous technical studies of design methodology. At the same time engineering design must be distinguished from aesthetic design as well as design by means of evolutionary processes in nature. Even within the realm of engineering design, studies such as those by Vincenti (1990), Louis Bucciarelli (1994), and Richard Buchanan and Victor Margolin (1995) have very different implications for assessing proposals for consumer, green, sustainable, or participatory design. With regard to technical functions, analyses have focused on the relation between functions in organisms, social institutions, and artifacts; on the relation between functional and physical descriptions of artifacts; and on the extent to which functions are determined by design or use.

A different sense for new beginnings has emerged in relation to prospects in the development of the new fields of bioengineering and biotechnology—especially when applied to humans. The leader in this case is the medical scientist and philosopher Leon Kass, the chair of the Bush administration's President's Council on Bioethics. In his turn Kass has tried to go outside the boundaries of standard bioethics in at least four ways: to promote thinking that enrolls more than professional bioethicists, that does more than piecemeal or specialized analyses, that references human nature as a norm, and that builds toward policy results. As in Beyond Therapy: Biotechnology and the Pursuit of Happiness (2003), Kass et al. at the council seek to raise broad issues about what it means to be human in the presence of possibilities for the reengineering not just of the external world but of the inner world of human birth, growth, and experience. He has been especially concerned about the possibilities for the deformation of humanity not from above by totalitarian governmental use of technology but from below by positive consumer endorsement of behaviors that would from a traditional perspective be assessed as temptations.

Beyond the policy-oriented work of Kass and colleagues, policy questions have become increasingly central not just as aspects of ethical responsibility but as issues in their own right. What precisely is technological policy, as opposed to technological politics? Does policy decision making take different forms in relation to science and to engineering? How are policies to be formulated and assessed?

The extent to which these turns in the philosophy of technology will define its future are questions that the professional community must examine. Any such examination will also need to include a self-criticism that considers the special responsibilities of a regionalization in philosophy that, more than the philosophy of science or of art, has as part of its heritage public responsibilities and a large measure of ethical concerns.

(The Nature of) Technology?
The question, What is technology? or What is the nature of technology?, is both a central question that philosophers of technology aim to answer and a question the answer to which determines the subject matter of philosophy of technology. One can think of philosophy of technology as the philosophical examination of technology, in the same way as the philosophy of science is the philosophical examination of science and the philosophy of biology the philosophical study of a particular subdomain of science. However, in this respect the philosophy of technology is in a similar situation as the philosophy of science finds itself in.

Central questions in the philosophy of science have long been what science is, what characterizes science and what distinguishes science from non-science (the demarcation problem). These questions have recently somewhat moved out of focus, however, due to the lack of acceptable answers. Philosophers of science have not been able to satisfactorily explicate the nature of science or to specify any clear-cut criterion by which science could be demarcated from non-science or pseudo-science. As philosopher of science Paul Hoyningen-Huene (2008: 168) wrote: "fact is that at the beginning of the 21st century there is no consensus among philosophers or historians or scientists about the nature of science."

The nature of technology, however, is even less clear than the nature of science. As philosopher of science Marx Wartofsky put it, ""Technology" is unfortunately too vague a term to define a domain; or else, so broad in its scope that what it does define includes too much. For example, one may talk about technology as including all artifacts, that is, all things made by human beings. Since we "make" language, literature, art, social organizations, beliefs, laws and theories as well as tools and machines, and their products, such an approach covers too much" (Wartofsky, 1979: 176). More clarity on this issue can be achieved by looking at the history of the term (for example, Nye, 2006: Chapter 1; Misa, 2009; Mitcham & Schatzberg, 2009) as well as at recent suggestions to define it.

Jacob Bigelow, an early author on technology, conceived of it as a specific domain of knowledge: technology was "an account [...] of the principles, processes, and nomenclatures of the more conspicuous arts" (Bigelow, 1829, quoted in Misa, 2009: 9; Mitcham & Schatzberg, 2009: 37). In a similar manner, Günter Ropohl (1990: 112; 2009: 31) defined "technology" as the 'science of technics' ("Wissenschaft von der Technik", where "Technik" denotes the domain of crafts and other areas of manufacturing, making, etc.). The important aspect of Bigelow's and Ropohl's definitions is that "technology" does not denote a domain of human activity (such as making or designing) or a domain of objects (technological innovations, such as solar panels), but a domain of knowledge. In this respect, their usage of the term is continuous with the meaning of the Greek "techne" (Section 1.a).

A review of a number of definitions of "technology" (Li-Hua, 2009) shows that there is not much overlap between the various definitions that can be found in the literature. Many definitions conceive of technology in Bigelow's and Ropohl's sense as a particular body of knowledge (thus making the philosophy of technology a branch of epistemology), but do not agree on what kind of knowledge it is supposed to be. On some definitions it is seen as firm-specific knowledge about design and production processes, while others conceive of it as knowledge about natural phenomena and laws of nature that can be used to satisfy human needs and solve human problems (a view which closely resembles Francis Bacon's).

Philosopher of science Mario Bunge presented a view of the nature of technology along the latter lines (Bunge, 1966). According to Bunge, technology should be understood as constituting a particular subdomain of the sciences, namely "applied science", as he called it. Note that Bunge's thesis is not that technology is applied science in the sense of the application of scientific theories, models, etc. for practical purposes. Although a view of technology as being "just the totality of means for applying science" (Scharff, 2009: 160) remains present among the general public, most engineers and philosophers of technology agree that technology cannot be conceived of as the application of science in this sense. Bunge's view is that technology is the subdomain of science characterized by a particular aim, namely application. According to Bunge, natural science and applied science stand side by side as two distinct modes of doing science: while natural science is scientific investigation aimed at the production of reliable knowledge about the world, technology is scientific investigation aimed at application. Both are full-blown domains of science, in which investigations are carried out and knowledge is produced (knowledge about the world and how it can be applied to concrete problems, respectively). The difference between the two domains lies in the nature of the knowledge that is produced and the aims that are in focus. Bunge's statement that "technology is applied science" should thus be read as "technology is science for the purpose of application" and not as "technology is the application of science."

Other definitions reflect still different conceptions of technology. In the definition accepted by the United Nations Conference on Trade and Development (UNCTAD), technology not only includes specific knowledge, but also machinery, production systems and skilled human labor force. Li-Hua (2009) follows the UNCTAD definition by proposing a four-element definition of "technology" as encompassing technique (that is, a specific technique for making a particular product), specific knowledge (required for making that product; he calls this technology in the strict sense), the organization of production and the end product itself. Friedrich Rapp, in contrast, defined "technology" even more broadly as a domain of human activity: "in simplest terms, technology is the reshaping of the physical world for human purposes" (Rapp, 1989: xxiii).

Thus, attempts to define "technology" in such a way that this definition would express the nature of technology, or only some of the principal characteristics of technology, have not led to any generally accepted view of what technology is. In this context, historian of science and technology Thomas J. Misa observed that historians of technology have so far resisted defining "technology" in the same way as "no scholarly historian of art would feel the least temptation to define "art", as if that complex expression of human creativity could be pinned down by a few well-chosen words" (Misa, 2009: 8). The suggestion clearly is that technology is far too complex and too diverse a domain to define or to be able to talk about the nature of technology. Nordmann (2008: 14) went even further by arguing that not only can the term "technology" not be defined, but also it should not be defined. According to Nordmann, we should accept that technology is too diverse a domain to be caught in a compact definition. Accordingly, instead of conceiving of "technology" as the name of a particular fixed collection of phenomena that can be investigated, Nordmann held that "technology" is best understood as what Grunwald & Julliard (2005) called a "reflective concept". According to the latter authors, "technology" should simply be taken to mean whatever we mean when we use the term. While this clearly cannot be an adequate definition of the term, it still can serve as a basis for reflections on technology in that it gives us at least some sense of what it is that we are reflection on. Using "technology" in this extremely loose manner allows us to connect reflections on very different issues and phenomena as being about – in the broadest sense – the same thing. In this way, "technology" can serve as the core concept of the field of philosophy of technology.

Philosophy of technology faces the challenge of clarifying the nature of a particular domain of phenomena without being able to determine the boundaries of that domain. Perhaps the best way out of this situation is to approach the question on a case-by-case basis, where the various cases are connected by the fact that they all involve technology in the broadest possible sense of the term. Rather than asking what technology is, and how the nature of technology is to be characterized, it might be better to examine the natures of particular instances of technology and in so doing achieve more clarity about a number of local phenomena. In the end, the results from various case studies might to some extent converge – or they might not.

Dominance
Theory of Technology Dominance Main dependent construct(s)/factor(s) TTD has two dependent factors:

1. Reliance - The extent to which and individual applies the intelligent decision aid and integrates the recommendations of that aid into his or her judgment.
2. Dominance - The state of decision making where the intelligent decision aid, as opposed to its user, takes primary control of a decision making process.

Main independent construct(s)/factor(s)
TTD has four independent factors:

1. Task Experience - The level of experience a decision maker has regarding the completion of a task as well as the extent to

which the decision maker has developed strategies for completing that particular task.

2. Task Complexity - The extent to which the cognitive abilities of the decision maker are challenged with completing a certain task. (In psychology this is often termed Task Difficulty.)
3. Decision Aid Familiarity - The extent to which the decision maker is comfortable with the intelligent decision aid based on prior experience and/or significant training with the aid (or similar aids).
4. Cognitive Fit – The extent to which the cognitive processes used with the decision aid to complete a task match the cognitive processes normally applied by the decision maker using the aid.

Concise description of theory

The Theory of Technology Dominance (TTD) posits that a decision maker may become reliant on an intelligent decision aid under two conditions:

1. The decision maker is low in task experience.
2. The decision maker is high in all factors (task experience, task complexity, decision aid familiarity, and cognitive fit).

According to TDD, reliance on an intelligent decision aid can create a long-term, de-skilling effect in the user as well as hinder that user's growth of knowledge and advancement in his or her domain. Furthermore, TDD states that a negative relationship exists between the user's expertise level and the risk of poor decision making when the expertise of the user and intelligent decision aid are mismatched. When the expertise of the user and the aid are matched, however, a positive relationship exists between reliance on the aid and improved decisions making.

Conceptually, TTD can be divided into three sections which are built on a total of eight testable propositions. The three sections are:

- Section 1: Addresses the factors that determine the likelihood that a decision maker will rely on an intelligent decision aid.
- Section 2: Addresses the conditions under which a decision maker is vulnerable to being dominated by the intelligent decision aid.
- Section 3: Addresses the long-term impact of intelligent decision aid use on de-skilling domain experts and impeding epistemological evolution.
- The eight testable propositions are (Arnold & Sutton, 1998):

Section 1 - Factors influencing reliance

- Proposition 1: "When users have a low to moderate level of experience, there is a negative relationship between task experience and reliance on a decision aid."
- Proposition 2: "There is a positive relationship between task complexity and reliance on a decision aid."
- Proposition 3: "When task experience and perceived task complexity are high, there is a positive relationship between decision aid familiarity and reliance on the decision aid."
- Proposition 4: "When task experience and perceived task complexity are high, there is a positive relationship between cognitive fit and reliance on the decision aid."

Section 2 – Conditions favorable for dominance

- Proposition 5: "When the expertise of the user and intelligent decision aid are mismatched, there is a negative relationship between the user's expertise level and the risk of poor decision making."
- Proposition 6: "When the expertise level of the user and intelligent decision aid are matched, there is a positive relationship between reliance on the aid and improved decisions making."

Section 3 – Long-term effects

- Proposition 7: "There is a positive relationship between continued use of an intelligent decision aid and the de-skilling of auditors' abilities for the domain in which the aid is used."
- Proposition 8: "There is negative relationship between the broad- based, long-term use of an intelligent decision aid in a given problem domain and the growth in knowledge and advancement of the domain."

Diagram/schematic of theory

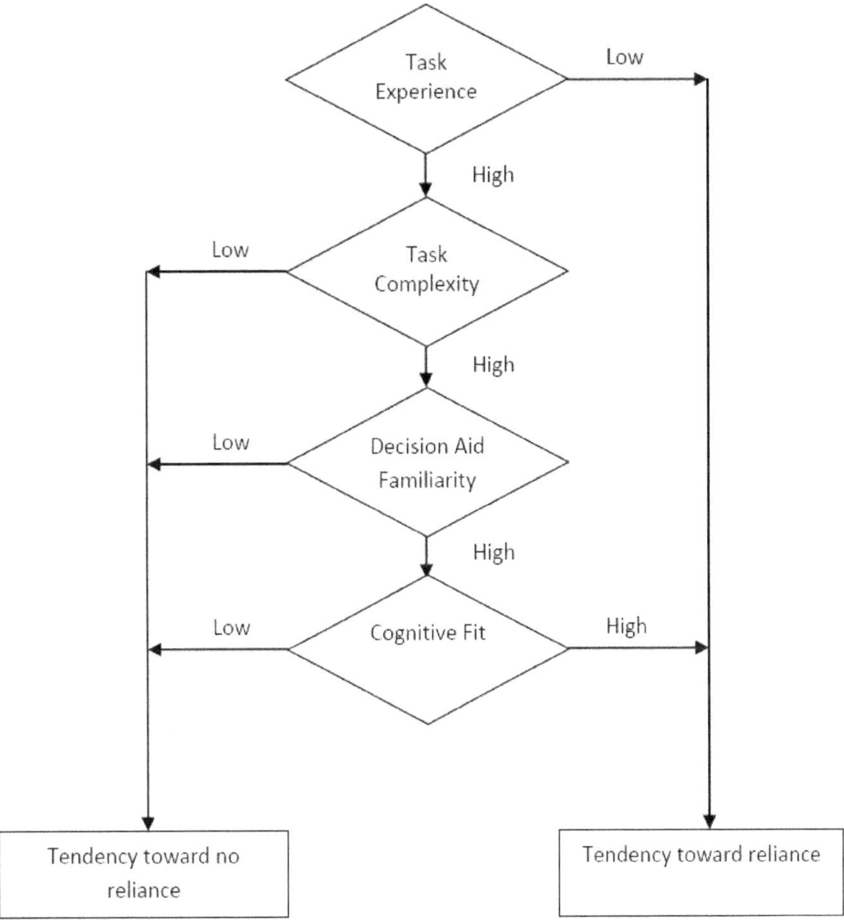

Recreated from Arnold and Sutton (1998)

Power and Social inequalities

Power and inequality determine the socioeconomic conditions of differentclasses.

Key Points

- Social stratification is a concept involving the classification of persons into groups based on shared socioeconomic conditions.
- Conflict theories, such as Marxism, focus on the inaccessibility of resources and lack of social mobility found in stratified societies.
- Social stratification has been shown to cause many social problems, including homicide, infant mortality, obesity, teenage pregnancies, emotional depression, teen suicide, and a high prison population.
- In modern Western societies, stratification is broadly organized into three main layers: upper class, middle class, and lower class.
- Conflict theories, such as Marxism, point to the inaccessibility of resources and lack of social mobility found in stratified societies.
- In Marxist theory, the capitalist mode of production consists of two main economic parts: the substructure and the Superstructure. Marx
- Social stratification has been shown to cause many social problems.

Key Terms

- **Marxist Theory**: An economic and sociopolitical worldview and method of socioeconomic inquiry centered upon a materialist interpretation of history, a dialectical view of social change, and an analysis–critique of the development of capitalism.
- **Conflict Theories**: Perspectives in social science that emphasize the social, political, or material inequality of a social group, critique the broad socio- political system, or otherwise detract from structural functionalism andideological conservatism.
- **Weberian**: Of or relating to Max Weber (1864–1920), influential Germansociologist and political economist.

Power and Inequality

In social science and politics, power is the ability to influence the behavior of people. The term authority is often used for power perceived as legitimate by the social structure. Power can be seen as evil or unjust, but the exercise of power is accepted as endemic to (or regularly found in) humans as social beings. French philosopher Michel Foucault (1926–1984) saw power as "a complex strategic situation in a given society social setting". Power may be held through authority, social class (material wealth), personal charisma, expertise or knowledge, persuasion, force (such as law or violence), and a myriad of other dynamics.

Because power operates both relationally and reciprocally, sociologists speak of the balance of power between people in a relationship. All parties to all relationships have some power; the sociological examination of power concerns itself with discovering and describing the relative strengths – equal or unequal, stable or subject to periodic change. Given that power is not innate and can be granted to others, to acquire power you must possess or control a form of power currency (such as wealth, social status, authority, etc.).

Social inequality and stratification

Social inequality refers to relational processes in society that have the effect of limiting or harming a group's social status, social class, and social circle. Areas of social inequality include access to voting rights, freedom of speech and assembly, the extent of property rights and access to education, health care, quality housing, traveling, transportation, vacationing and other social goods and services.

The reasons for social inequality can vary, but are often broad and far reaching. Social inequality can emerge through a society's understanding of appropriate gender roles, or through the prevalence of social stereotyping. They can also be established through discriminatory legislation. Social inequalities exist between ethnic or religious groups, classes and countries, making the concept a global phenomenon. In sociology, social stratification is a concept involving the classification of persons into groups based on shared socioeconomic conditions; it is a relational set of inequalities with economic, social, political and ideological dimensions. Theories of social stratification are based on four basic principles:

- Social stratification is a trait of society, not simply a reflection of individual differences.
- Social stratification carries over from generation to generation.
- Social stratification is universal but variable.
- Social stratification involves not just inequality but beliefs as well.

Classifications of stratification

In modern Western societies, stratification is broadly organized into three main layers: upper class, middle class, and lower class. The upper class in modern societies is the social class composed of the wealthiest members of society, who also wield the greatest political power. The upper class is generally contained within the wealthiest 1–2 percent of the population, with wealth passed from generation to generation. In Weberian socioeconomic terms, the middle class is the broad group of people in contemporary society who fall socioeconomically between the working class and upper class. The common measures of what constitutes middle class vary significantly between cultures. The working class describes the group of people employed in lower tier jobs, often including those in unemployment or otherwise possessing below-average incomes. Working classes are mainly found in industrialized economies and in urban areas of non-industrialized economies.

Social Stratification and Marxism

Conflict theories, such as Marxism, focus on the inaccessibility of resources and lack of social mobility found in stratified societies. Many sociological theorists have criticized the extent to which the working classes are unlikely to advance socioeconomically; the wealthy tend to hold political power which they use to exploit the proletariat inter-generationally.

In Marxist theory, the capitalist mode of production consists of two main economic parts: the substructure and the superstructure. Marx saw classes as defined by people's relationship to the means of productions in two basic ways: either they own productive property or they labor for others. The base comprehends the forces and relations of production: employer-employee work conditions, the technical division of labor, and property relations—into which people enter to produce the necessities and amenities of life. These relations determine society's other relationships and ideas, which are described as its superstructure. The superstructure of a society includes its culture, institutions, political power structures, roles, rituals, and state.

Social stratification has been shown to cause many social problems. A comprehensive study of major world economies revealed that homicide, infant mortality, obesity, teenage pregnancies, emotional depression, teen suicide, and prison population all correlate with higher social inequality.

There are three common characteristics of stratified systems:

1. Rankings apply to social categories of people who share a common characteristic without necessarily interacting or identifying with each other. The process of being ranked can be changed by the person being ranked, and it can differ based on race, gender, and social class.
2. People's life experiences and opportunities depend on their social category. This characteristic can be changed by the amount of work a person can put into their interests. The use of resources can influence others.
3. The ranks of different social categories change slowly over time. This has occurred frequently in the United States ever

since the American revolution—the U.S. Constitution has been altered several times to specify rights for everyone.

Democratization of technology
Democratization of technology refers to the process by which access to technology rapidly continues to become more accessible to more people. New technologies and improved user experiences have empowered those outside of the technical industry to access and use technological products and services. At an increasing scale, consumers have greater access to use and purchase technologically sophisticated products, as well as to participate meaningfully in the development of these products. Industry innovation and user demand have been associated with more affordable, user-friendly products. This is an ongoing process, beginning with the development of mass production and increasing dramatically as digitization became commonplace.

Thomas Friedman argued that the era of globalization has been characterized by the democratization of technology, democratization of finance, and democratization of information. Technology has been critical in the latter two processes, facilitating the rapid expansion of access to specialized knowledge and tools, as well as changing the way that people view and demand such access.

History
Scholars and social critics often cite the invention of the printing press as a major invention that changed the course of history. The force of the printing press rested not in its impact on the printing industry or inventors, but on its ability to transmit information to a broader public by way of mass production. This event is so widely recognized because of its social impact – as a democratizing force. The printing press is often seen as the historical counterpart to the Internet.

After the development of the Internet in 1969, its use remained limited to communications between scientists and within government, although use of email and boards gained popularity among those with access. It did not become a popular means of communication until the 1990s. In 1993 the US federal government opened the Internet to commerce and the creation of HTML formed the basis for universal accessibility.

Major innovations
The Internet has played a critical role in modern life as a typical feature of most Western households, and has been key in the democratization of knowledge. It not only constitutes arguably the most critical innovation in this trend thus far; it has also allowed users to gain knowledge of and access to other technologies. Users can learn of new developments more quickly, and purchase high-tech products otherwise only actively marketed to recognized experts. Some have argued that cloud computing is having a major effect by allowing users greater access through mobility and pay-as-you-use capacity.

Social media has also empowered and emboldened users to become contributors and critics of technological developments. The open-source model allows users to participate directly in development of software, rather than indirect participation, through contributing opinions. By being shaped by the user, development is directly responsive to user demand and can be obtained for free or at a low cost. In a comparable trend, arduino and littleBits have made electronics more accessible to users of all backgrounds and ages. The development of 3D printers has the potential to increasingly democratize production.

Cultural impact
This trend is linked to the spread of knowledge of and ability to perform high-tech tasks, challenging previous conceptions of expertise. Widespread access to technology, including lower costs, was critical to the transition to the new economy. Similarly, democratization of technology was also fuelled by this economic transition, which produced demands for technological innovation and optimism in technology-driven progress.

Since the 1980s, a spreading constructivist conception of technology has emphasized that the   social   and   technical   domains   are   critically intertwined. Scholars have argued that technology is non-neutral, defined contextually and locally by a certain relationship with society.

Andrew Feenberg, a central thinker in the philosophy of technology, argued that democratizing technology means expanding technological design to include alternative interests and values. When successful in doing so, this can be a tool for increasing inclusiveness. This also suggests an important participatory role for consumers if technology is to be truly democratic. Feenberg asserts that this must be achieved by consumer intervention in a liberated design process. Improved access to specialized knowledge and tools has been associated with an increase in the "do it yourself" (DIY) trend. This has also been associated with consumerization, whereby personal or privately owned devices and software are also used for business purposes. Some have argued that this is linked to reduced dependence on traditional information technology departments.

Astra Taylor, the author of the book The People's Platform: Taking Back Power and Culture in the Digital Age, argues, "The promotion of Internet-enabled amateurism is a lazy substitute for real equality of opportunity."

Industry impact
In some ways, democratization of technology has strengthened this industry. Markets have broadened and diversified. Consumer feedback and input is available at a very low or no cost. However, related industries are experiencing decreased demand for qualified professionals as consumers are able to fill more of their demands themselves. Users of a range of types and status have access to increasingly similar technology. Because of the decreased costs and expertise necessary to use products and software, professionals (e.g. in the audio industry) may experience loss of work.

In some cases, technology is accessible but sufficiently complex that most users without specialized training are able to operate it without necessarily understanding how it works. Additionally, the process of consumerization has led to an influx in the number of devices in businesses and accessing private networks that IT departments cannot control or access. While this can lead to lowered operating costs and increased innovation, it is also associated with security concerns that most businesses are unable to address at the pace of the spread of technology.

Political impact

At a demonstration at BMVIT, banners read, "Democracy needs anonymity – stop data retention" (left) and "Liberty dies with security" (right). Some scholars have argued that technological change will bring about a third wave of democracy. The Internet has been recognized for its role in promoting increased citizen advocacy and government transparency. Jesse Chen, a leading thinker in democratic engagement technologies, distinguishes the democratizing effects of technology from democracy itself. Chen has argued that, while the Internet may have democratizing effects, the Internet alone cannot deliver democracy at all levels of society unless technologies are purposely designed for the nuances of democracy, specifically the engagement of large groups of people in between elections in and beyond government.

The spread of the Internet and other forms of technology has led to increased global connectivity. Many scholars believe that it has been associated in the developing world not only with increased Western influence, but also with the spread of democracy through increased communication, efficiency, and access to information. Scholars have drawn associations between the level of technological connectedness and democracy in many nations.

Technology can enhance democracy in the developed world as well. In addition to increased communication and transparency, some electorates have implemented online voting to accommodate an increased number of citizens.

Public evaluation of science and technology

Although there was much technological progress in the Roman empire and during the Middle Ages, philosophical reflection on technology did not grow at a corresponding rate. Comprehensive works such as Vitruvius' De architectura (first century BC) and Agricola's De re metallica (1556) paid much attention to practical aspects of technology but little to philosophy.

In the realm of scholastic philosophy, there was an emergent appreciation for the mechanical arts. They were generally considered to be born of—and limited to— the mimicry of nature. This view was challenged when alchemy was introduced in the Latin West around the mid-twelfth century. Some alchemical writers such as Roger Bacon were willing to argue that human art, even if learned by imitating natural processes, could successfully reproduce natural products or even surpass them (Newman 2004). The result was a philosophy of technology in which human art was raised to a level of appreciation not found in other writings until the Renaissance. However, the last three decades of the thirteenth century witnessed an increasingly hostile attitude by religious authorities toward alchemy that culminated eventually in the denunciation Contra alchymistas, written by the inquisitor Nicholas Eymeric in 1396 (Newman 2004).

The Renaissance led to a greater appreciation of human beings and their creative efforts, including technology. As a result, philosophical reflection on technology and its impact on society increased. Francis Bacon is generally regarded as the first modern author to put forward such reflection. His view, expressed in his fantasy New Atlantis (1627), was overwhelmingly positive. This positive attitude lasted well into the nineteenth century, incorporating the first half-century of the industrial revolution.

For example, Karl Marx did not condemn the steam engine or the spinning mill for the vices of the bourgeois mode of production; he believed that ongoing technological innovation were necessary steps toward the more blissful stages of socialism and communism of the future.

A turning point in the appreciation of technology as a socio-cultural phenomenon is marked by Samuel Butler's Erewhon (1872), written under the influence of the Industrial Revolution, and Darwin's On the Origin of Species (1859). Butler's book gave an account of a fictional country where all machines are banned and the possession of a machine or the attempt to build one is a capital crime. The people of this country had become convinced by an argument that ongoing technical improvements are likely to lead to a 'race' of machines that will replace mankind as the dominant species on earth.

During the last quarter of the nineteenth century and most of the twentieth century a critical attitude predominated in philosophical reflection on technology. The representatives of this attitude were, overwhelmingly, schooled in the humanities or the social sciences and had virtually no first-hand knowledge of engineering practice. Whereas Bacon wrote extensively on the method of science and conducted physical experiments himself, Butler, being a clergyman, lacked such first-hand knowledge. Ernst Kapp, who was the first to use the term 'philosophy of technology' in his book Eine Philosophie der Technik (1877 [2018]), was a philologist and historian. Most of the authors who wrote critically about technology and its socio-cultural role during the twentieth century were philosophers of a general outlook, such as Martin Heidegger (1954 [1977]), Hans Jonas (1979 [1984]), Arnold Gehlen (1957 [1980]), Günther Anders (1956), and Andrew Feenberg (1999). Others had a background in one of the other humanities or in social science, such as literary criticism and social research in the case of Lewis Mumford (1934), law in the case of Jacques Ellul (1954 [1964]), political science in the case of Langdon Winner (1977, 1980, 1983) and literary studies in the case of Albert Borgmann (1984). The form of philosophy of technology constituted by the writings of these and others has been called by Carl Mitcham (1994) "humanities philosophy of technology", because it takes its point of departure from the social sciences and the humanities rather than from the practice of technology, and it approaches technology accepting "the primacy of the humanities over technologies" (1994: 39), since technology originates from the goals and values of humans.

Humanities philosophers of technology tend to take the phenomenon of technology itself largely for granted; they treat it as a 'black box', a given, a unitary, monolithic, inescapable phenomenon. Their interest is not so much to analyze and understand this phenomenon itself but to grasp its relations to morality (Jonas, Gehlen), politics (Winner), the structure of society (Mumford), human culture (Ellul), the human condition (Hannah Arendt), or metaphysics (Heidegger). In this, these philosophers are almost all openly critical of technology: all things considered, they tend to have a negative judgment of the way technology has affected human society and culture, or at least they single out for consideration the negative effects of technology on human society and culture. This does not necessarily mean that technology itself is pointed out as the principal cause of these negative developments. In the case of Heidegger, in particular, the paramount position of technology in modern society is rather a symptom of something more fundamental, namely a wrongheaded attitude towards Being which has been on the rise for almost 25 centuries. It is therefore questionable whether Heidegger should be considered as a philosopher of technology, although within the traditional view he is considered to be among the most important ones. Much the same could be said about Arendt, in particular her discussion of technology in The Human Condition (1958), although her position in the canon of humanities philosophy of technology is not as prominent.

To be sure, the work of these founding figures of humanities philosophy of technology has been taken further by a second and third generation of scholars— in particular the work of Heidegger remains an important source of inspiration— but who in doing so have adopted a more neutral rather than overall negative view of technology and its meaning for human life and culture. Notable examples are Ihde (1979, 1993) and Verbeek (2000 [2005]).

In its development, humanities philosophy of technology continues to be influenced not so much by developments in philosophy (e.g., philosophy of science, philosophy of action, philosophy of mind) but by developments in the social sciences and humanities. Although, for example, Ihde and those who take their point of departure with him, position their work as phenomenologist or postphenomenologist, there does not seem to be much interest in either the past or the present of this diffuse notion in philosophy, and in particular not much interest in the far from easy question to what extent Heidegger can be considered a phenomenologist. Of particular significance has been the emergence of 'Science and Technology Studies' (STS) in the 1980s, which studies from a broad social- scientific perspective how social, political, and cultural values affect scientific research and technological innovation, and how these in turn affect society, politics, and culture. For a detailed treatment Mitcham's 1994 book provides an excellent overview. Olsen, Selinger and Riis (2008) offer a collection of more recent contributions; Scharff and Dusek (2003 [2014]) and Kaplan (2004 [2009]) present comprehensive anthologies of texts from this tradition.

A Basic Ambiguity in the Meaning of Technology
Mitcham contrasts 'humanities philosophy of technology' to 'engineering philosophy of technology', where the latter refers to philosophical views developed by engineers or technologists as "attempts … to elaborate a technological philosophy" (1994: 17). Mitcham discusses only a handful of people as engineering philosophers of technology, however: Ernst Kapp, Peter Engelmeier, Friedrich Dessauer, and much more briefly Jacques Lafitte, Gilbert Simondon, Hendrik van Riessen, Juan David García Bacca, R. Buckminster Fuller and Mario Bunge. The label raises serious questions, however: several of them hardly classify as 'engineers or technologists' and it is also not very clear how the notion of 'a technological philosophy' should be understood. As philosophers these authors seem all to be rather isolated figures, whose work shows little overlap and who seem to be sharing mainly the absence of a 'working relation' with established philosophical disciplines. It is not so clear what sort of questions and concerns underlie the notion of 'engineering philosophy of technology'. A larger role for systematic philosophy could bring it quite close to some examples of humanities philosophy of technology, for instance the work of Jacques Ellul, where the analyses would be rather similar and the remaining differences would be ones of attitude or appreciation.

In the next section we discuss in more detail a form of philosophy of technology that we consider to occupy, currently, the position of alternative to the humanities philosophy of technology. It emerged in the 1960s and gained momentum in the past fifteen to twenty years. This form of the philosophy of technology, which may be called 'analytic', is not primarily concerned with the relations between technology and society but with technology itself. It expressly does not look upon technology as a 'black box' but as a phenomenon that should be studied in detail. It regards technology perhaps not in its entirety as a practice but as something grounded in a practice, basically the practice of engineering. It analyses this practice, its goals, its concepts and its methods, and it relates its findings to various themes from philosophy.

In focusing on technology as a practice sustained by engineers, similar to the way philosophy of science focuses on the practice of science as sustained by scientists, analytic philosophy of technology could be thought to amount to the philosophy of engineering. Indeed many of the issues related to design, could be singled out as forming the subject matter of the philosophy of engineering. The very title of Philosophy of Technology and Engineering Sciences (Meijers 2009), an extensive up-to-date overview, which contains contributions to all of the topics treated in the next section, expresses the view that technology and engineering do not coincide. Which is not to say, however, that the book offers a clear conception of what makes technology different from engineering, or more than engineering. In fact, the existence of humanities philosophy of technology and analytic philosophy of technology next to each other reflects a basic ambiguity in the notion of technology that the philosophical work that has been going on has not succeeded in clarifying. Technology can be said to have two 'cores' or 'dimensions', which can be referred to as instrumentality and productivity. Instrumentality covers the totality of human endeavours to control their lives and their environments by interfering with the world in an instrumental way, by using things in a purposeful and clever way. Productivity covers the totality of human endeavours to brings new things into existence that can do certain things in a controlled and clever way. For the study of instrumentality, however, it is in principle irrelevant whether or not the things that are made use of in controlling our lives and environments have been made by us first; if we somehow could rely on natural objects to always be available to serve our purposes, the analysis of instrumentality and its consequences for how we live our lives would not necessarily be affected. Likewise, for the analysis of what is involved in the making of artifacts, and how the notion of artifact and of something new being brought into existence are to be understood, it is to a large extent irrelevant how human life, culture and society are changed as a result of the artifacts that are in fact produced. Clearly, humanities philosophy of technology has until now been more attracted by the instrumentality core whereas analytic philosophy of technology has mainly gone for the productivity core. But technology as one of the basic phenomena ofmodern society, if not the most basic one, clearly is constituted by the processes centering on and involving both cores. It has proved difficult, however, to come toan overarching approach in which the interaction between these two dimensions of technology are adequately dealt with—no doubt partly due to the great differences in philosophical orientation and methodology associated with the twotraditions and their separate foci. To improve this situation is arguably the most urgent challenge that the field of philosophy of technology as a whole is facing, since the continuation of the two orientations leading their separate lives threatens its unity and coherence as a discipline in the first place. Notwithstanding its centrality and urgency, the ambiguity noted here seems hardly to be confronted directly in the literature. It is addressed by Lawson (2008, 2017) and by Franssen and Koller (2016).

After presenting the major issues of philosophical relevance in technology and engineering that are studied by analytic philosophers of technology in the next section, we discuss the problems and challenges that technology poses for the society in which it is practiced in the third and final section.

Analytic Philosophy of Technology

Introduction: Philosophy of Technology and Philosophy of Science as Philosophies of Practices It may come as a surprise to those new to the topic that the fields of philosophy of science and philosophy of technology show such great differences, given that few practices in our society are as closely related as science and technology. Experimental science is nowadays crucially dependent on technology for the realization of its research set-ups and for gathering and analyzing data. The phenomena that modern science seeks to study could never be discovered without producing them through technology.

Theoretical research within technology has come to be often indistinguishable from theoretical research in science, making engineering science largely continuous with 'ordinary' or 'pure' science. This is a relatively recent development, which started around the middle of the nineteenth century, and is responsible for great differences between modern technology and traditional, craft-like techniques. The educational training that aspiring scientists and engineers receive starts off being largely identical and only gradually diverges intoa science or an engineering curriculum. Ever since the scientific revolution of the seventeenth century, characterized by its two major innovations, the experimental method and the mathematical articulation of scientific theories, philosophical reflection on science has focused on the method by which scientific knowledge is generated, on the reasons for thinking scientific theories to be true, or approximately true, and on the nature of evidence and the reasons for accepting one theory and rejecting another. Hardly ever have philosophers of science posed questions that did not have the community of scientists, their concerns, their aims, their intuitions, their arguments and choices, as a major target. In contrast it is only recently that the philosophy of technology has discovered the community of engineers.

It might be claimed that it is up to the philosophy of technology, and not the philosophy of science, to target first of all the impact of technology—and with it science—on society and culture, because science affects society only through technology. This, however, will not do. Right from the start of the scientific revolution, science affected human culture and thought fundamentally and directly, not with a detour through technology, and the same is true for later developments such as relativity, atomic physics and quantum mechanics, the theory of evolution, genetics, biochemistry, and the increasingly dominating scientific world view overall. Philosophers of science overwhelmingly give the impression that they leave questions addressing the normative, social and culturalaspects of science gladly to other philosophical disciplines, or to historical studies.There are exceptions, however, and things may be changing; Philip Kitcher, to name but one prominent philosopher of science, has since 2000 written books on the relation of science to politics, ethics and religion (Kitcher 2001, 2011).

There is a major difference between the historical development of modern technology as compared to modern science which may at least partly explain this situation, which is that science emerged in the seventeenth century from philosophy itself. The answers that Galileo, Huygens, Newton, and others gave, by which they initiated the alliance of empiricism and mathematical description that is so characteristic of modern science, were answers to questions that had belonged to the core business of philosophy since antiquity. Science, therefore, kept the attention of philosophers. Philosophy of science is a transformation of epistemology in the light of the emergence of science. The foundational issues— the reality of atoms, the status of causality and probability, questions of space and time, the nature of the quantum world—that were so lively discussed during the end of the nineteenth and the beginning of the twentieth century are an illustration of this close relationship between scientists and philosophers. No such intimacy has ever existed between those same philosophers and technologists; their worlds still barely touch. To be sure, a case can be made that, compared to the continuity existing between natural philosophy and science, a similar continuity exists between central questions in philosophy having to do with human action and practical rationality and the way technology approaches and systematizes the solution of practical problems. To investigate this connection may indeed be considered a major theme for philosophy of technology. This continuity appears only by hindsight, however, and dimly, as the historical development is at most a slow convening of various strands of philosophical thinking on action and rationality, not a development into variety from a single origin. Significantly it is only the academic outsider Ellul who has, in his idiosyncratic way, recognized in technology the emergent single dominant way of answering all questions concerning human action, comparable to science as the single dominant way of answering all questions concerning human knowledge (Ellul 1954

[1964]). But Ellul was not so much interested in investigating this relationship as in emphasizing and denouncing the social and cultural consequences as he saw them. It is all the more important to point out that humanities philosophy of technology cannot be differentiated from analytic philosophy of technology by claiming that only the former is interested in the social environment of technology. There are studies which are rooted in analytic philosophy of science but address specifically the relation of technology to societyand culture, and equally the relevance of social relations to practices of technology, without taking an evaluative stand with respect to technology; an example is B. Preston 2012.

The Relationship Between Technology and Science

The close relationship between the practices of science and technology may easilykeep the important differences between the two from view. The predominant position of science in the philosophical field of vision made it difficult for philosophers to recognize that technology merits special attention for involving issues that do not emerge in science. This view resulting from this lack of recognition is often presented, perhaps somewhat dramatically, as coming down to a claim that technology is 'merely' applied science.

A questioning of the relation between science and technology was the central issue in one of the earliest discussions among analytic philosophers of technology.In 1966, in a special issue of the journal Technology and Culture, Henryk Skolimowski argued that technology is something quite different from science (Skolimowski 1966). As he phrased it, science concerns itself with what is, whereas technology concerns itself with what is to be. A few years later, in his well-known book The Sciences of the Artificial (1969), Herbert Simon emphasized this important distinction in almost the same words, stating that the scientist is concerned with how things are but the engineer with how things ought to be. Although it is difficult to imagine that earlier philosophers were blind to this difference in orientation, their inclination, in particular in the tradition of logical empiricism, to view knowledge as a system of statements may have led to a conviction that in technology no knowledge claims play a role that cannot also be found in science. The study of technology, therefore, was not expected to pose new challenges nor hold surprises regarding the interests of analytic philosophy.

In contrast, Mario Bunge (1966) defended the view that technology is applied science, but in a subtle way that does justice to the differences between science and technology. Bunge acknowledges that technology is about action, but an action heavily underpinned by theory—that is what distinguishes technology fromthe arts and crafts and puts it on a par with science. According to Bunge, theories in technology come in two types: substantive theories, which provide knowledge about the object of action, and operative theories, which are concerned with action itself. The substantive theories of technology are indeed largely applications of scientific theories. The operative theories, in contrast, are not preceded by scientific theories but are born in applied research itself. Still, as Bunge claims, operative theories show a dependence on science in that in such theories the method of science is employed. This includes such features as modeling and idealization, the use of theoretical concepts and abstractions, and the modification of theories by the absorption of empirical data through prediction and retrodiction.

In response to this discussion, Ian Jarvie (1966) proposed as important questions for a philosophy of technology what the epistemological status of technological statements is and how technological statements are to be demarcated from scientific statements. This suggests a thorough investigation of the various forms of knowledge occurring in either practice, in particular, since scientific knowledge has already been so extensively studied, of the forms of knowledge that are characteristic of technology and are lacking, or of much less prominence, in science. A distinction between 'knowing that'—traditional propositional knowledge—and 'knowing how'—non-articulated and even impossible-to- articulate knowledge—had been introduced by Gilbert Ryle (1949) in a different context. The notion of 'knowing how' was taken up by Michael Polanyi under the name of tacit knowledge and made a central characteristic of technology (Polanyi 1958). However, emphasizing too much the role of unarticulated knowledge, of 'rules of thumb' as they are often called, easily underplays the importance of rational methods in technology. An emphasis on tacit knowledge may also be ill- fit for distinguishing the practices of science and technology because the role of tacit knowledge in science may well be more important than current philosophyof science acknowledges, for example in concluding causal relationships on the basis of empirical evidence. This was also an important theme in the writings of Thomas Kuhn on theory change in science (Kuhn 1962).

The Centrality of Design to Technology

To claim, with Skolimowski and Simon, that technology is about what is to be or what ought to be rather than what is may serve to distinguish it from science but will hardly make it understandable why so much philosophical reflection on technology has taken the form of socio-cultural critique. Technology is an ongoingattempt to bring the world closer to the way one wishes it to be. Whereas science aims to understand the world as it is, technology aims to change the world. These are abstractions, of course. For one, whose wishes concerning what the world should be like are realized in technology? Unlike scientists, who are often personally motivated in their attempts at describing and understanding the world,engineers are seen, not in the least by engineers themselves, as undertaking their attempts to change the world as a service to the public.

The ideas on what is to beor what ought to be are seen as originating outside of technology itself; engineersthen take it upon themselves to realize these ideas. This view is a major source forthe widely spread picture of technology as being instrumental, as delivering instruments ordered from 'elsewhere', as means to ends specified outside of engineering, a picture that has served further to support the claim that technology is neutral with respect to values. This view involves a considerable distortion of reality, however. Many engineers are intrinsically motivated to change the world; in delivering ideas for improvement they are, so to speak, their own best customers. The same is true for most industrial companies, particularly in a market economy, where the prospect of great profits is another powerful motivator. As a result, much technological development is 'technology-driven'.

To understand where technology 'comes from', what drives the innovation process, is of importance not only to those who are curious to understand the phenomenon of technology itself but also to those who are concerned about its role in society. Technology or engineering as a practice is concerned with the creation of artifacts and, of increasing importance, artifact-based services. The design process, the structured process leading toward that goal, forms the core of the practice of technology. In the engineering literature, the design process is commonly represented as consisting of a series of translational steps; At the start are the customer's needs or wishes. In the first step these are translated into a list of functional requirements, which then define the design taskan engineer, or a team of engineers, has to accomplish.

The functional requirements specify as precisely as possible what the device to be designed mustbe able to do. This step is required because customers usually focus on just one ortwo features and are unable to articulate the requirements that are necessary to support the functionality they desire. In the second step, the functional requirements are translated into design specifications, which the exact physical parameters of crucial components by which the functional requirements are going to be met. The design parameters chosen to satisfy these requirements are combined and made more precise such that a blueprint of the device results. The blueprint contains all the details that must be known such that the final step to the process of manufacturing the device can take place. It is tempting to consider the blueprint as the end result of a design process, instead of a finished copy being this result. However, actual copies of a device are crucial for the purpose of prototyping and testing. Prototyping and testing presuppose that the sequence ofsteps making up the design process can and will often contain iterations, leading to revisions of the design parameters and/or the functional requirements. Even though, certainly for mass-produced items, the manufacture of a product for delivery to its customers or to the market comes after the closure of the design phase, the manufacturing process is often reflected in the functional requirements of a device, for example in putting restrictions on the number of different components of which the device consists. The complexity of a device willaffect how difficult it will be to maintain or repair it, and ease of maintenance or low repair costs are often functional requirements. An important modern development is that the complete life cycle of an artifact is now considered to be the designing engineer's concern, up till the final stages of the recycling and disposal of its components and materials, and the functional requirements of any device should reflect this.

From this point of view, neither a blueprint nor a prototype can be considered the end product of engineering design. The biggest idealization that this scheme of the design process contains is arguably located at the start. Only in a minority of cases does a design task originate in a customer need or wish for a particular artifact. First of all, as already suggested, many design tasks are defined by engineers themselves, for instance, by noticing something to be improved in existing products. But more often than not design starts with a problem pointed out by some societal agent, whichengineers are then invited to solve. Many such problems, however, are ill-defined or wicked problems, meaning that it is not at all clear what the problem is exactly and what a solution to the problem would consist in. The 'problem' is a situation that people—not necessarily the people 'in' the situation—find unsatisfactory, but typically without being able to specify a situation that they find more satisfactory in other terms than as one in which the problem has been solved. In particular it is not obvious that a solution to the problem would consist in some artifact, or some artifactual system or process, being made available or installed. Engineering departments all over the world advertise that engineering is problem solving, and engineers easily seem confident that they are best qualified to solvea problem when they are asked to, whatever the nature of the problem. This has led to the phenomenon of a technological fix, the solution of a problem by a technical solution, that is, the delivery of an artifact or artifactual process, whereit is questionable, to say the least, whether this solves the problem or whether it was the best way of handling the problem.

A candidate example of a technological fix for the problem of global warming would be the currently much debated option of injecting sulfate aerosols into the stratosphere to offset the warming effect of greenhouse gases such as carbon dioxide and methane. Such schemes of geoengineering would allow us to avoid facing the—in all likelihood painful—choices that will lead to a reduction of the emission of greenhouse gases into the atmosphere, but will at the same time allow the depletion of the Earth's reservoir of fossil fuels to continue. See for a discussion of technological fixing, e.g., Volti 2009: 26–32. Given this situation, andits hazards, the notion of a problem and a taxonomy of problems deserve to receive more philosophical attention than they have hitherto received.

These wicked problems are often broadly social problems, which would best be met by some form of 'social action', which would result in people changing their behavior or acting differently in such a way that the problem would be mitigated or even disappear completely. In defense of the engineering view, it could perhaps be said that the repertoire of 'proven' forms of social action is meager. The temptation of technical fixes could be overcome—at least that is how an engineer might see it—by the inclusion of the social sciences in the systematic development and application of knowledge to the solution of human problems. This however, is a controversial view. Social engineering is to many a specter to be kept at as large a distance as possible instead of an ideal to be pursued. Karl Popper referred to acceptable forms of implementing social change as 'piecemeal social engineering' and contrasted it to the revolutionary but completely unfounded schemes advocated by, e.g., Marxism. In the entry on Karl Popper, however, his choice of words is called 'rather unfortunate'. The notion of social engineering, and its cogency, deserves more attention that it is currently receiving.

An important input for the design process is scientific knowledge: knowledge about the behavior of components and the materials they are composed of in specific circumstances. This is the point where science is applied. However, much of this knowledge is not directly available from the sciences, since it often concerns extremely detailed behavior in very specific circumstances. Thisscientific knowledge is therefore often generated within technology, by the engineering sciences. But apart from this very specific scientific knowledge, engineering design involves various other sorts of knowledge. In his book What Engineers Know and How They Know It (Vincenti 1990), the aeronautical engineerWalter Vincenti gave a six-fold categorization of engineering design knowledge (leaving aside production and operation as the other two basic constituents of engineering practice). Vincenti distinguishes.

1. Fundamental design concepts, including primarily the operational principle and the normal configuration of a particular device;
2. Criteria and specifications;
3. Theoretical tools;
4. Quantitative data;
5. Practical considerations;
6. Design instrumentalities.

The fourth category concerns the quantitative knowledge just referred to, and the third the theoretical tools used to acquire it. These two categories can be assumed to match Bunge's notion of substantive technological theories. The status of the remaining four categories is much less clear, however, partly because they are less familiar, or not at all, from the well-explored context of science. Of these categories, Vincenti claims that they represent prescriptive forms of knowledge rather than descriptive ones. Here, the activity of design introduces an element of normativity, which is absent from scientific knowledge. Take such a basic notion as 'operational principle', which refers to the way in which the function of a device is realized, or, in short, how it works. This is still a purely descriptive notion. Subsequently, however, it plays a role in arguments that seek to prescribe a course of action to someone who has a goal that could be realized by the operation of such a device. At this stage, the issue changes from a descriptive to a prescriptive or normative one. An extensive discussion of the various kinds of knowledge relevant to technology is offered by Houkes (2009).

Although the notion of an operational principle—a term that seems to originate with Polanyi (1958)—is central to engineering design, no single clear-cut definition of it seems to exist. The issue of disentangling descriptive from prescriptive aspects in an analysis of the technical action and its constituents is therefore a task that has hardly begun. This task requires a clear view on the extent and scope of technology. If one follows Joseph Pitt in his book Thinking About Technology (1999) and defines technology broadly as 'humanity at work', then to distinguish between technological action and action in general becomes difficult, and the study of technological action must absorb all descriptive and normative theories of action, including the theory of practical rationality, and much of theoretical economics in its wake. There have indeed been attempts at such an encompassing account of human action, for example Tadeusz Kotarbinski's Praxiology (1965), but a perspective of such generality makes it difficult to arrive at results of sufficient depth. It would be a challenge for philosophy to specify the differences among action forms and the reasoning grounding them in, to single out three prominent fields of study, technology, organization and management, and economics.

A more restricted attempt at such an approach is Ilkka Niiniluoto's (1993). According to Niiniluoto, the theoretical framework of technology as the practice that is concerned with what the world should be like rather than is, the framework that forms the counterpoint to the descriptive framework of science, is design science. The content of design science, the counterpoint to the theories and explanations that form the content of descriptive science, would then be formed by technical norms, statements of the form 'If one wants to achieve X, one should do Y'. The notion of a technical norm derives from Georg Henrik von Wright's Norm and Action (1963). Technical norms need to be distinguished from anankastic statements expressing natural necessity, of the form 'If X is to be achieved, Y needs to be done'; the latter have a truth value but the former have not. Von Wright himself, however, wrote that he did not understand the mutual relations between these statements. Ideas on what design science is and can and should be are evidently related to the broad problem area of practical rationality—see this entries on practical reason and instrumental rationality—and also to means-ends reasoning, discussed.

Methodological Issues: Design as Decision Making

Design is an activity that is subject to rational scrutiny but in which creativity is considered to play an important role as well. Since design is a form of action, a structured series of decisions to proceed in one way rather than another, the form of rationality that is relevant to it is practical rationality, the rationality incorporating the criteria on how to act, given particular circumstances. This suggests a clear division of labor between the part to be played by rational scrutiny and the part to be played by creativity. Theories of rational action generally conceive their problem situation as one involving a choice among various course of action open to the agent.

Rationality then concerns the question how to decide among given options, whereas creativity concerns the generation of these options. This distinction is similar to the distinction between the context of justification and the context of discovery in science. The suggestion that is associated with this distinction, however, that rational scrutiny only applies in the context of justification, is difficult to uphold for technological design. If the initial creative phase of option generation is conducted sloppily, the result of the design task can hardly be satisfactory. Unlike the case of science, where the practical consequences of entertaining a particular theory are not taken into consideration, the context of discovery in technology is governed by severe constraints of time and money, and an analysis of the problem how best to proceed certainly seems in order. There has been little philosophical work done in this direction; an overview of the issues is given in Kroes, Franssen, and Bucciarelli (2009).

The ideas of Herbert Simon on bounded rationality (see, e.g., Simon 1982) are relevant here, since decisions on when to stop generating options and when to stop gathering information about these options and the consequences when they are adopted are crucial in decision making if informational overload and calculative intractability are to be avoided. However, it has proved difficult to further develop Simon's ideas on bounded rationality since their conception in the 1950s. Another notion that is relevant here is means-ends reasoning. In order to be of any help here, theories of means-ends reasoning should then concern notjust the evaluation of given means with respect to their ability to achieve given ends, but also the generation or construction of means for given ends. A comprehensive theory of means-ends reasoning, however, is not yet available; for a proposal on how to develop means-ends reasoning in the context of technical artifacts. In the practice of technology, alternative proposals for the realization of particular functions are usually taken from 'catalogs' of existing and proven realizations. These catalogs are extended by ongoing research in technology rather than under the urge of particular design tasks.

When engineering design is conceived as a process of decision making, governed by considerations of practical rationality, the next step is to specify these considerations. Almost all theories of practical rationality conceive of it as a reasoning process where a match between beliefs and desires or goals is sought. The desires or goals are represented by their value or utility for the decision maker, and the decision maker's problem is to choose an action that realizes a situation that, ideally, has maximal value or utility among all the situations that could be realized. If there is uncertainty concerning he situations that will be realized by a particular action, then the problem is conceived as aiming for maximal expected value or utility. Now the instrumental perspective on technology implies that the value that is at issue in the design process viewed as a process of rational decision making is not the value of the artifacts that are created. Those values are the domain of the users of the technology so created. They are supposed to be represented in the functional requirements defining the design task. Instead the value to be maximized is the extent to which a particular design meets the functional requirements defining the design task. It is in this sense that engineers share an overall perspective on engineering design as an exercise in optimization. But although optimization is a value-orientated notion, itis not itself perceived as a value driving engineering design.

The functional requirements that define most design problems do not prescribe explicitly what should be optimized; usually they set levels to be attained minimally. It is then up to the engineer to choose how far to go beyond meeting the requirements in this minimal sense. Efficiency, in energy consumption and use of materials first of all, is then often a prime value. Under the pressure of society, other values have come to be incorporated, in particular safety and, more recently, sustainability. Sometimes it is claimed that what engineers aim to maximize is just one factor, namely market success. Market success, however, canonly be assessed after the fact. The engineer's maximization effort will instead be directed at what are considered the predictors of market success. Meeting the functional requirements and being relatively efficient and safe are plausible candidates as such predictors, but additional methods, informed by market research, may introduce additional factors or may lead to a hierarchy among the factors.

Choosing the design option that maximally meets all the functional requirements (which may but need not originate with the prospective user) and all other considerations and criteria that are taken to be relevant, then becomes the practical decision-making problem to be solved in a particular engineering-design task. This creates several methodological problems. Most important of these is that the engineer is facing a multi-criteria decision problem. The various requirements come with their own operationalizations in terms of design parameters and measurement procedures for assessing their performance. This results in a number of rank orders or quantitative scales which represent the various options out of which a choice is to be made. The task is to come up with a final score in which all these results are 'adequately' represented, such that the option that scores best can be considered the optimal solution to the design problem. Engineers describe this situation as one where trade-offs have to be made: in judging the merit of one option relative to other options, a relative bad performance on one criterion can be balanced by a relatively good performance on another criterion. An important problem is whether a rational method for doing this can be formulated. It has been argued by Franssen (2005) that this problem is structurally similar to the well-known problem of social choice, for which Kenneth Arrow proved his notorious impossibility theorem in 1950, implying that no general rational solution method exists for this problem. This poses serious problems for the claim of engineers that their designs are optimal solutions, since Arrow's theorem implies that in most multi-criteria problems the notion of 'optimal' cannot be rigorously defined.

This result seems to except a crucial aspect of engineering activity from philosophical scrutiny, and it could be used to defend the opinion that engineering is at least partly an art, not a science. Instead of surrendering to the result, however, which has a significance that extends much beyond engineering and even beyond decision making in general, we should perhaps conclude insteadthat there is still a lot of work to be done on what might be termed, provisionally, 'approximative' forms of reasoning. One form of reasoning to be included here is Herbert Simon's bounded rationality, plus the related notion of 'satisficing'. Since their introduction in the 1950s (Simon 1957) these two terms have found wide usage, but we are still lacking a general theory of bounded rationality. It may be inthe nature of forms of approximative reasoning such as bounded rationality that a general theory cannot be had, but even a systematic treatment from which such an insight could emerge seems to be lacking.

Another problem for the decision-making view of engineering design is that in modern technology almost all design is done by teams. Such teams are composed of experts from many different disciplines. Each discipline has its own theories, itsown models of interdependencies, its own assessment criteria, and so forth, and the professionals belonging to these disciplines must be considered as inhabitantsof different object worlds, as Louis Bucciarelli (1994) phrases it. The different team members are, therefore, likely to disagree on the relative rankings and evaluations of the various design options under discussion. Agreement on one option as the overall best one can here be even less arrived at by an algorithmic method exemplifying engineering rationality. Instead, models of socialinteraction, such as bargaining and strategic thinking, are relevant here. An example of such an approach to an (abstract) design problem is presented by Franssen and Bucciarelli (2004).

To look in this way at technological design as a decision-making process is to view it normatively from the point of view of practical or instrumental rationality. At the same time it is descriptive in that it is a description of how engineering methodology generally presents the issue how to solve design problems. From that somewhat higher perspective there is room for all kinds of normative questions that are not addressed here, such as whether the functional requirements defining a design problem can be seen as an adequate representation of the values of the prospective users of an artifact or a technology, or by which methods values such as safety and sustainability can bestbe elicited and represented in the design process.

Metaphysical Issues: The Status and Characteristics of Artifacts

Understanding the process of designing artifacts is the theme in philosophy of technology that most directly touches on the interests of engineering practice. This is hardly true for another issue of central concern to analytic philosophy of technology, which is the status and the character of artifacts. This is perhaps not unlike the situation in the philosophy of science, where working scientists seem also to be much less interested in investigating the status and character of models and theories than philosophers are.

Artifacts are man-made objects: they have an author. The artifacts that are of relevance to technology are, in particular, made to serve a purpose. This excludes,within the set of all man-made objects, on the one hand byproducts and waste products and on the other hand works of art. Byproducts and waste products result from an intentional act to make something but just not precisely, although the author at work may be well aware of their creation. Works of art result from an intention directed at their creation (although in exceptional cases ofconceptual art, this directedness may involve many intermediate steps) but it is contested whether artists include in their intentions concerning their work an intention that the work serves some purpose. A further discussion of this aspect belongs to the philosophy of art. An interesting general account has been presented by Dipert (1993).

Technical artifacts, then, are made to serve some purpose, generally to be used for something or to act as a component in a larger artifact, which in its turn is either something to be used or again a component. Whether end product or component, an artifact is 'for something', and what it is for is called the artifact's function. Several researchers have emphasized that an adequate description of artifacts must refer both to their status as tangible physical objects and to the intentions of the people engaged with them. Kroes and Meijers (2006) have dubbed this view "the dual nature of technical artifacts"; its most mature formulation is Kroes 2012. They suggest that the two aspects are 'tied up', so to speak, in the notion of artifact function. This gives rise to several problems. One, which will be passed over quickly because little philosophical work seems to have been done concerning it, is that structure and function mutually constrain each other, but the constraining is only partial. It is unclear whether a general account of this relation is possible and what problems need to be solved to arrive there. There may be interesting connections with the issue of multiple realizability in thephilosophy of mind and with accounts of reduction in science; an example where this is explored is Mahner and Bunge 2001.

It is equally problematic whether a unified account of the notion of function as such is possible, but this issue has received considerably more philosophical attention. The notion of function is of paramount importance for characterizing artifacts, but the notion is used much more widely. The notion of an artifact's function seems to refer necessarily to human intentions. Function is also a key concept in biology, however, where no intentionality plays a role, and it is a key concept in cognitive science and the philosophy of mind, where it is crucial in grounding intentionality in non-intentional, structural and physical properties. Up till now there is no accepted general account of function that covers both the intentionality-based notion of artifact function and the non-intentional notion of biological function—not to speak of other areas where the concept plays a role, such as the social sciences. The most comprehensive theory, that has the ambition to account for the biological notion, cognitive notion and the intentionalnotion, is Ruth Millikan's 1984. The collection of essays edited by Ariew, Cumminsand Perlman (2002) presents a recent introduction to the general topic of definingthe notion of function in general, although the emphasis is, as is generally the case in the literature on function, on biological functions.

Against the view that, at least in the case of artifacts, the notion of function refersnecessarily to intentionality, it could be argued that in discussing the functions of the components of a larger device, and the interrelations between these functions, the intentional 'side' of these functions is of secondary importance only. This, however, would be to ignore the possibility of the malfunctioning of such components. This notion seems to be definable only in terms of a mismatch between actual behavior and intended behavior. The notion of malfunction also sharpens an ambiguity in the general reference to intentions when characterizing technical artifacts. These artifacts usually engage many people, and the intentionsof these people may not all pull in the same direction. A major distinction can be drawn between the intentions of the actual user of an artifact for a particular purpose and the intentions of the artifact's designer. Since an artifact may be used for a purpose different from the one for which its designer intended it to be used, and since people may also use natural objects for some purpose or other, one is invited to allow that artifacts can have multiple functions, or to enforce a hierarchy among all relevant intentions in determining the function of an artifact, or to introduce a classification of functions in terms of the sorts of determining intentions. In the latter case, which is a sort of middle way between the two otheroptions, one commonly distinguishes between the proper function of an artifact as the one intended by its designer and the accidental function of the artifact as the one given to it by some user on private considerations. Accidental use can become so common, however, that the original function drops out of memory.

Closely related to this issue to what extent use and design determine the functionof an artifact is the problem of characterizing artifact kinds. It may seem that we use functions to classify artifacts: an object is a knife because it has the function of cutting, or more precisely, of enabling us to cut. On closer inspection, however,the link between function and kind-membership seems much less straightforward. The basic kinds in technology are, for example, 'knife', 'aircraft' and 'piston'. The members of these kinds have been designed in order to be used to cut something with, to transport something through the air and to generate mechanical movement through thermodynamic expansion. However, one cannot create a particular kind of artifact just by designing something with the intention that it be used for some particular purpose: a member of the kind so createdmust actually be useful for that purpose. Despite innumerable design attempts and claims, the perpetual motion machine is not a kind of artifact. A kind like 'knife' is defined, therefore, not only by the intentions of the designers of its members that they each be useful for cutting but also by a shared operational principle known to these designers, and on which they based their design. This is, in a different setting, also defended by Thomasson, who in her characterization ofwhat she in general calls an artifactual kind says that such a kind is defined by the designer's intention to make something of that kind, by a substantive idea that the designer has of how this can be achieved, and by his or her largely successful achievement of it (Thomasson 2003, 2007). Qua sorts of kinds in which artifacts can be grouped, a distinction must therefore be made between a kind like 'knife' and a corresponding but different kind 'cutter'. A 'knife' indicates a particular waya 'cutter' can be made. One can also cut, however, with a thread or line, a weldingtorch, a water jet, and undoubtedly by other sorts of means that have not yet been thought of. A 'cutter' would then refer to a truly functional kind. As such, itis subject to the conflict between use and design: one could mean by 'cutter' anything than can be used for cutting or anything that has been designed to be used for cutting, by the application of whatever operational principle, presently known or unknown.

This distinction between artifact kinds and functional kinds is relevant for the status of such kinds in comparison to other notions of kinds. Philosophy of sciencehas emphasized that the concept of natural kind, such as exemplified by 'water' or 'atom', lies at the basis of science. On the other hand it is generally taken for granted that there are no regularities that all knives or airplanes or pistons answer to. This, however, is loosely based on considerations of multiple realizability that fully apply only to functional kinds, not to artifact kinds. Artifact kinds share an operational principle that gives them some commonality in physical features, and this commonality becomes stronger once a particular artifact kind is subdivided into narrower kinds. Since these kinds are specified in terms of physical and geometrical parameters, they are much closer to the natural kinds of science, in that they support law-like regularities;. A recent collection of essays that discuss the metaphysics of artifacts and artifact kinds is Franssen, Kroes, Reydon and Vermaas 2014.

Ethics of Technology

It was not until the twentieth century that the development of the ethics of technology as a systematic and more or less independent subdiscipline of philosophy started. This late development may seem surprising given the large impact that technology has had on society, especially since the industrial revolution. A plausible reason for this late development of ethics of technology is the instrumental perspective on technology. This perspective implies, basically, a positive ethical assessment of technology: technology increases the possibilities and capabilities of humans, which seems in general desirable. Of course, since antiquity, it has been recognized that the new capabilities may be put to bad use or lead to human hubris. Often, however, these undesirable consequences are attributed to the users of technology, rather than the technology itself, or its developers. This vision is known as the instrumental vision of technology resultingin the so-called neutrality thesis. The neutrality thesis holds that technology is a neutral instrument that can be put to good or bad use by its users. During the twentieth century, this neutrality thesis met with severe critique, most prominently by Heidegger and Ellul, but also by philosophers from the Frankfurt School, such as Horkheimer and Adorno (1947 [2002]), Marcuse (1964), and Habermas (1968 [1970]).

The scope and the agenda for ethics of technology to a large extent depend on how technology is conceptualized. The second half of the twentieth century has witnessed a richer variety of conceptualizations of technology that move beyond the conceptualization of technology as a neutral tool, as a world view or as a historical necessity. This includes conceptualizations of technology as a political phenomenon (Winner, Feenberg, Sclove), as a social activity (Latour, Callon, Bijkerand others in the area of science and technology studies), as a cultural phenomenon (Ihde, Borgmann), as a professional activity (engineering ethics, e.g., Davis), and as a cognitive activity (Bunge, Vincenti). Despite this diversity, the development in the second half of the twentieth century is characterized by two general trends. One is a move away from technological determinism and the assumption that technology is a given self-contained phenomenon whichdevelops autonomously to an emphasis on technological development being the result of choices (although not necessarily the intended result). The other is a move away from ethical reflection on technology as such to ethical reflection of specific technologies and to specific phases in the development of technology. Both trends together have resulted in an enormous increase in the number and scope of ethical questions that are asked about technology. The developments also imply that ethics of technology is to be adequately empirically informed, not only about the exact consequences of specific technologies but also about the actions of engineers and the process of technological development. This has also opened the way to the involvement of other disciplines in ethical reflections on technology, such as Science and Technology Studies (STS) and Technology Assessment (TA).

Approaches in the Ethics of Technology

Not only is the ethics of technology characterized by a diversity of approaches, it might even be doubted whether something like a subdiscipline of ethics of technology, in the sense of a community of scholars working on a common set of problems, exists. The scholars studying ethical issues in technology have diverse backgrounds (e.g., philosophy, STS, TA, law, political science) and they do not always consider themselves (primarily) ethicists of technology. To give the reader an overview of the field, three basic approaches or strands that might be distinguished in the ethics of technology will be discussed.

Cultural and political approaches

Both cultural and political approaches build on the traditional philosophy and ethics of technology of the first half of the twentieth century. Whereas cultural approaches conceive of technology as a cultural phenomenon that influences our perception of the world, political approaches conceive of technology as a political phenomenon, i.e., as a phenomenon that is ruled by and embodies institutional power relations between people.

Cultural approaches are often phenomenological in nature or at least position themselves in relation to phenomenology as post-phenomenology. Examples of philosophers in this tradition are Don Ihde, Albert Borgmann, Peter-Paul Verbeek and Evan Selinger (e.g., Borgmann 1984; Ihde 1990; Verbeek 2000 [2005], 2011). The approaches are usually influenced by developments in STS, especially the ideathat technologies contain a script that influences not only people's perception of the world but also human behavior, and the idea of the absence of a fundamental distinction between humans and non-humans, including technological artifacts (Akrich 1992; Latour 1992, 1993; Ihde & Selinger 2003). The combination of both ideas has led some to claim that technology has (moral) agency.

Political approaches to technology mostly go back to Marx, who assumed that thematerial structure of production in society, in which technology is obviously a major factor, determined the economic and social structure of that society. Similarly, Langdon Winner has argued that technologies can embody specific forms of power and authority (Winner 1980). According to him, some technologies are inherently normative in the sense that they require or are strongly compatible with certain social and political relations. Railroads, for example, seem to require a certain authoritative management structure. In other cases, technologies may be political due to the particular way they have been designed. Some political approaches to technology are inspired by (American) pragmatism and, to a lesser extent, discourse ethics. A number of philosophers, for example, have pleaded for a democratization of technological development and the inclusion of ordinary people in the shaping of technology (Winner 1983; Sclove 1995; Feenberg 1999).

Although political approaches have obviously ethical ramifications, many philosophers who have adopted such approaches do not engage in explicit ethicalreflection on technology. An interesting recent exception, and an attempt toconsolidate a number of recent developments and to articulate them into a more general account of what an ethics of technology should look like, is the volume Pragmatist Ethics for a Technological Culture (Keulartz et al. 2002). In this volume, the authors plead for a revival of the pragmatist tradition in moral philosophy because it is better fit to deal with a number of moral issues intechnology. Instead of focusing on how to reach and justify normative judgments about technology, a pragmatist ethics focuses on how to recognize and trace moral problems in the first place. Moreover, the process of dealing with these problems is considered more important than the outcome.

Engineering ethics

Engineering ethics is a relatively new field of education and research. It started offin the 1980s in the United States, merely as an educational effort. Engineering ethics is concerned with "the actions and decisions made by persons, individually or collectively, who belong to the profession of engineering" (Baum 1980: 1). According to this approach, engineering is a profession, in the same way as medicine is a profession.

Although there is no agreement on how a profession exactly should be defined, the following characteristics are often mentioned:

- A profession relies on specialized knowledge and skills that require a long period of study;
- The occupational group has a monopoly on the carrying out of the occupation;
- The assessment of whether the professional work is carried out in a competent way is done by, and it is accepted that this can only be done by, professional peers;
- A profession provides society with products, services or values that are useful or worthwhile for society, and is characterized by an ideal of serving society;
- The daily practice of professional work is regulated by ethical standards, which are derived from or relate to the society-serving ideal of the profession.

Typical ethical issues that are discussed in engineering ethics are professional obligations of engineers as exemplified in, for example, codes of ethics of engineers, the role of engineers versus managers, competence, honesty, whistle- blowing, concern for safety and conflicts of interest (Davis 1998, 2005; Martin & Schinzinger 2005; Harris, Pritchard, & Rabins 2008).
Recently, a number of authors have pleaded for broadening the traditional scope of engineering ethics (e.g., Herkert 2001;, van de Poel & Royakkers 2011). This callfor a broader approach derives from two concerns. One concern is that the traditional micro-ethical approach in engineering ethics tends to take the contextsin which engineers have to work for given, while major ethical issues pertain to how this context is 'organized'. Another concern is that the traditional micro- ethical focus tends to neglect issues relating to the impact of technology on society or issues relating to decisions about technology. Broadening the scope of engineering ethics would then, among others, imply more attention for suchissues as sustainability and social justice.

Ethics of specific technologies

The last decades have witnessed an increase in ethical inquiries into specific technologies. This may now be the largest of the three strands discussed, especially given the rapid growth in technology-specific ethical inquiries in the lasttwo decades. One of the most visible new fields is probably computer ethics (e.g., Moor 1985; Floridi 2010; Johnson 2009; Weckert 2007; van den Hoven & Weckert2008), with more recently a focus on robotics, artificial intelligence, machineethics, and the ethics of algorithms (Lin, Abney, & Jenkins 2017; Nucci & Santoni de Sio 2016; Mittelstadt et al. 2016; Bostrom & Yudkowsky 2014; Wallach & Allen 2009). But biotechnology has spurred dedicated ethical investigations as well (e.g., Sherlock & Morrey 2002; P. Thompson 2007). More traditional fields like architecture and urban planning have also attracted specific ethical attention (Fox 2000). More recently, nanotechnology and so-called converging technologies have led to the establishment of what is called nanoethics (Allhoff et al. 2007). Other examples are the ethics of nuclear deterrence (Finnis et al. 1988), nuclear energy (Taebi & Roeser 2015) and geoengineering (C. Preston 2016).

Obviously the establishment of such new fields of ethical reflection is a response to social and technological developments. Still, the question can be asked whether the social demand is best met by establishing new fields of applied ethics. This issue is in fact regularly discussed as new fields emerge. Several authors have for example argued that there is no need for nanoethics because nanotechnology does not raise any really new ethical issues (e.g., McGinn 2010). The alleged absence of newness here is supported by the claim that the ethical issues raised by nanotechnology are a variation on, and sometimes an intensification of, existing ethical issues, but hardly really new, and by the claim that these issues can be dealt with the existing theories and concepts from moral philosophy. For an earlier, similar discussion concerning the supposed new character of ethical issues in computer engineering.

The new fields of ethical reflection are often characterized as applied ethics, that is, as applications of theories, normative standards, concepts and methods developed in moral philosophy. For each of these elements, however, application is usually not straightforward but requires a further specification or revision. This is the case because general moral standards, concepts and methods are often not specific enough to be applicable in any direct sense to specific moral problems. 'Application' therefore often leads to new insights which might well result in the reformulation or at least refinement of existing normative standards, concepts and methods. In some cases, ethical issues in a specific field might require new standards, concepts or methods. Beauchamp and Childress for example have proposed a number of general ethical principles for biomedical ethics (Beauchamp & Childress 2001). These principles are more specific than general normative standards, but still so general and abstract that they apply to different issues in biomedical ethics. In computer ethics, existing moral concepts relating to for example privacy and ownership has been redefined and adapted to deal with issues which are typical for the computer age (Johnson 2003). New fields of ethical application might also require new methods for, for example, discerning ethical issues that take into account relevant empirical facts about these fields, like the fact that technological research and development usually takes place in networks of people rather than by individuals (Zwart et al. 2006). Another more general issue that applies to many new technologies is how to deal with the uncertainties about (potential) social and ethical impacts that typically surround new emerging technologies. Brey's (2012) proposal for an anticipatory ethics may be seen as a reply to this challenge. The issue of anticipation is also one of the central concerns in the more recent interdisciplinary field of responsible innovation (e.g., Owen et al. 2013).

Although different fields of ethical reflection on specific technologies might well raise their own philosophical and ethical issues, it can be questioned whether this justifies the development of separate subfields or even subdisciplines. One obvious argument might be that in order to say something ethically meaningful about new technologies, one needs specialized and detailed knowledge of a specific technology. Moreover such subfields allow interaction with relevant non-philosophical experts in for example law, psychology, economy, science and technology studies (STS) or technology assessment (TA). On the other side, it could also be argued that a lot can be learned from interaction and discussion between ethicists specializing in different technologies, and a fruitful interaction with the two other strands discussed above (cultural and political approaches and engineering ethics). Currently, such interaction in many cases seems absent, although there are of course exceptions.

Some Recurrent Themes in the Ethics of Technology

We now turn to the description of some themes in the ethics of technology. We focus on a number of general themes that provide an illustration of general issues in the ethics of technology and the way these are treated.

Neutrality versus moral agency

One important general theme in the ethics of technology is the question whether technology is value-laden. Some authors have maintained that technology is value-neutral, in the sense that technology is just a neutral means to an end, and accordingly can be put to good or bad use (e.g., Pitt 2000). This view might have some plausibility in as far as technology is considered to be just a bare physical structure. Most philosophers of technology, however, agree that technological development is a goal-oriented process and that technological artifacts by definition have certain functions, so that they can be used for certain goals but not, or far more difficulty or less effectively, for other goals. This conceptual connection between technological artifacts, functions and goals makes it hard to maintain that technology is value-neutral. Even if this point is granted, the value-ladenness of technology can be construed in a host of different ways. Some authors have maintained that technology can have moral agency. This claim suggests that technologies can autonomously and freely 'act' in a moral sense and can be held morally responsible for their actions.

The debate whether technologies can have moral agency started off in computer ethics (Bechtel 1985; Snapper 1985; Dennett 1997; Floridi & Sanders 2004) but has since broadened. Typically, the authors who claim that technologies (can) have moral agency often redefine the notion of agency or its connection to human will and freedom (e.g., Latour 1993; Floridi & Sanders 2004, Verbeek 2011). A disadvantage of this strategy is that it tends to blur the morally relevant distinctions between people and technological artifacts. More generally, the claim that technologies have moral agency sometimes seems to have become shorthand for claiming that technology is morally relevant. This, however, overlooks the fact technologies can be value-laden in other ways than by having moral agency (see, e.g., Johnson 2006; Radder 2009; Illies & Meijers 2009; Peterson & Spahn 2011). One might, for example, claim that technology enables (or even invites) and constrains (or even inhibits) certain human actions and the attainment of certain human goals and therefore is to some extent value-laden, without claiming moral agency for technological artifacts. A good overview of the debate can be found in Kroes and Verbeek 2014.

The debate about moral agency and technology is now particularly salient with respect to the design of intelligent artificial agents. James Moor (2006) has distinguished between four ways in which artificial agents may be or become moral agents:

1. Ethical impact agents are robots and computer systems that ethically impact their environment; this is probably true of all artificial agents.
2. Implicit ethical agents are artificial agents that have been programmed to act according to certain values.
3. Explicit ethical agents are machines that can represent ethical categories and that can 'reason' (in machine language) about these.
4. Full ethical agents in addition also possess some characteristics we often consider crucial for human agency, like consciousness, free will and intentionality.

It might perhaps never be possible to technologically design full ethical agents, and if it were to become possible it might be questionable whether it is morally desirable to do so (Bostrom & Yudkowsky 2014). As Wallach and Allen (2009) have pointed out, the main problem might not be to design artificial agents that can function autonomously and that can adapt themselves in interaction with the environment, but rather to build enough, and the right kind of, ethical sensitivity into such machines.

Responsibility
Responsibility has always been a central theme in the ethics of technology. The traditional philosophy and ethics of technology, however, tended to discuss responsibility in rather general terms and were rather pessimistic about the possibility of engineers to assume responsibility for the technologies they developed. Ellul, for example, has characterized engineers as the high priests of technology, who cherish technology but cannot steer it. Hans Jonas (1979 [1984]) has argued that technology requires an ethics in which responsibility is the central imperative because for the first time in history we are able to destroy the earth and humanity.

In engineering ethics, the responsibility of engineers is often discussed in relation to code of ethics that articulate specific responsibilities of engineers. Such codes of ethics stress three types of responsibilities of engineers: (1) conducting the profession with integrity and honesty and in a competent way, (2) responsibilities towards employers and clients and (3) responsibility towards the public and society. With respect to the latter, most US codes of ethics maintain that engineers 'should hold paramount the safety, health and welfare of the public'.

As has been pointed out by several authors (Nissenbaum 1996; Johnson & Powers 2005; Swierstra & Jelsma 2006), it may be hard to pinpoint individual responsibility in engineering. The reason is that the conditions for the proper attribution of individual responsibility that have been discussed in the philosophical literature (like freedom to act, knowledge, and causality) are often not met by individual engineers. For example, engineers may feel compelled to act in a certain way due to hierarchical or market constraints, and negative consequences may be very hard or impossible to predict beforehand. The causality condition is often difficult to meet as well due to the long chain from research and development of a technology till its use and the many people involved in this chain. Davis (2012) nevertheless maintains that despite such difficulties individual engineers can and do take responsibility.

One issue that is at stake in this debate is the notion of responsibility. Davis (2012), and also for example Ladd (1991), argue for a notion of responsibility that focuses less on blame and stresses the forward-looking or virtuous character of assuming responsibility. But many others focus on backward-looking notions of responsibility that stress accountability, blameworthiness or liability. Zandvoort (2000), for example has pleaded for a notion of responsibility in engineering that is more like the legal notion of strict liability, in which the knowledge condition for responsibility is seriously weakened. Doorn (2012) compares three perspectives on responsibility ascription in engineering—a merit-based, a right-based and a consequentialist perspective—and argues that the consequentialist perspective, which applies a forward-looking notion of responsibility, is most powerful in influencing engineering practice.

The difficulty of attributing individual responsibility may lead to the Problem of Many Hands (PMH). The term was first coined by Dennis Thompson (1980) in an article about the responsibility of public officials. The term is used to describe problems with the ascription of individual responsibility in collective settings. Doorn (2010) has proposed a procedurals approach, based on Rawls' reflective equilibrium model, to deal with the PMH; other ways of dealing with the PMH include the design of institutions that help to avoid it or an emphasis on virtuous behavior in organizations (van de Poel, Royakers, & Zwart 2015).

Design
In the last decades, increasingly attention is paid not only to ethical issues that arise during the use of a technology, but also during the design phase. An important consideration behind this development is the thought that during the design phase technologies, and their social consequences, are still malleable whereas during the use phase technologies are more or less given and negative social consequences may be harder to avoid or positive effects harder to achieve.

In computer ethics, an approach known as Value Sensitive Design (VSD) has been developed to explicitly address the ethical nature of design. VSD aims at integrating values of ethical importance in engineering design in a systematic way (Friedman & Kahn 2003). The approach combines conceptual, empirical and technical investigations. There is also a range of other approaches aimed at including values in design. 'Design for X' approaches in engineering aim at including instrumental values (like maintainability, reliability and costs) but they also include design for sustainability, inclusive design, and affective design (Holt & Barnes 2010). Inclusive design aims at making designs accessible to the whole population including, for example, handicapped people and the elderly (Erlandson 2008). Affective design aims at designs that evoke positive emotions with the users and so contributes to human well-being. Van de Hoven, Vermaas, and van de Poel 2015 gives a good overview of the state-of-the art of value sensitive design for various values and application domains.

If one tries to integrate values into design one may run into the problem of a conflict of values. The safest car is, due to its weight, not likely to be the most sustainability. Here safety and sustainability conflict in the design of cars. Traditional methods in which engineers deal with such conflicts and make trade- off between different requirements for design include cost-benefit analysis and multiple criteria analysis. Such methods are, however, beset with methodological problems like those discussed (Franssen 2005; Hansson 2007). Van de Poel (2009) discusses various alternatives for dealing with value conflicts in design including the setting of thresholds (satisficing), reasoning about values, innovation and diversity.

Technological risks
The risks of technology are one of the traditional ethical concerns in the ethics of technology. Risks raise not only ethical issues but other philosophical issues, such as epistemological and decision-theoretical issues as well (Roeser et al. 2012). Risk is usually defined as the product of the probability of an undesirable event and the effect of that event, although there are also other definitions around (Hansson 2004b). In general it seems desirable to keep technological risks as small as possible. The larger the risk, the larger either the likeliness or the impact of an undesirable event is. Risk reduction therefore is an important goal in technological development and engineering codes of ethics often attribute a responsibility to engineers in reducing risks and designing safe products. Still, risk reduction is not always feasible or desirable.

It is sometimes not feasible, because there are no absolutely safe products and technologies. But even if risk reduction is feasible it may not be acceptable from a moral point of view. Reducing risk often comes at a cost. Safer products may be more difficult to use, more expensive or less sustainable. So sooner or later, one is confronted with the question: what is safe enough? What makes a risk (un)acceptable?

The process of dealing with risks is often divided into three stages: risk assessment, risk evaluation and risk management. Of these, the second is most obviously ethically relevant. However, risk assessment already involves value judgments, for example about which risks should be assessed in the first place (Shrader-Frechette 1991). An important, and morally relevant, issue is also the degree of evidence that is needed to establish a risk. In establishing a risk on the basis of a body of empirical data one might make two kinds of mistakes. One can establish a risk when there is actually none (type I error) or one can mistakenly conclude that there is no risk while there actually is a risk (type II error). Science traditionally aims at avoiding type I errors. Several authors have argued that in the specific context of risk assessment it is often more important to avoid type II errors (Cranor 1990; Shrader-Frechette 1991). The reason for this is that risk assessment not just aims at establishing scientific truth but has a practical aim, i.e., to provide the knowledge on basis of which decisions can be made about whether it is desirable to reduce or avoid certain technological risks in order to protect users or the public.

Risk evaluation is carried out in a number of ways (see, e.g., Shrader-Frechette 1985). One possible approach is to judge the acceptability of risks by comparing them to other risks or to certain standards. One could, for example, compare technological risks with naturally occurring risks. This approach, however, runs the danger of committing a naturalistic fallacy: naturally occurring risks may (sometimes) be unavoidable but that does not necessarily make them morally acceptable. More generally, it is often dubious to judge the acceptability of the risk of technology A by comparing it to the risk of technology B if A and B are not alternatives in a decision.

A second approach to risk evaluation is risk-cost benefit analysis, which is based on weighing the risks against the benefits of an activity. Different decision criteria can be applied if a (risk) cost benefit analysis is carried out (Kneese, Ben-David, and Schulze 1983). According to Hansson (2003: 306), usually the following criterion is applied:

... a risk is acceptable if and only if the total benefits that the exposure gives rise to outweigh the total risks, measured as the probability-weighted disutility of outcomes.
A third approach is to base risk acceptance on the consent of people who suffer the risks after they have been informed about these risks (informed consent). A problem of this approach is that technological risks usually affect a large number of people at once. Informed consent may therefore lead to a "society of stalemates" (Hansson 2003: 300).

Several authors have proposed alternatives to the traditional approaches of risk evaluation on the basis of philosophical and ethical arguments. Shrader-Frechette (1991) has proposed a number of reforms in risk assessment and evaluation procedures on the basis of a philosophical critique of current practices. Roeser (2012) argues for a role of emotions in judging the acceptability of risks. Hansson has proposed the following alternative principle for risk evaluation:
Exposure of a person to a risk is acceptable if and only if this exposure is part of an equitable social system of risk-taking that works to her advantage. (Hansson 2003: 305).

Hansson's proposal introduces a number of moral considerations in risk evaluation that are traditionally not addressed or only marginally addressed. These are the consideration whether individuals profit from a risky activity and the consideration whether the distribution of risks and benefits is fair.

Some authors have criticized the focus on risks in the ethics of technology. One strand of criticism argues that we often lack the knowledge to reliably assess the risks of a new technology before it has come into use. We often do not know the probability that something might go wrong, and sometimes we even do not know, or at least not fully, what might go wrong and what possible negative consequences may be. To deal with this, some authors have proposed to conceive of the introduction of new technology in society as a social experiment and have urged to think about the conditions under which such experiments are morally acceptable (Martin & Schinzinger 2005; van de Poel 2016). Another strand of criticism states that the focus on risks has led to a reduction of the impacts of technology that are considered (Swierstra & te Molder 2012). Only impacts related to safety and health, which can be calculated as risks, are considered, whereas 'soft' impacts, for example of a social or psychological nature, are neglected, thereby impoverishing the moral evaluation of new technologies.

Computer and Information Ethics

This section surveys the field of computer and information ethics. The first section will define the field and will consider its aims and scope, its history, and major approaches and orientations. In the section thereafter, major topics in computer ethics will be surveyed, including privacy, security, free expression and content control, equity issues, intellectual property, and issues of moral responsibility. The final section will focus on the approaches of values in design and value sensitive design, which aim to analyze embedded values in computer software and systems, and to devise methodologies for incorporating values into the design process.

Approaches in Computer and Information ethics Computer ethics is a field of applied ethics that addresses ethical issues in the use, design and management of information technology and in the formulation of ethical policies for its regulation in society. Computer ethics, which has also been called cyberethics, took off as a field in the 1980s, together with the rise of the personal computer. Early work in the field had already started in the 1940s, soon after the invention of the computer. MIT Professor Norbert Wiener was a precursor of the field, already identifying many issues of computer ethics in his book The Human Use of Human Beings [Wiener, 1950]. The term "computer ethics" was first introduced in the mid-1970s by Walter Maner, who also promoted the idea of teaching computer ethics in computer science curricula [Maner, 1980]. The watershed year of 1985 saw the appearance of seminal publications by Jim Moor [1985] and Deborah Johnson [1985] that helped define the field. Since then, it has become a recognized field of applied ethics, with its own journals and conference series. In recent years, the field is sometimes also related to a more general field of information ethics, which includes computer ethics, media ethics, library ethics, and bioinformation ethics.

Why would there be a need for computer ethics, while there is no need for a separate field of ethics for many other technologies, like automobiles and appliances? Jim Moor [1985] has argued that the computer has had an impact like no other recent technology. The computer seems to impact every sector of society, and seems to require us to rethink many of our policies, laws and behaviors. According to Moor, this great impact is due to the fact that computers have logical malleability, meaning that their structure allows them to perform any activity that can be specified as a logical relation between inputs and outputs. Many activities can be specified in this way, and the computer therefore turns out to be an extremely powerful and versatile machine that can perform an incredible amount of functions, from word processor to communication device to gaming platform to financial manager.

The versatility of computers is an important reason for the occurrence of a computer revolution, or information revolution, which is now transforming many human activities and social institutions. Many important things that humans do, including many that raise moral questions like stealing from someone, defaming someone, or invading someone's privacy now also exist in electronic form. In addition, the computer also makes substantially new types of activities possible that are morally controversial, such as the creation of virtual child pornography for which no real children were abused. Because many of the actions made possible by computers are different and new, we often lack policies and laws to guide them. They generate what Moor has called policy vacuums, being the lack of clear policies or rules of conduct. The task of computer ethics, then, is to propose and develop new ethical policies, ranging from explicit laws to informal guidelines, to guide new types of actions that involve computers. Computer ethics has taken off since its birth in the mid-80s, and has established itself as a mature field with its own scientific journals, conferences and organizations.

The field initially attracted most of its interests from computer scientists and philosophers, with many computer science curricula nowadays requiring a course or module on computer ethics. However, given the wide implications for human action sketched by Moor, computer ethics is also of interest to other fields that focus on human behavior and social institutions, such as law, communication studies, education, political science and management. Moreover, computer ethics is also an important topic of debate in the public arena, and computer ethicists regularly contribute to public discussions regarding the use and regulating of computer technology. Computer ethics is sometimes defined as a branch of professional ethics similar to other branches like engineering ethics and journalism ethics. On this view, the aim of computer ethics is to define and analyze the moral and professional responsibilities of computer professionals. Computer professionals are individuals employed in the information technology branch, for example as hardware or software engineer, web designer, network or database administrator, computer science instructor or computer-repair technician.

Computer ethics, on this view, should focus on the various moral issues that computer professionals encounter in their work, for instance in the design, development and maintenance of computer hardware and software. Within this approach to computer ethics, most attention goes to the discussion of ethical dilemmas that various sorts of computer professionals may face in their work and possible ways of approaching them. Such dilemmas may include, for example, the question how one should act as a web designer when one's employer asks one to install spyware into a site built for a client, or the question to what extent software engineers should be held accountable for harm incurred by software malfunction. Next to the discussion of specific ethical dilemmas, there is also general discussion of the responsibilities of computer professionals towards various other parties, such as clients, employers, colleagues, and the general public, and of the nature and importance of ethical codes in the profession.

A recent topic of interest has been the development of methods for value- sensitive design, which is the design of software and systems in such a way that they conform to a desired set of (moral) values [Friedman, Kahn and Borning, 2006]. While the professional ethics view of computer ethics is important, manyin the field employ a broader conception that places the focus on general ethical issues in the use and regulation of information technology. This approach may be called the philosophical ethics approach to computer ethics. This conception holds, following Moor [1985], that computer ethics studies moral issues that are of broad societal importance, and develops ethical policies to address them. Such policies may regulate the conduct of organizations, groups and individuals and theworkings of institutions.

The philosophical approach focuses on larger social issues like information privacyand security, computer crime, issues of access and equity, and the regulation of commerce and speech on the Internet. It asks what ethical principles should guideour thinking about these issues, and what specific policies (laws, social and corporate policies, social norms) should regulate conduct with respect to them. Within this approach, some researchers focus on the development of ethicalguidelines for users of computer technology. Others place more emphasis on policy issues, and try to formulate ethical policies for organizations, government agencies or lawmakers. Still others focus on computer technologies themselves, and try to to identify and evaluate morally relevant features in their design. Some also focus on theoretical and metaethical issues.

Topics in Computer and Information Ethics
Introductions to computer ethics show considerable agreement on what the central issues for computer ethics are. They include ethical issues of privacy, security, computer crime, intellectual property, free expression, and equity and access, and issues of responsibility and professional ethics.

Privacy
Privacy is a topic that has received much attention in computer ethics from early on. Information technology is often used to record, store and transmit personal information, and it may happen that this information is accessed or used by third parties without the consent of the corresponding persons, thus violating their privacy. Privacy is the right of persons to control access to their personal affairs, such as their body, thoughts, private places, private conduct, and personal information about themselves. The most attention in computer ethics has gone toinformation privacy, which is the right to control the disclosure of personal data. Information technology can easily be used to violate this right.

Privacy issues come into play on the Internet, where cookies, spyware, browser tracking and access to the records of internet providers may be used to study the Internet behavior of individuals or to get access to their PCs. They also come into play in the construction of databases with personal information by corporations and government organizations, and the merging of such databases to createcomplex records about persons or to find matches across databases. Other topics of major concern include the privacy implications of video surveillance and biometric technologies, and the ethics of medical privacy and privacy in the workplace. It has also been studied whether people have a legitimate expectationto privacy in public areas, whether they can be freely recorded, screened and tracked whenever they appear in public and how the notion of "public" itself has changed in light of information technology.

Security and crime
Security has become a major issue in computer ethics, because of rampant computer crime and fraud, the spread of computer viruses, malware and spam, and national security concerns about the status of computer networks as breeding grounds for terrorist activity and as vulnerable targets for terrorist attacks. Computer security is the protection of computer systems against the unauthorized disclosure, manipulation, or deletion of information and against denial of service attacks. Breaches of computer security may cause harms and rights violations, including economic losses, personal injury and death, which may occur in so-called safety-critical systems, and violations of privacy and intellectual property rights.

Much attention goes to the moral and social evaluation of computer crime and other forms of disruptive behavior, including hacking (non-malicious break-ins into systems and networks), cracking (malicious break-ins), cybervandalism (disrupting the operations of computer networks or corrupting data), software piracy (the illegal reproduction or dissemination of proprietary software), and computer fraud (the deception for personal gain in online business transactions by assuming a false online identity or by altering or misrepresenting data). Another recently important security-related issue is how state interests in monitoring and controlling information infrastructures to better protect against terrorist attacks should be balanced against the right to privacy and other civil rights [Nissenbaum, 2005].

Free expression and content control
The Internet has become a very important medium for the expression of information and ideas. This has raised questions about whether there should be content control or censorship of Internet information, for example by governments or service providers. Censorship could thwart the right to free expression, which is held to be a basic right in many nations. Free expression includes both freedom of speech (the freedom to express oneself through publication and dissemination) and freedom of access to information.

Several types of speech have been proposed as candidates for censorship. These include pornography and other obscene forms of speech, hate speech such as websites of fascist and racist organizations, speech that can cause harm or undermine the state, such as information as to how to build bombs, speech that violates privacy or confidentiality, and libelous and defamatory speech. Studies in computer ethics focus on the permissibility of these types of speech, and on the ethical aspects of different censorship methods, such as legal prohibitions and software filters.

Equity and access The information revolution has been claimed to exacerbate inequalities in society, such as racial, class and gender inequalities, and to create a new, digital divide, in which those that have the skills and opportunities to use information technology effectively reap the benefits while others are left behind. In computer ethics, it is studied how both the design of information technologies and their embedding in society could increase inequalities, and how ethical policies may be developed that result in a fairer and more just distribution of their benefits and disadvantages. This research includes ethical analyses of the accessibility of computer systems and services for various social groups, studies of social biases in software and systems design, normative studies of education in the use of computers, and ethical studies of the digital gap between industrialized and developing countries.

Intellectual property Intellectual property is the name for information, ideas, works of art and other creations of the mind for which the creator has an established proprietary right of use. Intellectual property laws exist to protect creative works by ensuring that only the creators benefit from marketing them or making them available, be they individuals or corporations. Intellectual property rights for software and digital information have generated much controversy. There are those who want to ensure strict control of creators over their digital products, whereas others emphasize the importance of maintaining a strong public domain in cyberspace, and argue for unrestricted access to electronic information and for the permissibility of copying proprietary software. In computer ethics, the ethical and philosophical aspects of these disputes are analyzed, and policy proposals are made for the regulation of digital intellectual property in its different forms. Patentability of software is also a topic of major concern, which is problematic due to the non-tangible nature of software as well as the difficulty in specifying what counts as the identity of a piece of software (cf. Turner and Eden, forthcoming b).

Moral Responsibility

Society strongly relies on computers. It relies on them for correct information, for collaboration and social interaction, for aid in decision-making, and for the monitoring and execution of tasks. When computer systems malfunction or make mistakes, harm can be done, in terms of loss of time, money, property, opportunities, or even life and limb. Who is responsible for such harms? Computer professionals, end-users, employers, policy makers and others could all be held responsible for particular harms.

It has even been argued that intelligent computer systems can bear moral responsibility themselves [Dodig-Crnkovic and Persson, 2008]. In computer ethics, it is studied how the moral responsibility of different actors can be defined, and what kinds of decisions should be delegated to computers to begin with. It is studied how a proper assignment of responsibility can minimize harm and allows for attributions of accountability and liability.

Foundational Issues in Computer Ethics

Foundational, metaethical and methodological issues have received considerable attention in computer ethics. Many of these issues have been discussed in the context of the so-called foundationalist debate in computer ethics [Floridi and Sanders, 2002; Himma, 2007a]. This is an ongoing metatheoretical debate on the nature and justification of computer ethics and its relation to metaethical theories. Three questions central to the foundationalist debate are: "Is computer ethics a legitimate field of applied ethics?", "Does computer ethics raise any ethical issues that are new or unique?" and "Does computer ethics require substantially new ethical theories, concepts or methodologies different from those used elsewhere in applied ethics?".

The first question, whether computer ethics is a legitimate field of applied ethics, has often been discussed in the context of the other two questions, with discussants arguing that the legitimacy of computer ethics depends on the existence of unique ethical issues or questions in relation to computer technology. The debate on whether such issues exist has been called the uniqueness debate [Tavani, 2002].

In defense of uniqueness, Maner [1996] has argued that unique features of computer systems, like logical malleability, superhuman complexity and the ability to make exact copies, raise unique ethical issues to which no non-computer analogues exist. Others remain unconvinced that any computer ethics issue is genuinely unique. Johnson [2003] has proposed that issues in computer ethics are new species of traditional moral issues. They are familiar in that they involve traditional ethical concepts and principles like privacy, responsibility, harm and ownership, but the application of these concepts and principles is not straightforward because of special properties of computer technology, which require a rethinking and retooling of ethical notions and new ways of applying them. Floridi and Sanders [2002; Floridi, 2003] do not propose the existence of unique ethical issues but rather argue for the need of new ethical theory. They argue that computer ethics needs a metaethical and macrotheoretical foundation, which they argue be different from the standard macroethical theories like utilitarianism and Kantianism. Instead, they propose a macroethical theory they call Information Ethics, which assigns intrinsic value to information. The theory covers not just digital or analogue information, but in fact analyzes all of reality as having an informational ontology, being built out of informational objects.

Since informational objects are postulated to have intrinsic value, moral consideration should be given to them, including the informational objects produced by computers. In contrast to these various authors, Himma [2007a] has argued that computer technology does not need to raise new ethical issues or require new ethical theories to be a legitimate field of applied ethics. He argues that issues in computer ethics may not be unique and may be approached with traditional ethical theories, and that it nevertheless is a legitimate field because computer technology has given rise to an identifiable cluster of moral issues in much the same way like medical ethics and other fields of applied ethics.

Largely separately from the foundationalist debate, several authors have discussed the issue of proper methodology in computer ethics, discussing standard methods of applied ethics and their limitations for computer ethics [Van den Hoven, 2008;

Brey, 2000]. An important recent development that has methodological and perhaps also metaethical ramifications is the increased focus on cultural issues. In intercultural information ethics [Ess and Hongladarom, 2007;Brey, 2007], ethicists attempt to compare and come to grips with the vastlydifferent moral attitudes and behaviors that exist towards information and information technology in different cultures. In line with this development, Gorniak-Kocykowska [1995] and others have argued that the global character of cyberspace requires a global ethics which transcends cultural differences in value systems.

Other Topics

There are many other social and ethical issues that are studied in computer ethicsnext to these central ones. Some of these include the implications of IT for community, identity, the quality of work, and the quality of life, the relation between information technology and democracy, the ethics of Internet governance and electronic commerce, and the ethics of trust online. Many new ethical issues come up together with the development of new technologies or applications. Recently, much attention has been devoted to ethical aspects of social networking sites like Facebook, MySpace and Youtube, to ubiquitous computing and ambient intelligence, and to robotics and artificial agents. The constant addition of new products and services in information technology and theemergence of new uses and correlated social and cultural consequences ensures that the field keeps meeting new challenges.

Values and Computer Systems Design

Although most ethical commentary in the philosophical approach is directed at the use of computers by individuals and organizations, attention has also started to be paid to systems and software themselves. It has come to be recognized that the systems themselves are not morally neutral but contain values and biases in their design that must also be analyzed. Approaches of this sort have been called values in design approaches [Nissenbaum, 1998; Flanagan, Howe and Nissenbaum, 2007]. Values in design approaches hold that computer software and systems can be morally evaluated partially or wholly independently of actual uses of them. They can be said to embody values in the sense that they have a tendency to promote or sustain particular values when used. This may sound like technological determinism, but proponents usually do not subscribe to the strong determinist thesis that embodied values necessitate certain effects in whatever way the system is used.

Yet, they do hold a weak determinism according to which systems may embody values that systematically engender certain effects across a wide range of uses, atleast including typical or "normal" ways of using the system. For a system to embody a value, then, means that there is a tendency for that value to be promoted or realized when the system is used. This observation has led proponents to argue that more attention should be paid to ethical aspects in the design of computer systems rather than just their use.

Friedman and Nissenbaum [1996] have studied how values may enter into computer systems, with a focus on justice and bias. They argue that bias can enterinto computer systems in three ways. Preexisting bias emerges from the practices and attitudes of designers and the social institutions in which they function.Technical bias arises from technical constraints. Emergent bias arises after the design of the system, when a context of use emerges that is different from the one anticipated. These three origins of bias may be generalized to apply to other values as well. Brey [2000] has proposed a particular values in design approach termed disclosive computer ethics. He claims that a significant part of the effortof computer ethics should be directed at deciphering and subsequently evaluatingembedded moral values in computer software and systems. The focus should be on widely held public and moral values, such as privacy, autonomy, justice, and democracy. Research, Brey argues, should take place at three levels: the disclosure level, at which morally charged features of computer systems are detected and disclosed, the theoretical level, at which relevant moral theory is developed, and the application level, at which ethical theory is used in the evaluation of the disclosed morally charged features. He claims that such research should be interdisciplinary, involving ethicists, computer scientists and social scientists.

The approach of value-sensitive design [Friedman, Kahn and Borning, 2006; Friedman & Kahn, 2003] is not so much concerned with the identification and evaluation of values in computer systems, but rather with the development of methods for incorporating values into the design process. It is an approach to software engineering and systems development that builds on values in design approaches and studies how accepted moral values can be operationalized and incorporated into software and systems. Its proposed methodology integrates conceptual investigations into values, empirical investigations into the practices, beliefs and intentions of users and designers, and technical investigations into theway in which technological properties and mechanisms support or hinder the realization of values. It also seeks procedures to incorporate and balance the values of different stakeholders in the design process.

Biotechnology

The term "techno science" is increasingly being used to refer to such contemporary disciplines as information and communication technology, nanotechnology, artificial intelligence and to biotechnology. The popularity of the term is illustrated by the fact that even a group of social scientists reporting on the changing attitudes of European public towards biotechnology invokes the term to mark the departure of this particular field from the norms and values once held to be essential   to the ethos of science. The evident commercialization and industrialization of biotechnology, with the pursuitof private knowledge, patents and profits, hardly meets Merton's criteria of universalism, communism, disinterestedness and skepticism, or the public's expectations about the values, accountability and social responsibility of science. Biotechnology has become a techno science, a commercial enterprise accountable to financial markets and to shareholders. It is interesting to note thatthe public, according to these social scientists, have not yet fully accommodated to the new commercial realities of "techno science" and still entertain expectations about science that modern biotechnology is unlikely going to meet.

In the seventeenth century the philosophers Francis Bacon (1561–1626) and René Descartes (1596–1650) advocated a new way of doing science that would have the power to conquer nature for human benefit. (The old science had seemed to be more concerned with contemplating nature than controlling it.) In the contemporary world biotechnology is providing the technology for controlling andchanging living nature, including human nature. However, because biotechnological power over the living world offers not only the promise for doinggood but also an opportunity for doing evil, this has provoked an ethical debate over the modern scientific project for the mastery of nature through technology.

Biotechnology can be defined as the technical manipulation of living organisms or parts of those organisms to provide products and services to satisfy human desires. If it is defined in this broad way, one can see that biotechnology has been employed throughout human history.

Biotechnology in History
Biotechnology can be defined as the technical manipulation of living organisms or parts of those organisms to provide products and services to satisfy human desires. If it is defined in this broad way, one can see that biotechnology has been employed throughout human history.

The history of biotechnology can be divided into three periods: ancient, modern, and contemporary. Ancient biotechnology began more than 10,000 years ago with the emergence of agriculture in ancient Mesopotamia. Modern biotechnology began in the nineteenth century with the development of industrial microbiology. Contemporary biotechnology began in the 1970s with new techniques for genetic engineering. In each period one can see the power humans have acquired to manipulate nature. But one also can see the natural limits of this power, which is constrained by the natural potentialities available in wild plants and animals and the natural complexities of behavioral traits in the living world.

Ancient biotechnology began when human beings started to domesticate plants and animals for human use. Throughout most of the history of the human species,spanning approximately six million years, human beings fed themselves by gathering wild plants and hunting wild animals. Then some people in a few parts of the world began to produce food by cultivating domesticated plants and herding domesticated animals. As a consequence those farmers and herders bred for and selected genetic modifications in domesticated organisms that were moresuitable to human desires. Even in the early twenty-first century all of human civilization depends on this project in agricultural biotechnology.

The human power of domestication is limited, however, by the natural potentiality of wild plants and animals. Most plant and animal species in the wild are not suitable for domestication. For example, most wild plants are not good as a source of food because they are woody or do not produce fruit, leaves, or roots that are edible. Most wild animals are not susceptible to successful domesticationbecause they cannot be bred and herded in a manner that makes them useful for human beings. Although advances in biological knowledge have increased human biotechnological power over living nature, that power will always be limited by the potentialities found in nature.

Modern biotechnology arose in the nineteenth century as growing knowledge in the biological sciences was applied to the technological manipulation of the living world for human purposes. For example, the chemist Louis Pasteur's (1822–1895) microbiological explanation of fermentation as resulting from the activity of microscopic organisms allowed improvements in the brewing of beer and other industries that depend on using fermentation by yeast to produce food and beverages. Pasteur also showed that infectious diseases are caused by disease- producing microorganisms and perfected techniques for vaccination that would create immunity to some of those diseases. Later, in the twentieth century, the discovery of the ways in which some fungi produce antibiotics such as penicillin revolutionized the medical treatment of bacterial infections. In the early 2000s there are hundreds of pharmaceutical agents derived from fungal fermentation.

However, even modern biotechnology shows the technical limits set by nature. Bacteria vulnerable to fungal toxins can evolve to become resistant to thosetoxins. Indeed, bacteria have been so successful in evolving tolerance to antibiotics that there is a growing fear in the medical profession that the age of antibiotic protection against infectious diseases is reaching its end. The power of this aspect of biotechnology for controlling living nature is great but limited.

The contemporary biotechnology that began in the last half of the twentieth century arose from a deeper knowledge of genetics and molecular biology and has provided humans with greater power over the living world. Even so, contemporary biotechnology is limited in its technical means by the physical and chemical limits of nature. Contemporary biotechnology began in 1973 when Herbert Boyer and Stanley Cohen developed the technology for recombinant DNA, which allows scientists to alter DNA molecules and thus artificially create new forms of life. They did this by combining a number of discoveries. Bacteria protect themselves against certain viruses through the use of restriction enzymes that cut up viral DNA at specific sequences of nucleotide bases; this allows a scientist with the right restriction enzyme to cut out a specific genetic sequence. Bacteria contain plasmids, which are small loops of DNA that can pass from one bacterium to another. This allows bacteria to develop antibiotic resistance quickly if the genes for resistance are passed by plasmids. Boyer and Cohen showed how one could use a restriction enzyme to cut out a specific genetic sequence and then glue that sequence into a bacterial plasmid. That plasmid, with its new combination of genetic sequences, could be introduced into a bacterial cell. As the bacterial cell divided, it would produce copies of the recombinant plasmid, which then could be extracted from the bacteria.

An illustration of the value of this recombinant DNA technique is provided by the production of human insulin. People with diabetes do not have enough of the protein insulin to regulate blood-sugar levels. After the 1920s diabetic patients were treated with injections of insulin extracted from pigs and cattle. This is an example of modern biotechnology. Although pig and cow insulin is very similar to human insulin, there are enough differences that some people with diabetes have had allergic reactions. Contemporary biotechnology provided a solution to the problem by using recombinant DNA techniques. The human gene for insulin was identified and then could be inserted into a bacterial cell through a plasmid so that the bacterium would produce human insulin that could be harvested for use by human patients. In 1982 human insulin produced in genetically modified bacteria became the first drug of contemporary biotechnology to be approved by the U.S. Food and Drug Administration.

Contemporary biotechnology has developed hundreds of products with agricultural, environmental, and medical benefits. Agricultural biotechnology uses reliable techniques for genetic manipulation to produce new kinds of plants and animals to provide food that is cheaper and more nutritious. Environmental biotechnology is used to design genetically modified organisms that can clean up environmental pollution by consuming toxic materials. Medical biotechnology is used to devise new drugs and vaccines and therapeutic techniques that relieve or prevent suffering, cure disease, and enhance physical and mental well-being.

Ethical Issues

Despite its many benefits, biotechnology has provoked ethical controversy in six areas of moral concern: safety, liberty, justice, environmental nature, human nature, and religious beliefs. SAFETY. Safety is a moral concern for opponents of biotechnology who worry that its power disrupts the complex balance in living nature in ways that are likely to be harmful. Individuals such as Jeremy Rifkin (1977) and groups such as Greenpeace have warned that genetically modified crops and foods could endanger human health as well as the health of the environment. Critics of medical biotechnology fear that biotechnology medicine alters the human body and mind in radical ways that could produce harmful consequences—perhaps far into the future—in ways that are hard to foresee.

Proponents of biotechnology such as James Watson (2003) and Michael Fumento (2003) argue that its techniques are so precise and controlled that it tends to be far safer than older forms of technology. Breeders of plants and animals have genetically modified organisms for thousands of years without understanding exactly what they were doing. But biotechnology in the early 2000s provides a better understanding of and greater power over genetic mechanisms so that it is possible to minimize the risks. In fact, there is no clear evidence that any human being among the hundreds of millions who have been exposed has become sick from eating genetically modified foods. Similarly, the risks to human health from medical biotechnology can be reduced by means of careful testing and new techniques for designing drugs and therapies that are designed specifically for individual patients with unique genetic traits. Nevertheless, the history of unforeseen harm from all technologies justifies a cautious approach.

LIBERTY. Liberty is a moral concern for those who fear that biotechnology will give some people tyrannical power over others. The history of eugenics, in which governments used coercion to eliminate those judged to be biologically "unfit," illustrates the danger of encroachments on liberty. Libertarian proponents of biotechnology such as Fumento and Virginia Postrel (1998) insist that there should be no threat to liberty as long as biotechnology is chosen freely by individuals in a free market economy. But conservatives such as Leon Kass (2002) worry that people could be coerced informally by social pressure, employers, and insurance companies so that they will feel compelled to adopt biotechnology products and procedures. Moreover, Kass and others suggest that biotech can give parents the power to control the nature and behavior of their children in ways that threaten the liberty of the children.

JUSTICE. Justice is a moral concern for people who anticipate that biotechnology will be so expensive that only the richest individuals will benefit from it so that the rich will have an unjust advantage over the poor. Even proponents of biotechnology such as Lee Silver (1998) worry that reproductive biotechnology eventually could divide humanity into two separate species based on the wealth or poverty of their ancestors: the "genrich" who would be genetically designed to be superior and the "genpoor" who would be left behind as biologically inferior beings. Of course in some ways this problem is not unique to biotechnology because rich people always have unfair advantages over the poor, but the libertarian defenders of biotechnology foresee that in a free-market society prices for biotechnology products and services eventually will decline as a result of competition, and this will lessen the advantages of the rich over the poor. Similarly, critics of biotechnology argue that the rich nations of the world will benefit more from this new technology than will the poor nations, yet libertarians predict that international free trade will spread the advantages of biotechnology around the world.

ENVIRONMENTAL NATURE

Environmental nature is a moral concern for environmentalists such as Rifkin and Bill McKibben (2003). Those environmentalists predict that biotechnology will promote the replacement of the natural environment with a purely artificial world and that this will deprive human beings of healthy contact with wild nature. They also fear that introducing genetically modified organisms into the environment will produce monstrous forms of life that will threaten human beings and the natural world.

Proponents of biotechnology respond by noting that beginning with agriculture, human beings have been creating genetically modified organisms that transform the environment for thousands of years. All organisms modify their environments, sometimes with global effects. For example, the oxygen in the earth's atmosphere has been produced over billions of years by photosynthetic organisms. Biologists such as F. John Odling-Smee (2003) have called this "niche construction." So human beings are not unique in their capacity for changing their environments. Although this sometimes has produced disasters such as the extinction of plants and animals and the emergence of new disease-causing agents, people have learned to adjust to these dangers, and contemporary biotechnology provides more precise knowledge and techniques to recognize and avoid such dangers.

Moreover, environmental biotechnology is developing new organisms, such as bacteria genetically engineered to metabolize toxic wastes, to restore dangerous natural environments to a condition that is safe for human beings.

HUMAN NATURE

Human nature is a moral concern for anyone who fears that biotechnology could change or even abolish human nature. Both environmentalists such as Rifkin and McKibben and conservatives such as Kass and Francis Fukuyama (2002) worry that the biotechnological transformation of human nature will produce a "posthuman" world with no place for human dignity rooted in human nature. On the other side of this debate Nick Bolstrom (2003) and others in the World Transhumanist Association welcome the prospect of using biotechnology to move toward a "transhuman" condition. More moderate proponents of biotechnology dismiss both positions for being based on exaggerated views of the power of biotechnology.

In a report by the President's Council on Bioethics (2003) Kass and other members of the council contend that biotechnology expresses a willful lack of humility in pursuing a scientific mastery of nature that carries out the modern scientific project first described by Francis Bacon. When a physician uses medical therapy to restore the health of a patient, the physician cultivates the body's natural capacity for healing to serve the natural goal of health. Such medical treatment is guided in both its means and its ends by nature. But when biotechnologists use genetic engineering or psychotropic drugs to extend human bodily or mental powers beyond their normal range, they act not as nature's servant but as nature's master because they are forcing nature to serve their own willful desires.

As an example Kass and other members of the council point to the use of psychotropic drugs such as Prozac that alter the biochemistry of the brain to elevate mood. Using such drugs to cure severely depressed patients can be justified as therapy directed toward restoring normal mental health, but their use to change human personality radically—perhaps by inducing feelings of contentment that never yield to sadness—would violate the normal range of human mental experience set by nature. The ultimate aim of such a psychopharmacological science would be a drug-dependent fantasy of happiness that would be dehumanizing. Furthermore, scientists such as David Healy (2004) have warned that any drug powerful enough to change human personality is likely to have severely harmful side effects.

The President's Council (2003) warns against the excessive pride inherent in Bacon's project for mastering nature, which assumes that nature is mere material for humans to shape to their desires. Rather, it urges people to adopt an attitude of humility and respect and treat the natural world as a "gift." To respect the "giftedness" of the natural world is to recognize that the world is given to humans as something not fully under their control and that even human powers for changing the world belong to human nature as the unchanging ground of all change (Kass 2003).

Proponents of biotechnology could respond by defending Bacon's project as combining respect for nature with power over nature. At the beginning of the Novum Organon Bacon observed that "nature to be commanded must be obeyed" because "all that man can do is to put together or put asunder natural bodies," and then "the rest is done by nature working within" (Bacon 1955, p. 462). Kass has used the same words in explaining how the power of biotechnology is limited by the potentialities inherent in nature (Kass 1985).

Throughout the history of biotechnology—from the ancient Mesopotamian breeders of plants and animals, to Pasteur's use of microorganisms for fermentation and vaccination, to Boyer and Cohen's techniques for gene splicing—people have employed nature's properties for the satisfaction of human desires. Boyer and Cohen did not create restriction enzymes and bacterial plasmids but discovered them as parts of living nature. They then used those natural processes to bring about outcomes, such as the production of human insulin for persons with diabetes, that would benefit human beings. Biotechnology has the ability to change nature only insofar as it conforms to the laws of nature. To command nature people must obey it.

Baconian biotechnology is thus naturally limited in its technical means because it is constrained by the potentialities of nature. It is also naturally limited in its moral ends because it is directed toward the goals set by natural human desires. Kass and the President's Council (2003) acknowledge this by showing how biotechnology is employed to satisfy natural desires such as the desire of parents for happy children and the desire of all human beings for life and health. As they indicate, it is not enough to respect the "giftedness" of nature because some of the "gifts" of nature, such as diabetes and cancer, are undesirable. People accept some of nature's gifts and reject others on the basis of the desires inherent in human nature.

RELIGIOUS BELIEFS. To appreciate life as a gift that should elicit a feeling of humility rather than mastery is a religious emotion. Some of the moral concerns about biotechnology express the religious attitude that life is sacred and therefore the biotechnological manipulation of life shows a lack of reverence for the divinely ordained cosmic order. The biblical story of the Tower of Babel (Genesis 11:1–9) suggests that the human lust for technical power over the world provokes divine punishment.

In 1977 the environmentalist Jeremy Rifkin wrote a book attacking biotechnology with the title Who Should Play God?: The Artificial Creation of Life and What It Means for the Future of the Human Race. The title conveys the direction of his argument. The "creation of life" is proper only for God. For human beings to create life "artificially" is a blasphemous transgression of God's law that will bring punishment upon the human race. Rifkin often uses the imagery of the Frankenstein story. Like Doctor Frankenstein, biotech scientists are trying to take God's place in creating life, and the result can only be the creation of monsters. When people such as Rifkin use the phrase "playing God," they evoke a religious sense that nature is a sacred expression of God's will and therefore should not be changed by human intervention. Rifkin has said that "the resacralization of naturestands before us as the great mission of the coming age" (Rifkin 1983, p. 252).

In contrast to Rifkin, Bacon thought that regarding nature as sacred was a pagan idea contrary to biblical religion. In pagan antiquity the natural world was the sacred image of God, but the Bible teaches that God is the transcendent Creator of nature; therefore, God's mysterious will is beyond nature. Although nature declares God's power and wisdom, it does not declare the will and true worship ofGod. Bacon believed that true religion as based on faith in biblical revelation mustbe separated from true philosophy based on the rational study of nature's laws (Bacon 1955).

Some biblical theologians, such as Philip Hefner (2003) and Ted Peters (2003), have restated this Baconian claim that the biblical conception of God as thesupernatural creator of nature separates the sacred and the natural and thus denies pagan pantheism. They argue that because human beings have been created in God's image and God is the Creator, human beings must share somehow in God's creativity. The Bible declares that when God made humanity inhis image, this was to include "dominion" or "mastery" over all the earth, including all the animals (Genesis 1:26–28). Hefner reads the Bible as teaching that human beings are "created cocreators." As "created," humans are creatures and cannot create in the same way as God, who can create ex nihilo, "from nothing." However, as "cocreators" people can contribute to changes in creation. Of course, Hefner warns, people must do this as cautious and respectful stewards of God's creation, but it is not appropriate to worship nature as sacred and thus inviolable.

The theological idea of human beings as cocreators was affirmed by Pope John Paul II in his 1981 encyclical Laborem Exercens and criticized as a "remarkably bad idea" by the Protestant theologian Stanley Hauerwas (Houck and Williams 1983). In his 1991 encyclical Centesimus Annus the Pope stressed the importance ofhuman technological knowledge in improving the conditions of life (Novak 1993).

That God transcends nature, that nature is thus not sacred, that human beings as created in God's image share in God's creative activity, that human beings have the power and the duty to master nature by artful manipulation, and that they have the moral duty to do this as an activity of charity for the improvement of human life—all the precepts Bacon drew from the Bible to support his view of thenew science—have been accepted by some biblical believers. But many of those believers worry that modern science promotes an atheistic materialism that denies the dignity of human beings and of the natural world generally as God's Creation. In particular they worry about whether biotechnology expresses anunduly willful attitude toward the world as merely raw material for human manipulation and survival.

Environmental ethics Introduction
Environmental ethics is a sub-discipline of philosophy that deals with the ethical problems surrounding environmental protection. It aims to provide ethical justification and moral motivation for the cause of global environmental protection.
Body

- Environmental ethics focuses on questions concerning how we ought to inhabit the world; what constitutes a good life or a good society; and who, where, or what merits moral standing. The field emerged most significantly in the 1960s from an increasing awareness of the global environmental condition.
- It is concerned with the issue of responsible personal conduct with respect to natural landscapes, resources, species, and non-human organisms. It is a cluster of beliefs, values and norms regarding how humans should interact with the environment.

Issues involved in environmental ethics

a) **Consumption of natural resources:** Since humans are part of nature, sustainable use of resources can be achieved through cooperation with nature.
b) **Destruction of forests:** Big industries and multinational companies form themajor section which exploits forests unsustainably. However, the brunt of the destruction is faced by the poor and tribals who are the inhabitants of the forests. It leads to the loss of biodiversity, habitats and extinction of plants and animals.
c) **Environmental pollution:** Consequences of environmental pollution do not respect national boundaries. Moreover, the poor and weaker sections of society are disproportionately affected by negative effects of climate change.
d) **Anthropocentrism:** It refers to an ethical framework that grants "moral standing" solely to human beings. Thus, an anthropocentric ethic claims that only human beings are morally considerable in their own right, meaning that all the direct moral obligations we possess, including those we have with regard to the environment, are owed to our fellow human beings.
e) **Equity:** People living in the economically-advanced sections/ parts use greater amount of resources and energy per individual and also waste moreresources. This is at the cost of poor people who are resource-deprived.
f) **Animal rights:** The plants and animals that share the Earth with us too havea right to live and share the Earth's resources and living space. Animal welfare is relevant to environmental ethics because animals exist within thenatural environment and thus form part of environmentalists' concerns.

Measures to maintain environmental ethics

- The **"land ethic"** of Aldo Leopold: It demands that we stop treating the landas a mere object or resource. Land is not merely soil, instead, it is a fountain of energy, flowing through a circuit of soils, plants and animals.

- In order to preserve the relations within the land, Leopold claims that we must move towards a "land ethic", thereby granting moral standing to the land community itself, not just its individual members.

Deep ecology: There are eight principles or statements that are basic to deepecology:

- The well-being and flourishing of human and non-human life on Earth have value in themselves. These values are independent of the usefulness of the non-human world for human purposes.
- Richness and diversity of life forms contribute to the realization of these values and are also values in themselves.
- Humans have no right to reduce this richness and diversity except to satisfyvital needs.
- The flourishing of human life and cultures is compatible with a substantial decrease of the human population. The flourishing of non-human life requires such a decrease.
- Present human interference with the non-human world is excessive, and the situation is rapidly worsening.
- Policies must therefore be changed. These policies affect basic economic, technological and ideological structures.The resulting state of affairs will bedeeply different from the present.
- The ideological change is mainly that of appreciating life quality rather thanadhering to an increasingly higher standard of living.
- Those who subscribe to the foregoing points have an obligation directly orindirectly to try to implement the necessary changes.

The conservation ethics and traditional value systems: Since olden days, people have always valued mountains, rivers, forests, trees and several animals. Thus, much of nature was venerated and protected. Traditions held plants and animals as an important aspect of nature and were considered the basis of life-support systems and integral to bring about a harmonious life.

Virtue ethics: Virtue ethics is a way of thinking about how to behave well, which focuses on the character of moral agents and the nature of the good life. Virtue ethics is based on a positive view of human nature, one that takes into account that humans are strongly predisposed to recognize excellence in others (including non-human) whom they can take as role models and gain fulfillment from a life lived virtuously.

Conclusion
To cope with the issues of environmental ethics, human beings must reach some value consensus and cooperate with each other at the personal, national, regional, multinational and global levels. Global environmental protection depends on global governance. An environmental ethic is, therefore, typically a global ethic with a global perspective.

Nature as means or end
From the Latin natura (Gr. φύσις), a term with many related meanings in philosophy and with extensive applications in theology. Among philosophers it is commonly taken to mean the essence of a thing as this is the source of itsproperties or operations; more strictly, however, it is a primary and per se principle of motion and rest that is found in natural things as opposed to artifacts.It is sometimes used in the more restricted sense of human nature, for which meaning see man. Theologians use the term in opposition to grace or to supernature, particularly when discussing human nature, and in opposition to person, particularly in Trinitarian theology and Christology.

Since nature is the proper subject of the philosophy of nature, the major emphasis in this article is on nature as studied in natural philosophy. Topicstreated include the primary meanings of the concept, its development among the Greeks, modifications in it occasioned by the rise of modern science, an Aristotelian analysis of its meaning in natural philosophy, and various secondary meanings.

Primary Meanings. On Nature (Περὶ φύσεως) is the title under which the writings of the pre-Socratics have been handed down to posterity. Some doubt exists as towhat precisely was the first meaning, but it is generally admitted that at least an early and important use of the term φύσις was to designate the primordial stuffor underlying substratum persisting through all change. It is likely that the early Ionian philosophers imagined the world as developing in an orderly fashion from within, somewhat as a living being, and hence the primary substance would have been viewed, though indistinctly, as a source of activity. Thus φύσις was an intrinsic principle that accounted for the ceaseless change or becoming of things. Moreover, the very process of becoming, it seems, was itself called φύσις, a term that is etymologically related to φύω, to grow (cf. Lat. natura and nascor). Finally,at some later date the term was applied to the changing things themselves taken in their totality. This is possibly the most common sense of nature in modern usage and was probably the meaning of φύσις intended in the title Περί φύσεως.

Greek Development. The attempt of the Ionians of the 6th century b.c. to explain all becoming in terms of one material principle (e.g., water or air or fire) reached its logical conclusion in parmenides with the very denial of nature as process. For Parmenides all being must be one and exclude all nonbeing; as such it is perfectly immutable, and only as such is it knowable; all change is but sensory illusion. After Parmenides, there was an attempt to reconcile being, stable object of intellect, with the becoming of sensory experience. Fundamental reality remainedimmutable; it was, however, multiple: the four elements of empedocles; the"seeds," infinite in number, of anaxagoras; the atoms of Leucippus and democritus. These particles, in motion, combined and separated, and as such were principles of change and of a multiplicity of changing compounds. The atomists, with their homogeneous particles differing only in size and shape, interpreted all change in terms of movement in space ("void") and all sensible qualities, such as color, in terms of quantitative differences. They have been considered as forerunners to modern science. So too have the Pythagoreans, who, from the 6th century b.c., had been seeking to explain the world in the light of numbers.

The claim to find the ultimate explanation of reality in the random motions of corporeal elements, i.e., in nature and chance, was strongly opposed by plato. If nature means the primary source of becoming, what is truly nature, for him, couldonly be what is really first, and that is intelligence and art. Thus, with Plato, naturein the commonly accepted sense gave way to divine soul, and chance to divine direction (Laws 888E–899D). Finality, introduced as conscious design, was lodged in a principle (soul) distinct from the purely corporeal. Likewise, the intelligibility of sensible bodies was to be sought beyond them, in the changeless, purelyintelligible Ideas, of which they are imperfect imitations. The order of the sensibleworld could be seen, too, in terms of the a priori principles of pure number. As forthe changing imitations considered in themselves, of these there could be no science, but only a likely account.

Nature was reinstated as a true principle and a real source of explanation within the material universe by aristotle, who thus restored the philosophy of nature to the rank of a science (scientia). Aristotle continued the naturalist tradition of the pre-Socratics, his science being qualitative rather than mathematical, empirical rather than rationalist. It was far from being a mere return, however. After Plato there was form to be reckoned with. In Aristotle the natural world becomes intelligible in itself only because nature is identified with form in matter—with form now seen as the actuality of matter—even more properly than with matter itself. This form becomes the origin of activity, and matter, considered in itself, is reduced to a principle of mere passivity and receptivity. The realization of form in matter is the goal of natural activity, and although there are various combinations and separations of elements, it is always for the sake of a form; hence, the teleological view, as opposed to the mechanistic, remains dominant. But purpose is now found in the unconscious workings of form as well as in the conscious activities of rational soul. Although Aristotle conceived the natural universe as impregnated with and illuminated by form, for the ultimate explanation he too reached beyond nature. It is the desire to imitate the fully actual reality of Pure Form that, in the final analysis, explains all the ceaseless processes of nature.

Later Modifications. Both the Platonist and the Aristotelian view of nature extended into the Middle Ages. The early period was largely Neoplatonist, but in the 13th century the commentaries of St. albert the great and especially of St. thomas aquinas brought the Aristotelian doctrine of nature into the foreground.

In the 16th and 17th centuries, the rapid development of the new empirico- mathematical science was accompanied by an emphatic rejection of teleology: the conception of natures tending to ends. At first, change was Platonistically explained by an inherent, creative principle (natura naturans) animating and directing the world of nature (natura naturata)—terms that go back to the Latin translation of averroËs. Before long, however, under the influence of F. bacon, J. kepler, G. galilei, R. descartes, I. Newton, and others, the account became thoroughly mechanistic. With the rejection of the geocentric astronomy and the adoption of the universal law of gravitation, the qualitatively differentiated world of Aristotle gave place to a totally homogeneous universe. Purely qualitativedifferences, such as color, were considered to be functions of quantitative structure, and were soon dismissed as mere appearances to a sentient mind. Matter as potency was replaced by matter as mass and extension. All change was reduced to the motion of smallest parts in space; all causality, to prior events, i.e.,to prior motions, identical causes being followed by identical effects. The spontaneous activity of bodies gave way to the idea of force (impact, attraction) and the impulse toward ends was displaced by inertia, the disposition to remain always the same. Nature thus became, for the scientist and the philosopher of nature alike, a mechanical system of inert, homogeneous mass-bodies, situated in space and time, moved by external forces, and utterly devoid of all but quantitative properties.

In the 20th century, the adequacy of purely mechanistic principles of explanation has been seriously questioned for the biological and psychological sciences. Further, the scientific theories of evolution along with the physicist's conception of matter as energy have made more generally acceptable a view that was already to some degree in evidence in the philosophies of G. W. leibniz and G. W. F. hegel, viz, the idea of nature as internally active and engaged in process. This conception, to which in some instances has been added the idea of aim, has found philosophical expression in the works of such thinkers as H. bergson, S. alexander, and A.N. whitehead.

Aristotelian Analysis

A fuller presentation of the Aristotelian concept of nature, which has been generally adopted by scholastic thinkers, entails considering his definition of nature, nature as passive, nature as active, end as nature, and related concepts.

Definition of Nature

Aristotle (Phys. 192b 8–32) reached his definition of nature by way of a comparison of the things that exist by nature (viz, animals and their parts, plants and simple bodies) with those that exist by other causes, in particular by art. The former are seen to have within them a tendency to move, i.e., to change. The artifact as such has no such tendency. It has an inclination to change only accidentally insofar as it is made of a natural substance. Nature, then,concluded Aristotle, is the principle or cause of being moved and being at rest in that in which it is primarily, by reason of itself and not accidentally.

"Being moved" implies passivity. Strictly speaking, the principle that constitutes a thing as a mover is a nature only when the mover by its activity is itself moved. Also, motion here includes any kind of corporeal change, accidental or substantial; it excludes, however, spiritual operations, such as intellection. "Rest" implies the attainment of the end to which the movement was directed. The phrase "by reason of itself and not accidentally" excludes such cases as the doctor who cures himself. The art of medicine is, in this case, intrinsic but accidental to the one who is being cured, considered as such.

Nature as Passive
Nature, thus defined, was identified by Aristotle first (Phys. 193a 10–30) with matter taken as the substratum of change, i.e., as the passive, potential principle of being moved. In opposition to the pre-Socratics, Aristotle conceived of the ultimate material principle (primary matter) as being of itself bereft of all form, purely passive, pure potentiality. The matter, however, from which becoming proceeds, taken in its concrete existence, is always determined matter. The substantial form currently possessed, determining the matter in a particular way, always limits and defines matter's immediate potentialities. This is true both for the potency of primary matter for new substantial forms and more obviously for the accidental receptivities characteristic of any given being. Furthermore, since the form already possessed by the matter can be the source of certain activities as well, the matter on which a natural agent operates, just as it is never pure potency, need not be entirely passive. Its activity, in fact, may run contrary to the aim of the agent.

Nature as Active. It is especially with form, however, that Aristotle is concerned to identify nature (Phys. 193a 30-b 19). The ancients, not distinguishing the two principles of matter and form, had conceived of their primordial stuff as already determined and capable of activity. Once substantial form is disassociated from matter and recognized as principle of essential determination, source of activity, and end of generation, it becomes obvious that form more than matter deserves to be called nature. Nature, then, as active principle of movement, is substantial form. (Note that, although one says "Nature acts," strictly speaking it is the composite substance that acts in virtue of its nature.)

Form is the source of two different types of activity in nature. First and more obviously, form is the intrinsic source of the vital activities of the living body. As such, it is known as soul. And as such it is a nature, since, by these activities, the living being is itself moved. The soul, in fact, is the primary source of activity whereby one part of the heterogeneous composite moves another part. Moreover, all the vital activities are either movements themselves (e.g., growth) or essentially connected with movements (e.g., sensation) or they pre-suppose movements (e.g., intellection). The soul, however, is also the principle of generation, an activity that is essentially directed to another substance. But even as such, it is a nature, insofar as the movement takes place within the same species, if not within the same individual.

Second, form is the intrinsic source of the spontaneous activities characteristic of a given body, e.g., a chemical element. Inanimate bodies, not having differentiated parts, do not move themselves. Their activities, on the contrary, are directed to other bodies that in turn may affect them. The forms, in this case, satisfy the requirement of interiority in the definition of nature insofar as they are parts within a system of interrelated active and passive potencies.

In Aristotle's cosmology, however, there are certain movements of bodies that do arise from an intrinsic source (Phys. 254b 33–255b 31), as in his example of a body falling to the ground—a movement that does not appear to require an external agent. In this case, however, nature functions as a principle of activity without constituting the thing as a mover. The body, in fact, does not move itself, part moving part, as does the living thing. For Aristotle, rather, the movement arises spontaneously from the impulse of the form toward what is appropriate to it, which, in this instance, is a suitable environment.

End as Nature.
Whether a movement is natural or not cannot always be determined by sole reference to the active and passive principles. The determining factor is ultimately the end of becoming, and this too is nature.

Nature, in one sense, has been identified with the receptive and determinable principle. There are, however, in the world of nature, potencies that are not natural: the capacity of a natural body to take on an artificial form, or the capacity to be altered by some violent action. The natural potency differs from these in that it is a positive inclination to an act that perfects or fulfills the being so inclined, or else contributes to the good of the species or even to the good of the universe as a whole. The passive principle in nature, moreover, is normally related to a natural agent, through the activity of which it is brought to act. The activity of natural agents is accounted for by the tendency of the form in nature to actualize and bring to completion what is potential either within the same individual or beyond. The natural agent, then, actively tends to that good or perfection to which the potential principle is passively inclined. Furthermore, the natural agent, fixed in its species by its form, is also determined by this same principle with respect to specific goals, which it attains for the most part. Thus the acts to which it naturally directs matter by its activity are determinate acts. It is in this sense that a nature is said to act for an end. (Obviously, the end as a good is more easily recognized in the activity of living beings than it is in the workings of the inanimate world.) Consequently, it is the act or form, considered as the end to which a natural being tends either actively or passively, that determines whether a process is or is not in accordance with nature. And in those cases where the good of the whole is in opposition to the good of the individual (as in the case of corruption), it is the former that takes precedence as a determining principle.

The form considered as end, furthermore, is itself properly called nature. It is a principle of becoming, and one that, in the essential order of things, is prior even to the passive and active principles as such. It is also intrinsic, insofar as natural movements are for the sake of the form (finis cui) from which they spring. In fact, the natural form seeks its own preservation and development within the individual; it tends by generation to its own continuance, as a specific form, in other individuals; and ultimately, by realizing its specific ends, it contributes to the order and preservation of the universe, i.e., to the good of the whole of which it is a part.

Related Concepts. Art, violence, and chance are all active principles that presuppose nature but operate outside the order of natural finality.

Secondary Meanings

From nature meaning the form or essence that is the end of generation, the word has been extended to signify any essence whatsoever without reference at all to becoming. This sense, as applicable to any being, material or immaterial, is frequently conveyed by the terms definition and quiddity. A meaning somewhat closer to the original is that of essence as the source of any activity, whether of physical movement or of spiritual operation (De ente 1). This sense, too, is sometimes conveyed by the term substance.

Aldo-Leopold; land-ethics

When god-like Odysseus returned from the wars in Troy, he hanged all on one rope a dozen slave-girls of his household whom he- suspected of misbehavior during his absence. This hanging involved no question of propriety. The girls were property. The disposal of property was then, as now, a matter of expediency, not of right and wrong. Concepts of right and wrong were not lacking from Odysseus'. Greece: witness the fidelity of his wife through the long years before at last his black galleys clove the wine-dark seas for home. The ethical structure of that day covered wives, but had not yet been extended to human chattels. During the three thousand years which have since elapsed, ethical criteria have been extended to many fields of conduct, with corresponding shrinkages - in those judged by expediency only.

The Ethical Sequence

This extension of ethics, so far studied only by philosophers, is actually a process in ecological evolution. Its sequences may be described in ecological as well as in philosophical terms. An ethic, ecologically, is a limitation on freedom of action in the struggle for existence. An ethic, philosophically, is a differentiation of social from anti-social conduct. These are two definitions of one thing. The thing has its origin in the tendency of interdependent individuals or groups to evolve modes of co-operation. The ecologist calls these symbioses. Politics and economics are advanced symbioses in which the original free-for-all competition has been replaced, in part, by co-operative mechanisms with an ethical content. The complexity of co-operative mechanisms has increased with population density, and with the efficiency of tools. It was simpler, for example, to define the anti- social uses of sticks and stones in the days of the mastodons than of bullets and billboards in the age of motors. The first ethics dealt with the relation between individuals; the Mosaic Decalogue is an example. Later accretions dealt with the relation between the individual and society. The Golden Rule tries to integrate the individual to society; democracy to integrate social organization to the individual. There is as yet no ethic dealing with man's relation to land and to the animals and plants which grow upon it. Land, like Odysseus' slave-girls, is still property. The land-relation is still strictly economic, entailing privileges but not obligations.

The extension of ethics to this third element in human environment is, if I read the evidence correctly, an evolutionary possibility and an ecological necessity. It is the third step in a sequence. The first two have already been taken. Individual thinkers since the days of Ezekiel and Isaiah have asserted that the despoliation of land is not only inexpedient but wrong. Society, however, has not yet affirmed their belief. I regard the present conservation movement as the embryo of such an affirmation. An ethic may be regarded as a mode of guidance for meeting ecological situations so new or intricate, or involving such deferred reactions, that the path of social expediency is not discernible to the average individual. Animal instincts are modes of guidance for the individual in meeting such situations. Ethics are possibly a kind of community instinct in-the-making.

The Community Concept

All ethics so far evolved rest upon a single premise: that the individual is a member of a community of interdependent parts. His instincts prompt him to compete for his place in the community, but his ethics prompt him also to co- operate (perhaps in order that there may be a place to compete for). The land ethic simply enlarges the boundaries of the community to include soils, waters, plants, and animals, or collectively: the land.

This sounds simple: do we not already sing our love for and obligation to the land of the free and the home of the brave? Yes, but just what and whom do we love? Certainly not the soil, which we are sending helter-skelter downriver. Certainly not the waters, which we assume have no function except to turn turbines, float barges, and carry off sewage. Certainly not the plants, o£ which we exterminate whole communities without batting an eye. Certainly not the animals, of which we have already extirpated many of the largest and most beautiful species. A land ethic of course cannot prevent the. alteration, - management, and use of these `resources,' but it .does affirm their right to continued existence, and, at least in spots, their continued existence in a natural state.

In short, a land ethic changes the role of Homo sapiens from conqueror of the land-community- to plain member and citizen of it. It implies respect for his fellow=members, and also respect for the community as such. In human history, we have learned (I hope) that the conqueror role. is eventually self-defeating. Why? Because it is implicit in such a role that the conqueror knows, ex cathedra, just what makes the community clock tick; and just what and who is valuable, and what and who is worthless, in community life. It always turns out that he knows neither, and this is why his conquests eventually defeat themselves.

In the biotic community, a parallel situation exists. Abraham knew exactly what the land was for: it was to drip milk and honey into Abraham's mouth. At the present moment, the assurance with which we regard this assumption is inverse to the degree of our education: The ordinary citizen today assumes that science knows what- makes the community clock tick; the scientist is equally sure that he does not. He knows that the biotic mechanism is so complex that its workings may never be fully understood: That man is, in fact, only a member 'of a biotic team is shown by an ecological interpretation of history. Many historical events, hitherto explained solely in . terms of human enterprise, were actually biotic interactions between people and land. The characteristics of _ the land determined the facts quite as potently as the characteristics of the men who lived on it.

Consider, for example, the settlement of the Mississippi. valley.. In the years following the Revolution, three groups were contending for its control: the native Indian, the French and English traders, and the American settlers. Historians wonder what would have happened if the English at, Detroit had thrown a little more weight into the Indian side of those tipsy scales which decided the outcome of the colonial migration into the cane-lands of Kentucky. It is time now to ponder the fact that the caste-lands, when subjected to the particular mixture of forces represented by the cow, plow, fire, and axe of the pioneer, became bluegrass.

What if the plant succession inherent in this-dark and bloody ground had, under the impact of these forces, given us some worthless sedge, shrub, or weed? Would Boone and Kenton have held out? Would there have been any overflow into Ohio, Indiana, Illinois, and Missouri? Any Louisiana Purchase?- Any transcontinental union of new states? Any Civil War?

Kentucky was one sentence in the drama of history. We are commonly told what the human actors in this drama tried to do, but we are seldom told- that their success, or the lack of it, hung in large degree on the reaction of particular soils to the impact of the particular forces exerted by their occupancy. In the case of Kentucky, we do not even know where the bluegrass came from whether it is a native species, or a stowaway from Europe.

Contrast the cane-lands with what hindsight tells us about the Southwest, where the pioneers were equally brave, resourceful, and persevering.. The impact of occupancy here brought no bluegrass, or other plant fitted to withstand the bumps and buffetings of hard use. This region, when grazed by livestock, reverted through a series of more and more worthless grasses, shrubs, and weeds to a condition of unstable equilibrium. Each recession of plant types bred erosion; each increment to erosion bred a further recession of plants. The result today is a progressive and mutual deterioration, not only of plants and soils, but of the animal community subsisting thereon. The early settlers did not expect this: on the cienegas of New Mexico some even cut ditches to hasten it. So subtle has been its progress that few residents of the region are aware of it. It is quite invisible to the tourist who finds this wrecked landscape colorful and charming (as indeed it is, but it bears scant resemblance to what it was in 1848).

This same landscape was `developed' once before, but with quite different results. The Pueblo Indians settled the Southwest in pre-Colombian times, but they happened. not to be equipped with range live stock. Their civilization expired, but not because their land expired. In India, regions devoid of any sod- forming grass have been settled, apparently without wrecking the land, by the simple expedient of carrying the grass to the cow, rather than vice versa. (Was this the result of some deep wisdom, or was it just good luck? I do not know.) In short, the plant succession stared the course of history; the pioneer simply demonstrated, for good or ill, what successions inhered in the land. Is history taught in this spirit? It will be, once the concept of land as a community really penetrates our intellectual life.

The Ecological Conscience

Conservation is a state of harmony between men and land. Despite nearly a century of propaganda, conservation still proceeds at a snail's pace; progress still consists largely of letterhead pieties and convention oratory. On the back forty we still slip two steps backward for each forward stride. The usual answer to this dilemma is `more conservation education.' No one will debate this, but is it certain that only the volume of education needs stepping up? Is something lacking in the content as well? It is difficult to give a fair summary of its content in brief form, but, as I understand it, the content is substantially this: obey the law, vote right, join some organizations, and practice what conservation is profitable on your own land; the government will do the rest. Is not this formula too easy to accomplish anything worth while? It defines no right-or wrong, assigns no obligation, calls for no sacrifice, implies no change in the current philosophy of values. In respect of landuse, it urges only enlightened self-interest. Just how far will such education take us? An example will perhaps yield a partial answer.

By 1930 it had become clear to all except the ecologically blind that southwestern Wisconsin's topsoil was slipping seaward. In 1933 the farmers were told that if they would adopt certain remedial practices for five years, the public would donate CCC labor to install them, plus the necessary machinery and materials. The offer was widely accepted, but the practices were widely forgotten when the fiveyear contract period was up. The farmers continued only those practices that yielded an immediate and visible economic gain, for themselves.

This led to the idea that maybe farmers would learn more quickly if they themselves wrote the rules. Accordingly the Wisconsin Legislature in 1937 passed the Soil Conservation District Law. This said to farmers, in effect: We, the public, will furnish you free technical service and loan you specialized machinery, i f you ,wall unite your own rules for land-use. Each county „nay write its own rules, and these will have the force o f law. Nearly all the counties promptly organized to accept the proffered help, but after a decade of operation, no county has yet written a single rule. There has been visible progress in such practices as strip- cropping, pasture renovation, and soil liming, but none in fencing woodlots against grazing, and none in excluding plow and cow from steep slopes. The farmers, in short, have selected those remedial practices which were profitable anyhow, and ignored those which were profitable to the community, but not clearly profitable to themselves.

When one asks why no rules have been written, one is told that the community is not yet ready to support them; education must precede rules. But the education actually in progress makes no mention of obligations to land over and above those dictated by self-interest. The net result is that we have more education but less soil, fewer healthy woods, and as many floods as in 1937.

The puzzling aspect of such situations is that the existence of obligations over and above self-interest is taken for granted in such total community enterprises as thebetterment of roads, schools, churches, and baseball teams. Their existence is nottaken for granted, nor as yet seriously discussed, in bettering the behavior of the water that falls on the land, or in the preserving of the beauty or diversity of the farm landscape. Landuse ethics are still governed wholly by economic selfinterest,just as social ethics were a century ago.

To sum up: we asked the farmer to do what he conveniently could to save his soil,and he has done just that, and only that. The farmer who clears the woods off a 75 percent slope, turns his cows into the clearing, and dumps its rainfall, rocks, and soil into the community creek, is still (if otherwise decent) a respected member of society. If he puts lime on his fields and plants his crops on contour, heis still entitled to all the privileges and emoluments of his Soil Conservation District. The District is a beautiful piece of social machinery, but it is coughing along on two cylinders because we have been too timid, and too anxious for quicksuccess, to tell the farmer the true magnitude of his obligations. Obligations have no meaning without conscience, and - the problem we face is the extension of the social conscience from people to land.

No important change in ethics was ever accomplished without an internal change in our intellectual emphasis loyalties, affections, and convictions. The proof that- conservation has not yet touched these foundations of conduct lies in the factthat philosophy and religion have not yet heard of it. In our attempt to make conservation easy, we have made it trivial.

Substitutes for a Land Ethic
When the logic of history hungers for bread and we hand out a stone, we are at pains to explain how much the stone resembles bread. I now describe some of the stones which serve in lieu of a land ethic. One basic weakness in a conservation system based wholly on economic motives is that most members of the land community, have no economic value. Wildflowers and songbirds are examples. Of the 22,000 higher plants and animals native to Wisconsin, it isdoubtful whether more than 5 per cent can be sold, fed, eaten, or otherwise put to economic use. Yet members of the biotic community; and if (as I believe) its stability depends on its integrity, they are entitled to continuance. When one of these non-economic categories is threatened; and if we happen to love it, we invent subterfuges to give it economic importance. At the beginning of the century songbirds were supposed to be disappearing. Ornithologists jumped to the rescue with some distinctly shaky evidence to the effect that insects would eat us up if birds failed to control them. The evidence had to be economic inorder to be valid. It is painful to read these -circumlocutions today. We have no land ethic yet, but we have at least drawn nearer the point of admitting that birdsshould continue as a matter of biotic right, regardless of the presence or absence of economic advantage to us.

A parallel situation exists in respect of predatory mammals, raptorial birds, and fish-eating birds. Time was when biologists somewhat overworked the evidence that these creatures preserve the health of game by killing weaklings, or that theycontrol rodents for the farmer, or that they prey only on 'worthless' species. Here again, the evidence had to be economic in order to be valid. It is only in recent years that we hear the more honest argument that predators are members of thecommunity, and that no special interest has the right to exterminate them for the sake of a benefit, real or fancied, to itself. Unfortunately this enlightened view is still in the talk stage. In the field the extermination of predators goes merrily on: witness the impending erasure of the timber wolf by fiat of Congress, the Conservation Bureaus, and many state legislatures.

Some species of trees have been 'read out of the party by economics-minded foresters because they grow too slowly, or have too low a sale value to pay as - timber crops: white cedar, tamarack, cypress, beech, and hemlock are examples. In Europe, where forestry is ecologically - more advanced, the non-commercial tree species are recognized as members of the native forest community, to be preserved as such, within reason. Moreover some (like beech) have been found tohave a valuable function in building up soil fertility. The interdependence of the forest and its constituent tree species, ground flora, and fauna is taken for granted.

Lack of economic value is sometimes a character not only of species or groups,but of entire biotic communities: marshes, bogs, dunes, and 'deserts' are examples. Our formula in such cases is to relegate their conservation to government as refuges, monuments, or parks. The difficulty is that these communities are usually interspersed with more valuable private lands; the government cannot possibly own or control such scattered parcels. The net effect is that we have relegated some of them to ultimate extinction over large areas. If the private owner were ecologically minded, he would be proud to be the custodian of a reasonable proportion of such areas, which add diversity and beauty to his farm and to his community. In some instances, the assumed lack of profit in these 'waste' areas has proved to be wrong, but only after most of them had been done away with. The present scramble to reflood muskrat marshes is a case in point.

There is a clear tendency in American conservation to relegate to government all necessary jobs that private landowners fail to perform. Government ownership, operation, -subsidy, or regulation is now widely prevalent in forestry, range management, soil and watershed management, park and wilderness conservation, fisheries management, and migratory bird management, with more to come. Most of this growth in governmental conservation is proper and logical, some of it is inevitable. That I imply no disapproval of it is implicit in the fact that Ihave ,spent most of my life working for it. Nevertheless the question arises: What is the ultimate magnitude of the enterprise? Will the tax base carry its eventual ramifications? At what point will governmental conservation, like the mastodon, become handicapped by its own dimensions? The answer, if there is any, seems to be in a land ethic, or some other force which assigns more. obligation to the private landowner.

Industrial landowners and users, especially lumbermen and stockmen, are inclined to wail long and loudly about the extension of government ownership and regulation to land, but (with notable exceptions) they show little disposition to develop the only visible alternative: the voluntary practice of conservation on their own lands. When the private landowner is asked to perform some unprofitable act for the good of the community, he today assents only withoutstretched palm. If the act costs him cash this is fair and proper, but when it costs only fore-thought, open-mindedness, or time, the issue is at least debatable.The overwhelming growth of land-use subsidies in recent years must be ascribed, in large part, to the government's own agencies for conservation education: the land bureaus, the agricultural colleges,- and the extension services. As far as I can detect, no ethical obligation toward land is taught in these institutions.

To sum up: a system of conservation based solely on economic self-interest is hopelessly .lopsided. It tends to ignore, and thus eventually to eliminate, many elements in the land community that lack commercial value, but that are (as far as we know) essential to its healthy functioning. It assumes, falsely, I think, that the economic   -parts of the biotic cluck will function without the uneconomic parts. It tends to relegate to government many functions eventually too large, too complex, or too widely dispersed to be performed by government. An ethical obligation on the part of the private owner is the only visible remedy for these situations.

The Land Pyramid
An ethic to supplement and guide the economic relation to land presupposes the existence of some mental image of land as a biotic mechanism. We can be ethical only in relation to something we can see, feel, understand, love, or otherwise have faith in. The image commonly employed in conservation education is `the balance of nature.' For reasons too lengthy to detail here, this figure of speech * fails to describe accurately what little we know about the land mechanism.- A much truer image is the one employed in ecology: the biotic pyramid. I shallfirst sketch the pyramid as a symbol of develop some of its implications in terms of land-use.

Plants absorb energy from the sun. This energy flows through a circuit called the biota, which map be represented by a pyramid consisting of layers. The bottom layer is the soil. A plant layer rests on the soil, an insect layer on the plants, a bird and rodent layer on the insects, and so on up through various animal groups to the apex layer, which consists of the larger carnivores. The species of a layer are alike not in where they came from, or in what they look like, but rather in what they eat. Each successive layer depends on those below it for food and often for other services, and each in turn furnishes food and services to those above.Proceeding upward, each successive layer decreases in numerical abundance.Thus, for every carnivore there are hundreds of his prey, thousands of their prey, millions of insects, uncountable plants. The pyramidal form of the system reflects this numerical progression from apex to base. Man shares an intermediate layer with the bears, raccoons, and squirrels which eat both meat and vegetables.

The lines of dependency for food and other services are called food chains. Thus soil-oak-deer-Indian is a chain that has now been largely converted to soilcorn- cow-farmer. Each species, including ourselves, is a link in many chains. The deer eats a hundred plants other than oak, and the cow a hundred plants other than corn. Both; then, are links in a hundred chains. The pyramid is a tangle of chains so complex as to seem disorderly, yet the stability of the system proves it to be a highly organized structure. Its functioning depends on the cooperation and competition of its diverse parts.

In the beginning; the pyramid of life was low and squat; the food chains short andsimple. Evolution has added layer after layer, link after link. Man is one of thousands of accretions to the height and complexity of the pyramid. Science has given us many doubts, .but it has given us at least one certainty: the trend ; of evolution .is to elaborate and diversify the biota. Land, then, is not merely soil; itis a fountain of energy flowing through a circuit of soils, plants, and animals. Food chains are the living channels which conduct energy upward; death and decay return it to the. soil. The circuit is not closed; some energy is dissipated in decay, some is added by absorption from the air, some is stored in soils, peats and longlived forests; but it is a sustained circuit, like a slowly augmented revolving fund of life. There is always a net loss by downhill wash, but this is normally small and offset by the decay of rocks. It is deposited in the ocean and, in the course of geological time, raised to form new lands and new pyramids.

The velocity and character of the upward flow of energy depend on the complex structure of the plant and animal community, much as the upward flow of sap in atree depends on its complex cellular organization. Without this complexity, normal circulation would presumably not occur. Structure means the characteristic numbers, as well as the characteristic kinds and functions, of the component species. This interdependence between the .complex structure of the land and its smooth functioning as -an, energy unit is one of its basic attributes.

When a change occurs in one part: of the circuit, may other parts must adjust themselves to it. Change does not . necessarily obstruct or divert the flow of energy; evolution is a long series of self-induced changes, the net result of which has been to elaborate the flow, mechanism, and to lengthen. the circuit. Evolutionary changes; however, are usually slow and local. Man's invention of tools has enabled him to make changes of unprecedented violence, rapidity, and scope.

One change is in the composition of floras and faunas. The larger predators are lopped off the apex of the pyramid; food chains, for the first time in history, become shorter rather than longer. Domesticated species from other lands are substituted for wild ones, and wild ones are moved to new habitats. In this world-wide pooling of faunas and floras, some species get out of bounds as pests and diseases, others are, extinguished. Such effects are seldom intended or foreseen; they represent unperfected and often untraceable readjustments in the structure.Agricultural science is largely a race between the emergence of new pests and theemergence of new techniques for their control.

Another change touches the flow of energy through plants and `animals and its return to the soil. Fertility is the ability of soil to receive, store, and release energy. Agriculture, by overdrafts on the soil, or by too radical a substitution of domestic for native species in the superstructure; may derange the channels of flow or deplete storage. Soils depleted of their storage, or of the organic matter which anchors it, wash away faster than they form. This is erosion. Waters, like soil; are part of the energy circuit. Industry, by polluting waters or obstructing them with dams, may exclude the plants and -animals necessary to keep energy incirculation.

Transportation brings about another basic change: the plants or animals grown in one region are now consumed and returned to-the soil in another. Transportationtaps the energy stored in rocks, and in the air, and uses it elsewhere; thus we fertilize the garden with nitrogen gleaned by the guano birds from the fishes of seas on the other side of the Equator. Thus the formerly localized and self- contained circuits are pooled on a world-wide scale.

The process of altering the pyramid for human occupation releases stored energy,and this often gives rise, during the pioneering period; to a deceptive exuberance of plant and animal life, both wild and tame. These releases of biotic capital tend to becloud or postpone the penalties of violence.

This thumbnail sketch of land as an energy circuit conveys three basic ideas:

1. That land is not merely soil.
2. That the native plants and animals kept the energy circuit open; others may ormay not.
3. That man-made changes are of -a different order than evolutionary changes,and have effects more comprehensive than is intended or foreseen.

These ideas, 'collectively; raise two- basic issues: Can the land adjust itself to the new order? Can the desired alterations be accomplished with less violence? Biotas seem to differ in their capacity . to sustain violent conversion. Western Europe, for example, carries- a far different pyramid than Caesar found there. Some large animals are lost; swampy forests have become meadows or plowland;many new plants and animals are introduced, some of which escape as pests; the remaining natives are greatly changed in distribution and abundance. Yet the soil is still there and, with the help of imported nutrients, still fertile; the waters flow normally; the new structure seems to function and to persist. There is no visible stoppage or derangement of the circuit.

Western Europe, then, has a resistant biota. Its inner processes are tough, elastic, resistant to strain. No matter how violent the alterations, the pyramid, so far, has developed some new modus vivendi which preserves its habitability for man, and for most of the other natives. Japan seems to present another instance of radical conversion without disorganization. Most other civilized regions, and some as yet barely touched by civilization, display various stages of disorganization, varying from initial symptoms to advanced wastage: In Asia Minor and North Africa diagnosis is confused by climatic changes, which may have been either the cause or the effect of advanced wastage. In the United States the degree of disorganization varies locally; it is worst in the Southwest, the Ozarks, and parts ofthe South, and least in New England and the Northwest. Better land-uses may stillarrest it in the less :advanced regions. In parts of Mexico, South America, South Africa, and Australia a violent and accelerating wastage is in progress, but I cannotassess the prospects.

This almost world-wide display of disorganization in the land seems to be similar to disease in an animal, except that it never culminates in complete disorganization or death. The land _ recovers, but at some reduced level of complexity, and with a reduced carrying capacity for people, plants, and animals: Many biotas currently regarded as lands of opportunity' are in fact already subsisting on exploitative agriculture, i.e. they have already exceeded their sustained carrying capacity. Most of South America is overpopulated in this sense.

In arid regions we attempt to offset the process of wastage by reclamation, but it is only too evident that the prospective longevity of reclamation projects is often short. In our own West, the best of them may not last a century.

The combined evidence of history and ecology seems to support one general deduction: the less violent the man-made changes, the greater the probability of successful readjustment in the pyramid. Violence, in turn, varies with human population density; a dense population requires a more violent conversion. In thisrespect, North America has a better chance for permanence than Europe, if she can contrive to limit her density.

This deduction runs counter to our current philosophy, which assumes that because a small increase in density enriched human life, that an indefinite increase will enrich it indefinitely. Ecology knows of no density relationship that holds for indefinitely wide limits. All gains from density are subject to a law of diminishing returns.

Whatever may be the equation for men and land, it is improbable that we as yet know all its terms. Recent discoveries in mineral and vitamin nutrition reveal unsuspected dependencies in the up-circuit: incredibly minute quantities of certain substances determine the value of soils to plants, of plants to animals. What of the down-circuit? What of the vanishing species, the preservation of which we now regard as an esthetic luxury? They helped build the soil; in what unsuspected ways may they be essential to its maintenance? Professor Weaver proposes that we use prairie flowers to reflocculate the wasting soils of the dust bowl; who knows for what purpose cranes and condors, otters and grizzlies may some day be used?

Land Health and the A-B Cleavage

A land, ethic, then, reflects the existence of an ecological conscience, and this in turn reflects a conviction of individual responsibility for the -health of 'the land. Health is the capacity of . the land for self-renewal. Conservation is our effort to understand and preserve this capacity. Conservationists are notorious for their dissensions. Superficially these seem to add up to mere confusion, but a more careful scrutiny reveals a single plane of cleavage common to many specialized fields. In each field one group (A) regards the land as soil, and its function as commodity-production; another group (B) regards the land as a biota, and its. function as something broader. How much broader is admittedly in a state of doubt and confusion. In my own field, forestry, group A is quite content to grow trees like cabbages, with cellulose as the sic forest commodity. It feels no inhibition against violence; its ideology is agronomic. Group B, on the other hand, sees forestry as fundamentally different from agronomy because it, employs natural species, and manages a natural environment rather than creating an artificial one. Group B prefers natural reproduction on principle. It worries on biotic as well as economic grounds about the loss of species like chestnut, and the threatened lugs of the white pines. It worries about a whole series of secondary forest Functions: wildlife, recreation, watersheds, wilderness areas. To my mind, Group B feels the stirrings of an ecological conscience.

In the wildlife field, a parallel cleavage exists. For Group A the basic commodities are sport and meat; the yardsticks of production are ciphers of take in pheasants and trout. Artificial propagation is acceptable as a permanent as well as a temporary recourseif its unit costs permit. Group B, on the other hand, worries about a whole series of biotic side-issues. What is the cast in predators of producing a game crop? Should we have further recourse to exotics? How can management restore the shrinking species, like prairie grouse, already hopeless as shootable game? How can management restore the threatened ratites, like trumpeter-swan and whooping crane? Can management principles be extended to wildflowers? Here again it is dear to me that we have the same A-B cleavage as in forestry.

In the larger field of agriculture I am less competent to speak, but there seem to be somewhat parallel cleavages. Scientific agriculture was actively developing before ecology was born, hence a slower. penetration of ecological concepts might be expected. Moreover the farmer, by the very nature of his techniques, must modify the biota more radically than the forester or the wildlife manager. Nevertheless, there are many discontents in agriculture which seem to add up toa new vision of biotic farming.'

Perhaps the most important of these is the new evidence that poundage ortonnage is no measure of the food-value of farm crops; the products of fertile soil may be qualitatively as well as quantitatively superior. We can bolster poundage from depleted soils by pouring on imported fertility, but we are riot necessarily bolstering food-value. The possible ultimate ramifications of this idea are so immense that I must leave their exposition to abler pens.

The discontent that labels itself `organic farming,' while bearing some of the earmarks of a cult, is nevertheless biotic in its direction, particularly in its insistence on the importance of soil flora and fauna.

The ecological fundamentals of agriculture are just as poorly known to the public as in other fields of land-use. For example, few educated people realize that the marvelous advances in technique made during recent decades are improvements in the pump, rather than the well. Acre for acre, they have barely sufficed to offset the sinking level of fertility.

In all of these cleavages, we see repeated the same basic paradoxes: man the conqueror versus man the biotic citizen; science the sharpener of his sword versus science the searchlight on his universe; land the slave and servant versus land the collective organism. Robinson's injunction to Tristram may well be applied, at this juncture, to Homo Sapiens as a species in geological time
Whether you will or not You are a King, Tristram, for you are one Of the time- tested few that leave the world, When they are gone, not the same place it was. Mark what you leave.

The Outlook
It is inconceivable to me that an ethical relation to land can exist without love, respect, and admiration for land, and a high regard for its value. By value, I of course men something far broader than mere economic value; I mean value in thephilosophical sense. Perhaps the most serious obstacle impeding the. evolution of a land ethic is the fact that our educa headed away from, rather than toward, an intense consciousness of land. Your true modem is separated from the land by many middlemen, and by innumerable physical gadgets. He has no vital relation to it; to him it is the space between citieson which crops grow. Turn him loose for a day on the land, and if the spot does not happen to be a golf links or a `scenic' area, he is bored stiff. If crops could be raised by hydroponics instead of farming, it would suit him very well. Synthetic substitutes for wood, leather, wool, and other natural land products suit him better than the originals. In short, land is something he has `outgrown.'

Almost equally serious as an obstacle to a land ethic is the attitude of the farmer for whom the land is still an adversary, or a taskmaster that keeps him in slavery. Theoretically, the mechanization of farming ought to cut the farmer's chains, but whether it really does is debatable. One of the requisites for an ecological comprehension of land is an understandingof ecology, and this is by no means co-extensive with `education'; in fact, much higher education seems deliberately to avoid ecological concepts. An understanding of ecology does not necessarily originate in courses bearing ecological labels; it is quite as likely to be labeled geography, botany, agronomy, history, or economics. This is as it should be, but whatever the label, ecological training is scarce.

The case for a land ethic would appear hopeless but for the minority which is in obvious revolt against these `modern' trends.

The `key-log' which must be moved to release the evolutionary process for an ethic is simply this: quit thinking about decent land-use as solely an economic problem. Examine. each question in terms of what is ethically and esthetically right, as well as what is economically expedient. A thing is right when it tends to preserve the integrity, stability, and beauty of the biotic community. It is wrong when it tends otherwise.

It of course goes without saying that economic feasibility limits the tether of what can or cannot be done for land. It always has and it always will. The fallacy the economic determinists have tied around our collective neck, and which we now need to cast off, is the belief that economics determines all landuse. This is simply not true. An innumerable host of actions and attitudes, comprising perhaps the bulk of all land relations, is determined by the land-users' tastes and predilections, rather than by his purse. The bulk of all land relations hinges on investments of time, forethought, skill, and faith rather than on investments of cash. As a land-user thinketh, so is he.

I -have purposely presented the land ethic as a product of social evolution because nothing so important as an ethic is ever 'written.' Only the most superficial student of history supposes that Moses 'wrote' the Decalogue; it evolved in the minds of a thinking community, and Moses wrote a tentative summary of it for a 'seminar.' We say tentative because evolution never stops.

The evolution of a land ethic is an intellectual as well as emotional process. Conservation is paved with good intentions which prove to be futile, or even dangerous, because they are devoid of critical understanding either of the land, or of economic landuse. We think it is a truism that as the ethical frontier advances from the individual to the community, its intellectual content increases.
The mechanism of operation is the same fur any ethic: social approbation for right actions: social disapproval for wrong actions. By and large, our present problem is one of attitudes and implements. We are remodeling the AI with a steam-shovel, and we are proud of our yardage. We
shall hardly relinquish the shovel, which after--all has many good points, but we are in need of gentler and more objective criteria for its successful use.

Deep Ecology
"Deep ecology" was born in Scandinavia, the result of discussions between Næss and his colleagues Sigmund Kvaløy and Nils Faarlund; for a historical survey and commentary on the development of deep ecology). All three shared a passion for the great mountains. On a visit to the Himalayas, they became impressed with aspects of "Sherpa culture" particularly when they found that their Sherpa guides regarded certain mountains as sacred and accordingly would not venture onto them. Subsequently, Næss formulated a position which extended the reverence the three Norwegians and the Sherpas felt for mountains to other natural things in general.

The "shallow ecology movement", as Næss (1973) calls it, is the "fight against pollution and resource depletion", the central objective of which is "the health and affluence of people in the developed countries." The "deep ecology movement", in contrast, endorses "biospheric egalitarianism", the view that all living things are alike in having value in their own right, independent of their usefulness to others. The deep ecologist respects this intrinsic value, taking care, for example, when walking on the mountainside not to cause unnecessary damage to the plants.

Inspired by Spinoza's metaphysics, another key feature of Næss's deep ecology is the rejection of atomistic individualism. The idea that a human being is such an individual possessing a separate essence, Næss argues, radically separates the human self from the rest of the world. To make such a separation not only leads to selfishness towards other people, but also induces human selfishness towards nature. As a counter to egoism at both the individual and species level, Næss proposes the adoption of an alternative relational "total-field image" of the world. According to this relationalism, organisms (human or otherwise) are best understood as "knots" in the biospherical net. The identity of a living thing is essentially constituted by its relations to other things in the world, especially its ecological relations to other living things. If people conceptualise themselves and the world in relational terms, the deep ecologists argue, then people will take better care of nature and the world in general.

As developed by Næss and others, the position also came to focus on the possibility of the identification of the human ego with nature. The idea is, briefly, that by identifying with nature We can enlarge the boundaries of the self beyond my skin. My larger—ecological—Self (the capital "S" emphasizes that we are something larger than our body and consciousness), deserves respect as well. To respect and to care for my Self is also to respect and to care for the natural environment, which is actually part of me and with which I should identify. "Self- realization", in other words, is the reconnection of the shriveled human individual with the wider natural environment. Næss maintains that the deep satisfaction that we receive from identification with nature and close partnership with other forms of life in nature contributes significantly to our life quality. (One clear historical antecedent to this kind of nature spiritualism is the romanticism of Jean-Jacques Rousseau as expressed in his last work, the Reveries of the Solitary Walker).

When Næss's view crossed the Atlantic, it was sometimes merged with ideas emerging from Leopold's land ethic;. But Næss—wary of the apparent totalitarian political implications of Leopold's position that individual interests and well-being should be subordinated to the holistic good of the earth's biotic community—has always taken care to distance himself from advocating any sort of "land ethic". Some critics have argued that Næss's deep ecology is no more than an extended social-democratic version of utilitarianism, which counts human interests in the same calculation alongside the interests of all natural things (e.g., trees, wolves, bears, rivers, forests and mountains) in the natural environment. However, Næss failed to explain in any detail how to make sense of the idea that oysters or barnacles, termites or bacteria could have interests of any morally relevant sort at all. Without an account of this, Næss's early "biospheric egalitarianism"—that all living things whatsoever had a similar right to live and flourish—was an indeterminate principle in practical terms. It also remains unclear in what sense rivers, mountains and forests can be regarded as possessors of any kind of interests. This is an issue on which Næss always remained elusive.

Biospheric egalitarianism was modified in the 1980s to the weaker claim that the flourishing of both human and non-human life have value in themselves. At the same time, Næss declared that his own favoured ecological philosophy— "Ecosophy T", as he called it after his Tvergastein mountain cabin—was only one of several possible foundations for an environmental ethic. Deep ecology ceased to be a specific doctrine, but instead became a "platform", of eight simple points, on which Næss hoped all deep green thinkers could agree. The platform was conceived as establishing a middle ground, between underlying philosophical orientations, whether Christian, Buddhist, Daoist, process philosophy, or whatever, and the practical principles for action in specific situations, principles generated from the underlying philosophies. Thus the deep ecological movement became explicitly pluralist.

While Næss's Ecosophy T sees human Self-realization as a solution to the environmental crises resulting from human selfishness and exploitation of nature,some of the followers of the deep ecology platform in the United States and Australia further argue that the expansion of the human self to include non- human nature is supported by the Copenhagen interpretation of quantum theory,which is said to have dissolved the boundaries between the observer and the observed. These "relationalist" developments of deep ecology are, however, criticized by some feminist theorists. The idea of nature as part of oneself, one might argue, could justify the continued exploitation of nature instead. For one is presumably more entitled to treat oneself in whatever ways one likes than to treat another independent agent in whatever ways one likes. According to some feminist critics, the deep ecological theory of the "expanded self" is in effect a disguised form of human colonialism, unable to give nature its due as a genuine "other" independent of human interest and purposes.

Meanwhile, some third-world critics accused deep ecology of being elitist in its attempts to preserve wilderness experiences for only a select group of economically and socio-politically well-off people. The Indian writer Ramachandra.

Guha (1989, 1999) for instance, depicts the activities of many western-based conservation groups as a new form of cultural imperialism, aimed at securing converts to conservationism (cf. Bookchin 1987 and Brennan 1998a). "Green missionaries", as Guha calls them, represent a movement aimed at further dispossessing the world's poor and indigenous people. "Putting deep ecology in its place," he writes, "is to recognize that the trends it derides as "shallow" ecology might in fact be varieties of environmentalism that are more apposite, more representative and more popular in the countries of the South." Although Næss himself repudiates suggestions that deep ecology is committed to any imperialism. Guha's criticism raises important questions about the application of deep ecological principles in different social, economic and cultural contexts.Finally, in other critiques, deep ecology is portrayed as having an inconsistent utopian vision.

Peter Singer; Animal Rights
Moral philosopher and Princeton professor Peter Singer described what he called a "momentous revolution in thinking" regarding animal welfare during a talk in the Ames Courtroom at the Harvard Law School on Friday.

During the event, entitled "Ethics and Animals: Where are We Now," Singer described the economically-driven processes of factory farming and mass-fishing and the laws that the European Union and United Kingdom have implemented in the past decade to strictly regulate the treatment of animals during those practices.

But, Singer cautioned, while the world has come a long way, outlooks surroundingthe ethics and the treatment of animals have not been pushed as far as he thinks they could.
"Animals have interests," Singer said. "When these are similar to ours, or their pain is on a similar level, why give them less consideration?"

Singer cited the Bible, in which God grants the humans dominion over the animals, as the first documentation of humanity's obligation to animals. He said that he thinks "dominion" has come to be interpreted as the right "to do as we will," rather than as responsible stewardship.

"The question is not 'Can they reason?' nor 'Can they talk?' but 'Can they suffer?'" said Singer, quoting the logic used by nineteenth-century philosopher Jeremy Bentham, Bentham's ideology has also been applied to discussions about slaves, infants, and those with cognitive disabilities.

The case for animal consciousness and the need to acknowledge their interests, Singer said, is evidenced by the similarities between animals and humans— anatomically, physiologically, and behaviorally. He also pointed to the shared evolutionary history between the two. "We are animals," Singer said, citing Darwin's theory of evolution.

Singer, a professor of bioethics at Princeton and the University of Melbourne, is the author of the controversial book Animal Liberation, which asserts that animals' interests should be given equal weight to those of humans. The book drew criticism upon its release in 1975.

Friday's talk was part of a series sponsored by the Petrie-Flom Center for Health Law Policy, Biotechnology, and Bioethics at the Law School. Singer also spoke laterin the day in the Science Center about effective altruism—a utilitarian stance on how best to affect change in the world.

"If God were a utilitarian, Singer would be his patron saint," Law School professor and Petrie-Flom Center co-director Glenn Cohen said in his introduction.

Medical-Ethics: Surrogacy
"Surrogacy is often thought to be a 'treatment' option for the infertile or an alternative to adoption, and so to be celebrated in fulfilling people's desires to be parents. However, surrogacy also brings a wealth of more complex ethical issues around gender, labour, payment, exploitation and inequality."

Payment
Take the issue of payment: surrogacy involves literal labour (physical and often emotional effort in both gestating and birthing). However, many see it as distinct from labour (working in a factory or teaching a class). This raises an ethical question around whether surrogacy is different from other kinds of paid work and, if it isn't, shouldn't we remunerate surrogates?

Some philosophers argue that surrogacy is unique when compared to other work.For instance, they claim that women are intimately connected to their reproductive capacities and bodies (so pregnancy and birth are special and shouldnot be bought), or that being pregnant requires an unusual time commitment (unlike other kinds of work, the woman works for 24 hours a day, seven days a week, for nine months).

Others argue that there is equivalence to traditional work. Various occupations demand control over the body (ballerinas and astronauts are heavily controlled in what they can eat and how much they exercise, just as surrogates are) andlongevity of work (writing a book can take longer than gestating and delivering a baby). All this work should be paid, so the argument goes.

Gender
Ethics also come into play when thinking about the gendered nature of surrogacy and intended parenting. Biologically, the surrogate has to be someone with the capacity to gestate and give birth – usually a woman. As gendered labour, surrogacy triggers important feminist concerns, such as about bodily autonomy, vulnerability, inequality and rights.

For example, whether women who are surrogates maintain autonomy over their body when they are carrying a foetus for another individual or couple, or when decisions are being made about what happens to that foetus when there is disagreement. I think about the complexity of these sorts of questions and defendthe importance of protecting and promoting women's autonomy in my broader work on feminist conceptions of autonomy.

Intended parenthood raises feminist concerns too, such as on gendered roles and expectations. This includes whether women in particular feel that being mothersis critical to being 'proper' women (and hence why they might pursue surrogacy if they cannot carry their own children). Likewise, women might feel breastfeedingis what 'real' mothers (and women) do (and why intended mothers – ie, women who are not pregnant – might want to induce lactation).

Interestingly, at SUK's annual conference in September, it was noted that lactation can be induced in men using a similar process as for non-pregnantwomen. (It has been used for a transgender woman who wanted to breastfeed recently too). For feminists worried about unequal gender roles in parenting in general, this could be further ammunition for dispelling myths about women as 'natural' carers because of their biological capacities.

Exploitation
A final ethical issue to mention is exploitation. The UK, Ukraine, US, Australia and India have different regulations about surrogacy. Some countries see the surrogate, while others the intended mother, as the legitimate mother. Some favour altruistic forms of surrogacy, while others allow commercial forms. Some countries give parental rights to intended parents before or at the birth of the child, while others only after six weeks.

There are good reasons to worry about a country-specific approach to surrogacy, as outlined in the recent. In particular, the country-specific approach opens up the potential to exploit legal loopholes, intended parents, and, ultimately those doing the majority of the labour – surrogates.

Despite the inevitable difficulties of securing global agreement, concerns about exploitation – of all parties, but especially the most vulnerable – provides a significant reason to push for a global approach to surrogacy arrangements.

These are just three ethical puzzles of surrogacy. All of the themes, and more beyond, require careful consideration since what we think about each is not just philosophically intriguing but is likely to have implications for how we believe our practice, laws and policy should be shaped. As the UK is currently reviewing its legislation on surrogacy, giving attentive thought to these issues is a particularly timely demand on all of us.

Social, ethical, medical & legal aspects of surrogacy:
An Indian Scenario
On examining the thousands of years old records of Indian Vedic literature and based on the discoveries of today's science dealing with molecules, genes and DNA it appears that the motherhood is an instinct driven physiological phenomena. Instinct of motherhood is the most powerful desire that exists in all the living creatures that include all animals and humans. According to ancient Indian philosophy the biological purpose of life is to propagate once own traits (genes) and all living creatures are here on a transition phase to pass their own traits (genes) to the next generation. Propagation is the ultimate purpose of any species,

therefore, birth of an offspring is always dependent on the factors that lead to high chances of survival of the offspring. For example, birds migrate thousands of kilometers to find out suitable place where environment can support the high chances of survival of their offsprings. In the Canadian Inuit Community which is 300 miles north of Arctic Circle, the seasonality was reported till 1970. But due to modernization and decline of traditional life-style the seasonality in this community has not been reported in the later years.

Infertility is generally known as a social stigma in India. It is hypothesized that the agony and trauma of infertility is best felt and described by the infertile couples themselves. Though, infertility does not claim the life of an individual but it inflicts devastating influence on life of an individual for not fulfilling the biological role of parenthood for no fault of his or her own. It is also known that in general, Indian society has got a very stable family structure, strong desire for children and particularly for son to carry forth the lineage or Vansh. With the enormous advances in the field of medicine, the infertility can now be treated using the new medical technologies collectively called as Assisted Reproductive Technology (ART) such as in vitro fertilization (IVF) or intracytoplasmic sperm injection.

(ICSI), etc. The birth of the world's first child, Louise Brown on July 25, 1978, through the technique of in vitro fertilization was a path-breaking step in control of infertility; and is considered as one of the most important medical advances of the last century. In October 1978, Dr Subhash Mukherjee, Kolkata (India) announced the birth of country's first test tube baby. Dr Mukherjee and his team used the cryopreserved embryo.

There are different types of infertility and in some cases it would be physically or medically impossible/ undesirable to carry a baby to term and hence, to fulfill the desire of such infertile couple to have a child, the surrogacy comes as an important option.

Surrogacy
In Latin "Surrogatus" means a substitute i.e. a person appointed to act in the place of another. As per the Black's Law Dictionary surrogacy means the process of carrying and delivering a child for another person. The New Encyclopedia Britannica defines surrogacy as a practice in which a woman bears a child for a couple unable to produce children in the usual way. According to Warnock Report (1984) HF&E, surrogacy is the practice whereby one woman carries a child for another with the intension that the child should be handed over after birth.

There are two types of surrogacy practices prevailing in India: (i) Traditional/Natural/Partial surrogacy; and (ii) Gestational surrogacy.

Like in other countries, in India also, the following two types of surrogacy arrangements are being practiced:

Altruistic surrogacy: Where the surrogate mother receives no financial rewards for her pregnancy or the relinquishment of the child to the genetic parents except necessary medical expenses.
Commercial surrogacy: Where the surrogate mother is paid over and above the necessary medical expenses.

Surrogacy is the union of science, society, services and person that make it a reality. Surrogacy leads to a win-win situation for both the infertile couple and the surrogate mother. The infertile couple is able to fulfill their most important desire and the surrogate mother receives the suitable reward.

To give a womb for rent means to nurture the fertilized egg of another couple in your womb and give birth to the child with a specific intention, the intention here being either money, or service, or because of altruistic reasons.

Bhadaraka has described the following misconceptions regarding a surrogate mother:

1.	She is not the genetic mother of the child whom she nurtures and gives birth to.
2.	She is not the wife of the father of the child to whom she gives birth.
3.	This is a scientific idea, a scientific process. There is no need for any physical contact.
4.	She is not an asocial woman.
5.	This is not an illegal practice.
6.	She is not forced into this. She herself decides whether she wants to become a surrogate mother or not.
7.	She has no claim or rights over the child that is born.
8.	"This is my child", "this child is my inheritance" - she cannot articulate such thoughts, because of social, scientific and legal restrictions.
9.	She is not a woman who sells children.
10.	She is not responsible for the child (once the child is born).
11.	Surrogacy is a mutually beneficial concept of providing services.

It is necessary to mention here that the couple's insistence does not agree with what science believes. It does not matter as to which religion the surrogate belongs, as the child is genetically of the couple. Religion is interpreted according to the conditions, education, time and the circumstances.

Surrogacy is a social act of highest level of service which is scientific and brims with goodwill. A person's opinion based on a lack of information should not harm others. Like medicine is prescribed for treatment of a disorder, in the same way surrogacy is also a method of treatment.

Bhadaraka reported that the majority of the Indian society considered surrogate mother as an amalgam of religion, culture and science with following noble services: (i) She shows a strong inclination to society by doing something novel, (ii) She abolishes the stigma of infertility from the society, (iii) She fulfils her duty by doing something worthwhile for the society, and (iv) She is an example of a model woman in society.

As per the proposed draft Assisted Reproductive Technology (Regulation) Bill the surrogacy and related terms are defined in the following ways: (i) Surrogacy means an arrangement in which a woman agrees to a pregnancy, achieved through assisted reproductive technology, in which neither of the gametes belong to her or her husband, with the intention to carry it to term and hand over the child to the person or persons for whom she is acting as a surrogate; (ii) Surrogate mother means a woman who agrees to have an embryo generated from the sperm of a man who is not her husband and the oocyte of another woman, implanted in her to carry the pregnancy to full term and deliver the child to its biological parents; and (iii) Surrogacy agreement means a contract between the persons availing of assisted reproductive technology and the surrogate mother.

Issues related with surrogacy

Surrogacy, by ART, should be considered only for those infertile women for whom it would be physically or medically impossible/ undesirable to carry a baby to the term. Surrogate mother should sign an agreement with the commissioning couple which shall have legal bindings on both the parties. Before signing the agreement, the written consent of her spouse shall be required. A woman seeking or agreeing to act as a surrogate shall be medically tested for diseases such as sexually transmitted diseases or otherwise, as may be necessary, and all other communicable diseases which may endanger the health of the child or children, and must declare in writing that she has not received a blood transfusion or a blood product in the last six months. The commissioning parent(s) shall ensure that the surrogate and the child or children she delivers are appropriately insured until the time the child is handed over to the commissioning parent(s) or any other person as per the agreement and till the surrogate is free of all health complications arising out of surrogacy. Surrogate mother must register as a patient in her own name in the hospital after signing the appropriate agreement. While registering, the surrogate mother must mention that she is a surrogate mother and should provide all the necessary information about the commissioning parents. Surrogate mother should not use or register in the name of the commissioning couple for whom she is acting as surrogate as this would pose legal issues, particularly in the untoward event of maternal death.

The birth certificate shall be in the name of the commissioning parents. The ART clinic should also provide a certificate to the commissioning parents giving the name and address of the surrogate mother. All the expenses of surrogate mother during the period of pregnancy and postnatal care relating to pregnancy should be borne by the commissioning couple. The surrogate mother would also be entitled a monitory compensation from the commissioning couple for agreeing to act as a surrogate. The exact value of the compensation should be decided by discussion between the commissioning couple. and the prospective surrogate mother or an appropriate formula may be developed by the Government to calculate the minimum compensation to be paid to the surrogate mother. A surrogate mother should never donate her own oocyte to the commissioning couple. Surrogate mother as well as the donor shall relinquish all parental rights related with the offsprings in writing.

Background of proposed draft ART (Regulation) Bill

After the birth of the first scientifically well documented test tube baby in 1986 in India, there was mushrooming of IVF clinics in the country. The services offered by some of these IVF clinics were questionable. The reason for this was a lack of ART guidelines as well as legislation on ART in the country, no accreditation, supervisory and regulatory body and no control of Government. Therefore, the Indian Council of Medical Research (ICMR) developed draft National Guidelines for Accreditation, Supervision & Regulation of ART Clinics in India in 2002. The draft document was then subjected to extensive public debate throughout the country (in seven cities; New Delhi, Jodhpur, Mumbai, Bangalore, Chennai, Hyderabad & Kolkata) where more than four thousand people participated. To obtain the opinion of the people on the various issues where the consensus of all the members of the Committee could not be established, a prescribed proforma was designed and given to the participants (85% general public, 13% Indian doctors and 2% international doctors).

Based on the opinion of this survey (Table), comments and suggestions received from the various stakeholders including National Commission for Women and National Human Right Commission, the National Guidelines were finalized and after the approval of the Drafting Committee the revised document was submitted to the Ministry of Health & Family Welfare, Government of India. The Ministry of Health & Family Welfare examined these guidelines and after slight modifications published the National Guidelines for Accreditation, Supervision & Regulation of ART Clinics in India as National Guidelines of Government of India in 2005.

Table
Opinion of the people on various issues obtained during the public debates

Sl. no.	Issues	Opinion of the people (%)					
		Doctor			General public		
		Yes	No	No opinion	Yes	No	No opinion
1	Whether surrogacy should be allowed in the Country?	96	2	2	92	3	5
2	Whether commercial surrogacy should be allowed in the Country?	80	15	5	72	24	4
3	Whether relatives/friends should be allowed to act as a surrogate mother?	45	52	3	14	83	3
4	Whether the identity of the donor should be known to the infertile couple?	37	58	5	7	89	4
5	Whether relatives/friends should be allowed for gamete donation?	44	54	2	8	91	1
6	Whether you are satisfied or agreed with the points mentioned under the heading "How may sperm and oocytes donors be sourced?"	54	42	4	81	15	4

On obtaining the feedback from different States of the country it was noticed thatthese National Guidelines were not being followed properly in the country. Therefore, the Indian Council of Medical Research developed draft Assisted Reproductive Technology (Regulation) Bill in 2008 with the help of a Drafting Committee of ICMR. The draft Assisted Reproductive Technology (Regulation) Bill-2008 was again subjected to extensive public debate not only throughout the country but globally by placing the draft Bill on the websites of the Ministry of Health & Family Welfare, Government of India and of the ICMR. Based on the comments received from various stakeholders including the comments from other countries and as per the recommendations of the Drafting Committee, the draft Assisted Reproductive Technology (Regulation) Bill was revised and finalized.The finalized version of draft Assisted Reproductive Technology (Regulation) Bill- 2010 was sent to the Ministry of Health & Family Welfare, and has now been revised by the Ministry of Law & Justice as Assisted Reproductive Technology (Regulation) Bill - 2013. The Assisted Reproductive Technology (Regulation) Bill- 2014 has now become a part of the Cabinet Note.

Conclusion

The draft Assisted Reproductive Technology (Regulation) Bill proposes to establish National Board, State Boards and National Registry of Assisted Reproductive Technology (ART) in India for accreditation and supervision of ART clinics and ART Banks, ensuring that services provided by these are ethical and that the medical, social and legal rights of all those concerned including surrogate mother are protected with maximum benefit to all the stakeholders within a recognized framework of ethics and good medical practices.

The doctor-patient relationshipIntroduction

The doctor-patient relationship plays an essential role in ordering the health care system and medical ethics, and since it is a form of communication, it necessitatesethical, philosophical, psychological, and sociological considerations. The present paper aims to evaluate the essence of the doctor-patient relationship in order to re-examine its conceptual framework. In the first part, the philosophical, psychological and sociological significance of this relationship is explored, and in the final section, the theoretical implications will be discussed. It seems that despite the imbalance in the relationship between doctors and patients resulting from the greater significance of the physicians' ethics, organization of this relationship is not possible without enhancing patient ethics.

Simultaneous consideration of sociological, psychological and philosophicaldimensions of the doctor-patient relationship can contribute to developing theoretical foundations and multidisciplinary bases for establishing practical ethical codes. The result will eventually be a more effective interaction between the two.

A) The Philosophical Essence of the Doctor-Patient Relationship

In investigating the philosophical essence of the doctor-patient relationship, three points should be taken into consideration. First, ethical demands in doctor-patientinteractions must have distinct definitions and terms; second, the phenomenological ethical debates on this issue need to be explored; and third, modern topics in the philosophy of the relationship should be considered, and relationships with the others should be analyzed from different perspectives.

Ethical Demands

Various organizations and professions differ in their attitudes towards ethical demands, recommendations, norms, values and judgments. The threecomponents of inclusion, priority and severity are presented below as the criteria for judgment in ethical issues.

1. **Inclusion:** The main questions to answer in regard to this component are: "What are the ethical limits?" and "Should all of our actions be judged ethically oronly some of them are included in the scope of ethical judgment?" In other words, is it enough to avoid doing the wrong thing, or is doing right among our moral duties too? It seems that the doctors' moral du-

ties include doing the right thing as well. This important matter is embedded within the principles of beneficence and non-maleficence.

2. **Priority:** The component of priority relies on the answers to the following questions: "If what morality is demanding is in conflict with our personal interests (for example it concerns our self, family, friends and so on), which side should we take? Should we always take the ethical side and forget about our personal interests? Or personal interests could have priority over moral obligations?" Nigel and Stalker explain that autonomy and our personal integrity have priority over what morality is demanding from us, or as Kagan and Singer say, demandingness of morality can even affect autonomy and our personal integrity. It seems that on the one hand the altruism of a practitioner as a professional should be based on the priority of patients' interests, and on the other hand it should safeguard the practitioner's own autonomy.

3. **Severity:** The main questions here are: Can ethics press extreme and costly demands from us? Or are the obligations of morality lighter and easier in the way that most people could overcome?" Apparently if ethics are founded on costly demands, we will be more likely to fail to fulfill our ethical duties.

Based on the above-mentioned considerations and classifications, three macro- positions emerge in the ethical relationship, including: maximal ethics, ordinary ethics, and minimal ethics.

Maximal Ethics: Maximal ethics include all the three components discussed above. In this type of ethics, ethical inclusion does not have any limits and covers all human actions. Extremist moralities consider ethical inclusion to be an absolute matter that covers all life styles and signify that no human action should be outside of this infinite circle.

Ordinary Ethics: This is the sort of ethics that most people believe in, and because of its affinity to the contemporary human life, it is also referred to as "common ethics". Here what ethics demands from us are boundaries. In other words, moderate ethics often state that after performing our obligations and moral duties, in a relatively wild range of personal interests we can start selecting. Thus, our actions are not always subject to moral judgment.

Minimal Ethics : This type of ethics is contradicted with maximal ethics. According to minimalists, the only forbidden action is intentional harassment. Followers of minimal ethics believe in a wide range of choices and selection areas; they recognize only a limited range of constraints and are in favor of acting upon personal interests.

It is a growing concern in medical ethics that the doctor-patient relationship is not approached in a sufficiently broad way and that this overly narrow medical perspective leaves doctors, nurses and other health care professionals badly equipped to deal with ethical dilemmas. Phenomenology could broaden this perspective and serve as a strong basis to understand moral sensitivity. Two notions in phenomenology have a central role in understanding the concept of the doctor-patient relationship: intentionality and first-person point of view.

Intentionality and first-person point of view

One of the basic concepts of phenomenology is attainment of phenomenal intentionality, which occurs when a person recognizes earlier assumptions and adopts a perspective. Some thinkers like Franz Brentano believe that intentionality and the phenomenological approach can be applied to the first- person point of view. For instance the first sighting of a beautiful landscape elevates us in a way that may not happen in later encounters. The reason is that later encounters are accompanied by presuppositions of the observer, who will be more used to the landscape. It seems that the phenomenological approach can be applied to the doctor-patient relationship. Doctors must reexamine and restrict assumptions toward patients, and at the same time value intentionality in order not to fall into habits.

Moral Sensitivity

Moral sensitivity may be enhanced in two ways. First, through reinforcing the phenomenological approach by renewing the first sight experience, that is, in each re-identification (of the patient for instance), priorities should be observed. Second, since any situation could come to a fork and ethical conflicts may rise, the adverse impacts should be considered and every situation must be regarded from an ethical perspective. Although at commencement moral sensitivity appears to overlap with maximal ethics, it is of particular importance especially in heterogeneous communications such as the doctor-patient relationship. It may be added that enhancing moral sensitivity even seems to be the target of the phenomenology of ethics in the doctor-patient relationship.

Communication with Others

The term "communication" can be defined through the philosophical approaches of great thinkers such as Levinas, Marcel and Buber who set their philosophical arguments in the relationship between "me" and "the other". Levinas insists on the maximum responsibility of any other; Marcel assists on turning the me-that relationship to the me-you relationship and replacing absence with presence; Buber finds God in "Thou".

B) The Psychological Essence of The Doctor-Patient Relationship

In terms of psychology, the doctor-patient relationship is imbalanced as the doctor has superiority over the patient. Such imbalanced relationships may give rise to various patterns of communication behavior. Psychologists have distinguished the following four communication behavior patterns based on components such as honesty, perspicuity, respect and inhibition:

1) Submissiveness

Submissive persons are shy, and although they speak honestly, they are usually taciturn and cannot express themselves perspicuously. They are also afraid of being judged or offending others, so they are incapable of making eye contact while speaking. Their voices are weak and unsteady, and they speak hesitantly. Submissive people avoid conflict rather than try to resolve it. They speak indirectly and in general terms because they cannot express themselves openly and may quickly feel depressed and vulnerable. People with this behavioral pattern admittedly let others abuse them and treat them disrespectfully. These patterns work both for doctors and patients. Patients who evade their responsibilities and encourage physicians to patriarchy in the process of therapy, or doctors who are not able to say "no" to patients easily consent to inappropriate and ineffective treatments.

2) Dominance
Domineering people feel insecure and believe that they do not possess good qualities. Accordingly, they try to deceive others and take advantage. Domineering persons do not have the perspicuity and honesty necessary for earning their wishes. They express themselves in general terms and sometimes their voices shake. These people use others to achieve their goals and make light of this inhibition and deception, so they take away another person's autonomy and freedom. This behavioral pattern is often seen in doctors and sometimes among patients as well. Doctors who prefer patient satisfaction to authority thus create a false autonomy for the patients and will eventually be dominated by them, and patients with this behavioral pattern impair the healing process by inhibition and deception.

3) Aggressiveness
The target of aggressive and domineering people is very similar and that is exploitation and domination of others. Their difference is that a domineering person achieves this aim by secrecy and cheating, while an aggressive person follows it frankly and openly. Unlike the domineering type, aggressive people are honest and straightforward; they are horrible listeners, always accuse others, get angry soon, get confused by criticism, and are usually grim in appearance. They have loud voices and look hostile, and in conflicts, they tend to destroy their opponents. This pattern is seen among both physicians and patients. Impatient physicians that do not listen, shout all the time and sometimes make irreparable mistakes during the healing process, or patients with lower anger thresholds who create tension in medical environments belong in the category of aggressivepeople.

4) Assertiveness
Assertiveness is the most creative behavioral pattern of communication. Assertivepeople respect themselves and others, and observe the authority of all sides. They are both honest and frank, and do not accuse themselves or others. Their approach to matters is problem-oriented, that is, when dealing with a problem, instead of accusing themselves and others, they think of a solution. They listen effectively and speak appropriately and understandably. During conflict they emphasize conversation. Their arguments are clear, specified, objective, fair and respectful, and eventually they are the most successful communicators. Issues such as breaking bad news, wasted treatments and medical mistakes are easy andsolvable with this type of behavioral pattern. While submissiveness, dominance and aggression lead to lose-lose situations in long term, assertiveness, is a helpful behavioral pattern and finally results in win-win solutions.

Based on the above-mentioned notions, the following practical hints should be outlined:

1. **Psychic Distance:** An important topic in aesthetics and artistic criticism that is also related to ethics is psychic distance. In aesthetics, this refers to the distance that should exist between a work of art and the viewer, so that aesthetic entente is created and art is not confused with reality. Omitting the psychic distance and forming deep sympathy and psychological identification with the work of art obstructs artistic judgment and aesthetic approach. In medical ethics, the concept seems to be important while encountering patients. Reduction of psychic distance and excessive sympathy with patients prevent an effective doctor-patient relationship as a fundamental element of treatment.

2. **Body Language**: Nonverbal communication skills are referred to as body language. This type of communication is very important in the doctor-patient relationship due to factors such as the limited visiting time, and linguistic and discourse differences.

3. **Truth-Telling versus Pain Relief**: One of the oldest ethical challenges is the painand suffering that can be caused by telling the truth. On the other hand, we can bring comfort and relief to patients by lying to them. Physicians can employ various methods at their discretion, but it seems that health care systems are more inclined toward telling the truth, and doctors must try to maintain a balancebetween the two.

4. **Emotional Quotient (EQ):** Unlike intelligence quotient that does not improve after the second decade of life, emotional quotient can continue to improve till the end. Emotional quotient refers to the ability to control emotions, sentiments and unwanted desires. People with high intelligence quotient dealing with people with lower intelligence quotient are susceptible to reckless, impulsive behavior and may gradually lose their EQ. In order to improve the doctor-patient relationship, health providers must be instructed in techniques to promote their emotional quotient.

C) The Sociological Essence of the Doctor-Patient Relationship
Unlike the psychological approach, the sociological approach to the doctor- patient relationship examines the essence of this (individualistic) relationship in a social context. In other words, the sociological approach regards the doctor- patient relationship beyond a merely mutual connection and therefore external elements are considered particularly important.
In order to investigate this relationship from the sociological perspective, communicative actions serve as a valid basis. They have been included among the most important sociological criteria in the last few decades as a set of social actions oriented

towards reaching entente. The target of communication action theory is to subvert a single prophetic and patriarchal individu-alism in human interactions. Jürgen Habermas has developed this notion in his famous book The Theory of Communicative Action, and his ideas are quite often presented in ethical manuscripts and medical ethics books. In this book Habermas distin-guishes and characterizes his theory by drawing a distinction between instrumental action and communicative action.

Instrumental Action

Jürgen Habermas states, "We call an action oriented to success instrumentalwhen we consider it in the light of following the rules of rational choice and assessthe efficiency of influencing the decisions of a rational opponent. By contrast, I shall speak of communicative action whenever the actions of the agents involved are coordinated not through egocentric calculations of suc-cess but through acts aiming at reaching an understanding. In communicative action the participants are not primarily orient-ed to their own individual successes; they pursue their individual goals under the condition that they can harmonize their plans of action on the basis of common situation definitions. In this respect, negotiating the definitions of the situation is an essential element of the interpretive accomplishments required for communicative action".

Reducing an individual to only one of the functions of his or her integrity is called instrumentalism. The function of a ticket sell-er in a bus station is just like that of amachine and therefore his human dimension could easily be overlooked. In the doctor-patient relationship both sides (especially the doctor) are susceptible to perceive others as mere instruments. The power that is practiced over patients by"medical gazing" makes them abject by reducing them to bodies that are examined simply to locate illness. Three fundamental concepts in sociology and philosophy have been purposed to deal with instrumentalism:

1) Teleological view of others by emphasizing the task:
In his works on the Golden Rule, Kant argues that instrumental action is inconsistent with socialization and human dignity, and proposes to regard others as an acme, not an instrument. The universal version of this rule is that you should like for others whatever you like for yourself and vice versa. One concrete technique for applying this rule is that human beings constantly put themselves inother people's positions and see the world from their perspectives.

2) The distinction between mysterious looks and issue makers:
Martin Buber and Gabriel Marcel emphasize the difference between the I-Thou and I-It relationship. In the former, a human is a mystery that unfolds and in the latter, an issue that resolves.

3) Maximum responsibility toward others:
Emmanuel Levinas states, "We are responsible for each other, and me more so...".This approach considers responsibility to-ward others as an unconditional matter, but does not require others to be equally responsible in return.

Communicative Action

Communicative action is allegedly an action focused on entente. Whoever wants to be successful in reaching entente should be prepared to bring up claims. Habermas states that the communication between a speaker and a listener is constituted by the existence of three universally valid claims: the claims for truth, rightness and truthfulness. The terms of these claims in the doctor-patient relationship accurately reveal the sociological essence of this relationship. Doctorsshould speak understandably and beware of ambiguity and opacity in their speech. On the other hand, they should make true statements and propositions, scientific and other. They should be honest and have faith in what they say, and ultimately they can use their discretion to determine the content of their relationship with patients.

Analysis

To clarify the concept of relationship and connectedness, we used a hybrid concept analysis including: identifying essential attributes, critiquing the existing definitions, examining boundaries and identifying antecedents. On the basis of the compara-tive concept analysis, the doctor-patient relationship is an interdisciplinary notion and a mono-disciplinary approach will re-duce this relationship to communicative skills.

Discussion and Conclusion

The doctor-patient relationship has greater impact on the health system than it may seem at first. In this paper, three novel dimensions of the doctor-patient relationship were deeply explored. The philosophical approach emphasizes the importance of promoting moral sensitivity. Communicating with others entails considerations rooted in the human soul that provoke great philosophical concerns. The psychological approach emphasizes learning about behavioral patterns, enhancing the intelligence quotient, and creating a balance between truth-telling and pain relief. Finally, the sociological approach demonstrates that the doctor-patient relationship is part of a macro social relationship in a community and discovers various aspects beyond the two-person relationship.

Abortion

An overview of the moral and legal aspects of abortion and evaluates the most important arguments. The central moral aspect concerns whether there is any morally relevant point during the biological process of the development of the fetus from its beginning as a unicellular zygote to birth itself that may justify not having an abortion after that point. Leading candidates for the morally relevant point are: the onset of movement, consciousness, the ability to feel pain, and viability. The central legal aspect of the abortion conflict is whether fetuses have abasic legal right to live, or, at least, a claim to live. The most important argument with regard to this conflict is the potentiality argument, which turns on whether the fetus is potentially a human per-son and thus should be protected. The question of personhood depends on both empirical findings and moral claims.

Preliminary Distinctions

One of the most important issues in biomedical ethics is the controversy surrounding abortion. This controversy has a long history and is still heavily discussed among researchers and the public—both in terms of morality and in terms of legality. The following basic questions may characterize the subject in more detail: Is abortion morally justifiable? Does the fetus (embryo, conceptus, and zygote) have any moral and/or legal rights? Is the fetus a human person and, thus, should be protected? What are the criteria for being a person? Is there any morally relevant break along the biological process of development from the unicellular zygote to birth? This list of questions is not meant to be exhaustive, but it describes the issues of the following analysis.

1) Three Views on Abortion

There are three main views: first, the extreme conservative view (held by the Catholic Church); second, the extreme liberal view (held by Singer); and third, moderate views which lie between both extremes. Some opponents (anti- abortionists, pro-life activists) holding the extreme view, argue that human personhood begins from the unicellular zygote and thus – according to the religious stance – one should not have an abortion by virtue of the imago dei of the human being (for example, Schwarz 1990). To have an abortion would be, by definition, homicide. The extreme liberal view is held by proponents (abortionists). They claim that human personhood begins immediately after birth or a bit later (Singer). Thus, they consider the relevant date is at birth or a short time later (say, one month). The proponents of the moderate views argue that there is a morally relevant break in the biological process of development – from the unicellular zygote to birth – which determines the justifiability and non- justifiability of having an abortion. According to them, there is a gradual process from being a fetus to being an infant where the fetus is not a human being but a human offspring with a different moral status.

The advantage of the extreme conservative view is the fact that it defines human personhood from the beginning of life (the unicellular zygote); there is no slippery slope. However, it seems implausible to say that the zygote is a human person. The advantage of the extreme liberal view is that its main claim is supported by a common philosophical usage of the notion "personhood" and thus seems more sound than the extreme conservative view because the offspring is far more developed; as the unicellular zygote. This view also faces severe problems; for example, it is not at all clear where the morally relevant difference is between the fetus five minutes before birth and a just born offspring. Some moderate views have commonsense plausibility especially when it is argued that there are significant differences between the developmental stages. The fact that they also claim for a break in the biological process, which is morally relevant, seems to be a relapse into old and unjustified habits. As Gillespie stresses in his article "Abortion and Human Rights" (1984, 94-102) there is no morally relevant break in the biological process of development. But, in fact, there are differences, which make a comparative basis possible without having to solve the problem of drawing a line. How should one decide?

2) The Standard Argument

The standard argument is the following practical syllogism:

- The killing of human beings is prohibited.
- A fetus is a human being.
- The killing of fetuses is prohibited.

Hence, abortion is not allowed since homicide is prohibited. It seems obvious to question the result of the practical syllogism since one is able to argue against both premises. First, there are possible situations where the first premise could be questioned by noting, for example that killing in self-defense is not prohibited. Second, the second premise could also be questioned since it is not at all clear whether fetuses are human beings in the sense of being persons, although they are of course human beings in the sense of being members of the species of homo sapiens. Consecutively, one would deny that fetuses are persons but admit that a young two year old child may be a person. Although, in the end, it may be difficult to claim that every human being is a person. For example, people with severe mental handicaps or disorder seem not to have personhood. That is, if personhood is defined with regard to specific criteria like the capacity to reason, or to have consciousness, self-consciousness, or rationality, some people might be excluded. But, in fact, this does not mean that people with severe mental handicaps who lack personhood can be killed. Even when rights are tied to the notion of personhood, it is clearly prohibited to kill disabled people. Norbert Hoerster, a well-known German philosopher, claims that fetuses with severe handicaps can be – like all other fetuses – aborted, as born human beings with severe handicaps they have to be protected and respected like all other human beings, too (1995, 159).

3) The Modified Standard Argument

However, it seems appropriate to modify the standard argument and to use a more sophisticated version. Replace the notion "human being" with "human life form." The new practical syllogism is:

- The killing of human life forms is prohibited.
- A fetus is a human life form.
- The killing of fetuses is prohibited.

The objection against the first premise of the standard argument still holds for the new more sophisticated version. But, the second modified premise is much stronger than the previous one because one has to determine what a human life form really is. Is a fetus a human life form? But, even if the fetus is a human life form, it does not necessarily follow that it should be protected by that fact, simpliciter. The fetus may be a human life form but it hardly seems to be a person (in the ordinary sense of the notion) and thus has no corresponding basic right to live. However, as already stated, this kind of talk seems to go astray because the criteria for personhood may be suitable for just-borns but not appropriate for fetuses, embryos, or unicellular zygotes, like some biological (human being), psychological (self-consciousness), rational (ability to reasoning), social (sympathy/love), or legal (being a human life form with rights) criteria may indicate (for example, Jane English 1984). Jane English persuasively argues in "Abortion and the Concept of a Person" that even if the fetus is a person, abortion may be justifiable in many cases, and if the fetus is no person, the killing of fetuses may be wrong in many cases.

Personhood

What does it mean to claim that a human life form is a person? This is an important issue since the ascription of rights is at stake. I previously stated that it is unsound to say that a fetus is a person or has personhood since it lacks, at least, rationality and self-consciousness. It follows that not every human being is also a person according to the legal sense, and, thus, also lacks moral rights (extreme case). The fetus is by virtue of his genetic code a human life form but this does not mean that this would be sufficient to grant it legal and moral rights. Nothing follows from being a human life form by virtue of one's genes, especially not that one is able to derive legal or moral rights from this very fact (for example, speciesism). Is a human person exclusively defined by her membership of the species Homo sapiens sapiens and thus should be protected? To accept this line of argumentation would entail the commitment of the existence of normative empirical features. It seems premature to derive the prohibition to kill a life form from the bare fact of its genetic feature – including the human life form – unless one argues that human beings do have the basic interest of protecting their offspring. Is a human life form a moral entity? This seems to be a good approach. The argument runs as follows: It seems plausible to claim that human beings create values and, if they have the basic interest of protecting their offspring, human beings may establish a certain morality by which they can argue, for example, for the prohibition of abortions. The moral judgment can be enforced through legal norms.

To be more precise about the assumption of the existence or non-existence of normative, empirical features: Critics of the view to tie the right to live and the biological category of being a human being claim that the protagonists effect the is-ought fallacy. Why is it unsound to take the bare fact of being a member of the biological species Homo sapiens as a solid basis for granting the right to live? The linkage seems only justified when there are sound factual reasons. If there are none, the whole line of reasoning would "hang in the air" so that one could also easily argue for the right to live for cats and dogs. Only factual relevant features may be important for the linkage. What could these relevant features look like?

Jane English presents in her article "Abortion and the Concept of a Person" several features of personhood which characterize the human person. Her notion of personhood can be grouped into five sectors (English 1984, pp. 152):

(i)   the biological sector (being a human being, having extremities, eating and sleeping);
(ii)   the psychological sector (perception, emotions, wishes and interests, ability to communicate, ability to make use of tools, self-consciousness);
(iii)   the rational sector (reasoning, ability to make generalizations, to make plans, learning from experience);
(iv)   the social sector (to belong to different groups, other people, sympathy and love); and
(v)   the legal sector (to be a legal addressee, ability to make contracts, to be a citizen). According to English, it is not necessary for a human life form to comply with all five sectors and different aspects to count as a person. A fetus lies right in the penumbra where the concept of personhood is hard to apply. There is no core of necessary and sufficient features that could be ascribed to a human life form in order to be sure that these features constitute a person (English 1984, 153).

Mary Anne Warren claims that a human life form should qualify as a person when, at least, some of the following aspects (especially i-iii) are at stake: (i) consciousness and the ability to feel pain; (ii) reasoning; (iii) a self-motivated activity; (iv) ability to communicate; and (v) the existence of a self-concept (for example, individual, racial) and self-consciousness (Warren 1984, 110-113). Warren argues that the fetus is no person since it lacks the criteria of personhood and, thus, an abortion is justified.

The aim is not to give an airtight definition of the concept of personhood. The main question is whether a fetus could qualify as a person. The following can be stated: The fetus is a human offspring but is not a legal, social, and rational person in the ordinary sense of the notions. Some aspects of the psychological sector for example, the ability to feel and perceive can be ascribed to the fetus but not to the embryo, conceptus, or the (unicellular) zygote. It seems implausible to say that a fetus (or embryo, conceptus, zygote) is a person, unless one additionally claims that the genetic code of the fetus is a sufficient condition. However, this does not mean, in the end, that one could always justify an abortion. It only shows that the fetus could hardly be seen as a human person.

It is hard to keep the legal and moral aspects of the conflict of abortion apart. There are overlaps which are due to the nature of things since legal considerations are based on the ethical realm. This can also be seen according to the notion person. What a person is is not a legal question but a question which is to be decided within a specific ethics. If one characterizes the notion of a person along some criteria, then the question of which criteria are suitable or not will be discussed with regard to a specific moral approach (for example, Kantianism, utilitarianism, virtue ethics). The relevant criteria, in turn, may come from different areas like the psychological, rational, or social sphere. If the criteria are settled, this influences the legal sector because the ascription of legal rights – especially the right to live in the abortion debate – is tied to persons and respectively to the concept of personhood.

Moral Aspects of the Abortion Conflict

The main question with regard to the moral sphere concerns identification of the right developmental point of the fetus (or the embryo, conceptus, zygote) to decide which break may morally justify an abortion or not (proponents of the moderate view and the extreme liberal view claim that there is such a break). The main arguments in the debate will be evaluated in the following. Before we analyze the arguments, it is necessary to say something about moral rights.

a) Moral Rights
Some authors claim that the talk of moral rights and moral obligations is an old never-ending tale. There are no "moral rights" or "moral obligations" per se; at least, in the sense that there are also moral rights and moral obligations apart from legal rights and legal obligations. There is no higher ethical authority which may enforce a specific moral demand. Rights and obligations rest on law. According to ethics, one should better say "moral agreements" (for example, Gauthier). The proponents claim that moral agreements do have a similar status to legal rights and legal obligations but stress that no person has an enforceable demand to have her moral rights prevail over others. The suitability is the essential aspect of the metaphysics of rights and obligations. Only the formal constraint establishes rights and obligations within a given society (for example, Hobbes); the informal constraint within a given society – though it may be stronger – is not able to do so. Without a court of first instance there are no rightsand obligations. Only by using the legal system is one able to establish specific moral rights and specific moral obligations. Those authors claim that there are no absolute moral rights and moral obligations which are universally valid; moral agreements are always subjective and relative. Hence, there are also no(absolute) moral rights which the fetus (embryo, conceptus, or zygote) may call for. The only solution may be that the survival of the fetus rests on the will of the human beings in a given moral society. According to their view, it is only plausible to argue that an abortion is morally reprehensible if the people in a given society do have a common interest not to abort and make a moral agreement which is enforced by law.

b) At Birth
Proponents of the liberal view contend that the morally significant break in the biological development of the fetus is at birth. This means that it is morallypermitted to have an abortion before birth and morally prohibited to kill the offspring after birth. The objection against this view is simple because thereseems to be no morally relevant difference between a short time (say five minutes) before birth and after it. Factually, the only biological difference is the physical separation of the fetus from the mother. However it seems unsound to interpret this as the morally significant difference; the bare evidence with regard to the visibility of the offspring and the physical separation (that is, the offspring is no longer dependent on the woman's body) seems insufficient.

c) Viability
Proponents of the moderate view often claim that the viability criterion is a hot candidate for a morally significant break because the dependence of the nonviable fetus on the pregnant woman gives her the right to make a decision about having an abortion. The aspect of dependence is insufficient in order to determine the viability as a possible break. Take the following counter-example: Ason and his aged mother who is nonviable without the intensive care of her son; the son has no right to let his mother die by virtue of her given dependence. However, one may object that there is a difference between "needing someone to care for you" and "needing to live off a particular person's body." Furthermore,one may stress that the nonviable and the viable fetus both are potential human adults. But as below the argument of potentiality is flawed since it is unclear how actual rights could be derived from the bare potentiality of having such rights at a later time. Hence, both types of fetuses cannot make claim for a right. There is also another objection that cannot be rebutted: the viability of the fetus regarding the particular level of medical technology. On the one hand, there is a temporal relativity according to medical technology. The understanding of what constitutes the viability of the fetus has developed over time according to the technical level of embryology in the last centuries and decades. Today, artificial viability allows physicians to rescue many premature infants who would have previously died. On the other hand, there exists a local relativity according to the availability of medical supplies in and within countries which determines whether the life of a premature infant will be saved. The medical supply may vary greatly. Consequently, it seems inappropriate to claim that viability as such should be regarded as a significant break by being a general moral justification againstabortions.

d) First Movement
The first movement of the fetus is sometimes regarded as a significant break because proponents stress its deeper meaning which usually rests on religious or non-religious considerations. Formerly the Catholic Church maintained that the first movement of the fetus shows that it is the breathing of life into the human body (animation) which separates the human fetus from animals. This line of thinking is out-of-date and the Catholic Church no longer uses it. Another point is that the first movement of the fetus that women experience is irrelevant since the real first movement of the fetus is much earlier. Ultrasonic testing shows that the real first movement of the fetus is somewhere between the 6th and 9th week.But even if one considers the real first movement problems may arise. The physical ability to move is morally irrelevant. One counter-example: What about an adult human being who is quadriplegic and is unable to move? It seems out of the question to kill such people and to justify the killing by claiming that people who are disabled and simply lack the ability to move are, therewith, at other people's disposal.

e) Consciousness and the Ability to Feel Pain
In general, proponents of moderate views believe that consciousness and the ability to feel pain will develop after about six months. However the first brain activities are discernable after the seventh week so that it is possible to conclude that the fetus may feel pain after this date. In this respect, the ability to suffer is decisive for acknowledging a morally significant break. One may object to this claim, that the proponents of this view redefine the empirical feature of "the ability to suffer" as a normative feature (is-ought fallacy). It is logically unsound toconclude from the bare fact that the fetus feels pain that it is morally reprehensible or morally prohibited per se to abort the fetus.

f) Unicellular Zygote
Proponents of the extreme conservative view claim that the morally significant break in the biological development of the fetus

is given with the unicellular human zygote. They argue that the unicellular zygote is a human person, and thus, it is prohibited to have an abortion because one kills a human being (for example, Schwarz).

The extreme conservative proponents argue that biological development from the fetus to a human being is an incremental process which leaves no room for a morally significant break (liberals deny this line of thinking). If there is no morally significant break, then the fetus has the same high status of a newborn, or the newborn has the same low status of the fetus.
To many opponents of the "extreme" conservative position, it seems questionable to claim that a unicellular zygote is a person. At best, one may maintain that the zygote will potentially develop into a human being. Except the potentiality argument is flawed since it is impossible to derive current rights from the potential ability of having rights at a later time. Opponents (for example, Gert) also object to any attempt to base conclusions on religious considerations that they believe cannot stand up to rational criticism. For these reasons, they argue that the conservative view should be rejected.

g)   Thomson and the Argument of The Sickly Violinist
Judith Jarvis Thomson presents an interesting case in her landmark article "A Defense of Abortion" (1971) in order to show that, even if the fetus has a right to live, one is still able to justify an abortion for reasons of a woman's right to live/integrity/privacy. Thomson's famous example is that of the sickly violinist: You awake one morning to find that you have been kidnapped by a society of music lovers in order to help a violinist who is unable to live on his own by virtue of his ill-health. He has been attached to your kidneys because you alone have the only blood type to keep him alive. You are faced with a moral dilemma because the violinist has a right to live by being a member of the human race; there seems to be no possibility to unplug him without violating this right and thus killing him. However, if you leave him attached to you, you are unable to move for months, although you did not give him the right to use your body in such a way (Thomson 1984, 174-175).

First, Thomson claims that the right to live does not include the right to be given the means necessary for survival. If the right to live entails the right to those means, one is not justified in preventing the violinist from the on-going use of one's kidneys. The right to the on-going use of the kidneys necessarily implies that the violinist's right to his means for survival always trumps the right to another person's body. Thomson refuses this and claims that "the fact that for continued life that violinist needs the continued use of your kidneys does not establish that he has a right to be given the continued use of your kidneys" (Thomson 1984, 179). She argues that everybody has a right of how his own body is used. That is, the violinist has no right to use another person's body without her permission. Therefore, one is morally justified in not giving the violinist the use of one's own kidneys.

Second, Thomson contends that the right to live does not include the right not to be killed. If the violinist has the right not to be killed, then another person is not justified in removing the plug from her kidneys although the violinist has no right to their use. According to Thomson, the violinist has no right to another person's body and hence one cannot be unjust in unplugging him: "You surely are not being unjust to him, for you gave him no right to use your kidneys, and no one else can have given him any such right" (Thomson 1984, 180). If one is not unjust in unplugging oneself from him, and he has no right to the use of another person's body, then it cannot be wrong, although the result of the action is that the violinist will be killed.

Legal Aspects of the Abortion Conflict
What is the legal status of the fetus (embryo, conceptus, and zygote)? Before the question is answered, one should pay some attention to the issue of the genesis of a legal system. Which ontological status do legal rights have? Where do they come from? Usually we accept the idea that legal rights do not "fall from the blue sky" but are made by human beings. Other conceptions which had been provided in the history of human kind are:

1. rights rest on God's will;
2. rights rest on the strongest person; or
3. rights rest on a specific human feature like a person's wisdom or age.

However, let us take the following description for granted: There is a legal community in which the members are legal entities with (legal) claims and legal addressees with (legal) obligations. If someone refuses the addressee's legal obligation within such a system, the legal entity has the right to call the legal instance in order to let his right be enforced. The main question is whether the fetus (or the embryo, conceptus, zygote) is a legal person with a basic right to live or not and, furthermore, whether there will be a conflict of legal norms, that is a conflict between the fetus' right to live and the right of self-determination of the pregnant woman (principle of autonomy). Is the fetus a legal entity or not?

The Account of Quasi-Rights
It was previously stated that the fetus as such is no person and that it seems unsound to claim that fetuses are persons in the ordinary sense of the notion. If rights are tied to the notion of personhood, then it seems appropriate to say that fetuses do not have any legal rights. One can object that animals of higher consciousness have some "rights" or quasi-rights because it is prohibited to kill them without good reason (killing great apes and dolphins for fun is prohibited in most countries). Their "right" not to be killed is based on the people's will and their basic interest not to kill higher developed animals for fun. But, it would be wrong to assume that those animals are legal entities with "full" rights, or that they have only "half" rights. Thus, it seems reasonable to say that animals have "quasi-rights." There is a parallel between the so-called right of the fetus and the quasi-rights of some animals: both are not persons in the normal sense of the notion but it would cause us great discomfort to offer them no protection and to deliver them to the vagaries of the people. According to this line of argument, it seems sound to claim that fetuses also have quasi-rights. It does not follow that the quasi-rights of the fetuses and the quasi-rights of the animals are iden-

tical; people would normally stress that the quasi-rights of fetuses are of more importance than that of animals.

However, there are some basic rights of the pregnant woman, for example, the right of self-determination, the right of privacy, the right of physical integrity, and the right to live. On the other hand, there is the existential quasi-right of the fetus, that is, the quasi-right to live. If the presumption is right that legal rights are tied to the notion of personhood and that there is a difference between rights and quasi-rights, then it seems right that the fetus has no legal right but "just" a quasi-right to live. If this is the case, what about the relation between the existential quasi-right of the fetus and the basic legal rights of the pregnant woman? The answer seems obvious: quasi-rights cannot trump full legal rights. The fetus has a different legal status that is based on a different moral status (see above). On this view there is no legal conflict of rights.

The Argument of Potentiality
Another important point in the debate about the ascription of legal rights to the fetus is the topic of potential rights. Joel Feinberg discusses this point in his famous article "Potentiality, Development, and Rights" (1984, 145-151) and claims that the thesis that actual rights can be derived from the potential ability of having such rights is logically flawed because one is only able to derive potential rights from a potential ability of having rights. Feinberg maintains that there may be cases where it is illegal or wrong to have an abortion even when the fetus does not have any rights or is not yet a moral person. To illustrate his main argument – that rights do not rest on the potential ability of having them – Feinberg considers Stanley Benn's argument which I slightly modified:

If person X is President of the USA and thus is Commander in Chief of the army, then person X had the potential ability to become the President of the USA and Commander in Chief of the army in the years before his rule.

But, it does not follow that:
The person X has the authority to command the army as potential President of the USA.
Thus, it seems incorrect to derive actual rights from the bare potential ability to have legal rights at a later time. It should be added that Benn – despite his criticism on the argument of potential rights – also claims that there are valid considerations which do not refer to the talk of rights and may provide plausible reasons against infanticide and late abortions even when fetuses and newborns are lawless beings with no personhood.

A Pragmatic Account
There is always a chance that women get pregnant when they have sex with their (heterosexual) partners. There is not a 100% certainty of not getting pregnant under "normal circumstances"; there is always a very small chance even by using contraception to get pregnant. However, what does the sphere of decisions look like? A pregnancy is either deliberate or not. If the woman gets deliberately pregnant, then both partners (respectively the pregnant woman) may decide to have a baby or to have an abortion. In the case of having an abortion there may be good reasons for having an abortion with regard to serious health problems, for example, a (seriously) disabled fetus or the endangerment of the woman's life. Less good reasons seem to be: vacation, career prospects, or financial and social grievances. If the pregnancy is not deliberate, it is either self-caused in the sense that the partners knew about the consequences of sexual intercourses and the contraception malfunctioned or it is not self-caused in the sense of being forced to have sex (rape). In both cases the fetus may be aborted or not. The interesting question concerns the reasons given for the justification of having an abortion.
There are at least two different kinds of reasons or justifications: The first group will be called "first order reasons"; the second "second order reasons." First order reasons are reasons of justifications which may plausibly justify an abortion, for example, (i) rape, (ii) endangerment of the woman's life, and (iii) a serious mentally or physically disabled fetus. Second order reasons are reasons of justifications which are, in comparison to first order reasons, less suitable in providing a strong justification for abortion, for example, (i) a journey, (ii) career prospects, (iii) by virtue of financial or social grievances.

a) First Order Reasons
i. Rape
It would be cruel and callous to force the pregnant woman who had been raped to give birth to a child. Judith Jarvis Thomson maintains in her article "A Defense of Abortion" that the right to live does not include the right to make use of a foreign body even if this means having the fetus aborted (Thomson 1984, pp. 174 and pp. 177). Both the fetus and the raped woman are "innocent," but this does not change "the fact" that the fetus has any rights. It seems obvious in this case that the raped woman has a right to abort. Forcing her not to abort is to remind her of the rape day-by-day which would be a serious mental strain and should not be enforced by law or morally condemned.

However, this assumption would be premature from John Noonan's viewpoint according to his article "An Almost Absolute Value in History" (Noonan 1970, 51- 59). He claims that the fetus as human [is] a neighbor; his life [has] parity with one's own [...] [which] could be put in humanistic as well as theological terms: do not injure your fellow man without reasons. In these terms, once the humanity of the fetus is perceived, abortion is never right except in self-defense. When life must be taken to save life, reason alone cannot say that a mother must prefer a child's life to her own. With this exception, now of great rarity, abortion violates the rational humanist tenet of the equality of human lives.

Hence, the woman has no right to abort the fetus even if she had been raped and got pregnant against her will. This is the consequence of Noonan's claim since he only permits having an abortion in self-defense while Thomson argues that women, in general, have a right to abort the fetus when the fetus is conceived as an intruder (for example, due to rape). But, it remains unclear what Noonan means by "self-defense." At the end of his article he states that "self-sacrifice carried to the point of death seemed in extreme situations not without meaning. In the less extreme cases, preference for one's own interests to the life of anotherseemed to express cruelty or selfishness irreconcilable with the demands of love"

(Noonan 1970). On this view, even in the standard case of self-defense — for example, either the woman's life or the life of the fetus — the pregnant woman's death would not be inappropriate and in less extreme cases the raped woman would express cruelty or selfishness when she aborts the fetus — a judgment not all people would agree with.

ii. Endangerment of the Woman's Life
Furthermore, there is no good reason to proceed with a pregnancy when the woman's life is in serious danger. Potential life should not be more valued then actual life. Of course, it is desirable to do everything possible to rescue both but it should be clear that the woman's life "counts more" in this situation. To force her at the risk of her life means to force her to give up her right of self-defense and her right to live. There seems to be no good reason to suspend her basic right of self-defense.

iii.Serious Mentally or Physically Disabled Fetuses
It is hard to say when exactly a fetus is seriously mentally or physically disabled because this hot issue raises the vital question of whether the future life of the disabled fetus is regarded as worth living (problem of relativity). Hence, there are simple cases and, of course, borderline cases which lie in the penumbra and are hard to evaluate. Among the simple cases take the following example: Imagine a human torso lacking arms and legs that will never develop mental abilities like self-consciousness, the ability to communicate, or the ability to reason. It seems quite obvious to some people that such a life is not worth living. But what about the high number of borderline cases? Either parents are not entitled to have a healthy and strong offspring, nor are the offspring entitled to become healthy andstrong. Society should not force people to give birth to seriously disabled fetuses or morally worse to force mothers who are willing to give birth to a disabled fetusto have an abortion (for example, Nazi Germany). It seems clear that a rather small handicap of the fetus is not a good reason to abort it.

Often radical groups of disabled persons claim that, if other people hold the view that it is all right to abort fetuses with (serious) genetic handicaps, the same people therewith deny the basic right to live of disabled adults with serious handicaps. This objection is unreasonable since fetuses in contrast to adult humanbeings have no basic interest in continuing to live their lives. Disabled fetuses maybe aborted like other fetuses, disabled (adult) human persons have to be respected like other people.

b)   Second Order Reasons
i.   A Journey to Europe
With regard to the reasons of justification according to the second group, there is a specific view which is based on the argument that it is the decision of the woman to have an abortion or not.
There is a related view that rests on the assumption of the pregnant woman who claims that the fetus is a part of her body like a limb so that she has the right to do what ever she wants to do with the fetus. The argument is wrong. The fetus is certainly not a simple part of the pregnant woman but, rather, a dependent organism that relies on the woman.

The following example, the journey to Europe from North America, is based on the feminist argument but it is somewhat different in stressing another point in the line of argumentation: A young woman is pregnant in the seventh month and decides to make a journey to Europe for a sight-seeing tour. Her pregnancy is an obstacle to this and she decides to have an abortion. She justifies her decision by claiming that it will be possible for her to get pregnant whenever she wants but she is only able to make the journey now by virtue of her present career prospects. What can be said of her decision? Most authors may feel a deep discomfort not to morally condemn the action of the woman or not to reproach her for her decision for different reasons. But, there seems only two possible answers which may count as a valid basis for morally blaming the woman for her decision: First, if the young woman lives in a moral community where all membershold the view that it is immoral to have an abortion with regard to the reason given, then her action may be morally reprehensible. Furthermore, if the (moral) agreement is enforced by law, the woman also violated the particular law for which she has to take charge of. Second, one could also blame her for not showing compassion for her potential child. People may think that she is a callous person since she prefers to make the journey to Europe instead of giving birth to her almost born child (seventh month). If the appeal to her mercy fails, one will certainly be touched by her "strange" and "inappropriate" action. However, the community would likely put some informal pressure on the pregnant woman to influence her decision not to have an abortion. But some people may still contend that this social pressure will not change anything about the fact that the fetus has no basic right to live while claiming that the woman's decision is elusive.

ii. Financial and Social Reasons
A woman got pregnant (not deliberately) and wants to have an abortion by virtue of her bad financial and social background because she fears that she will be unable to offer the child an appropriate life perspective. In this case, the community should do everything possible to assist the woman if she wants to givebirth to her child. Or, some may argue, that society should offer to take care ofher child in special homes with other children or to look for other families whoare willing to house another child. According to this line of thinking, people may claim that the financial or social background should not be decisive for having an abortion if there is a true chance for help.

c)   First Order Reasons vs. Second Order Reasons
There is a difference between the first order reasons and the second order reasons. We already saw that the first order reasons are able to justify an abortion while the second order reasons are less able to do so. That is because people think that the second order reasons are weaker than the reasons of the first group. It seems that the human ability to show compassion for the

fetus is responsible for our willingness to limit the woman's basic right of autonomy where her reasons are too elusive. However, one may state that there are no strong compulsive reasons which could morally condemn the whole practice of abortion. Some people may not unconvincingly argue that moral agreements and legal rights are due to human beings so that reasons for or against abortion are always subjective and relative. According to this view, one is only able to contend the "trueness" or "wrongness" of a particular action in a limited way. Of course, there are other people who argue for the opposite (for example, Kantians, Catholic Church). One reason why people have strong feelings about the conflict of abortion is that human beings do have strong intuitive feelings, for example, to feel compassion for fetuses as helpless and most vulnerable human entities. But moral intuitionism falls short by being a valid and objective basis for moral rights.

In the end, it is a question of a particular moral approach whether one regards an abortion as morally justifiable or not. But not every approach is justified. There is no anything goes.

Public Policy and Abortion

One of the most difficult issues is how to make a sound policy that meets the needs of most people in a given society without focusing on the extreme conservative view, or the extreme liberal view, or the many moderate views on the conflict of abortion. The point is simple, one cannot wait until the philosophical debate is settled, for maybe there is no one solution available. But, in fact, people in a society must know what the policy is; that is, they have to know when and under what circumstances abortion is permitted or altogether prohibited. What are the reasons for a given policy? Do they rest on religious beliefs or do they depend on cultural claims? Whose religious beliefs and whose cultural claims? Those beliefs and claims of most people or of the dominant group in a given society ? What about the problem of minority rights? Should they be respected or be refused? These are hard questions; no one is able to yet give a definite response.

But, of course, the problem of abortion has to be "solved," at least, with regard to practical matters. This means that a good policy does not rest on extreme views but tries to cover as many points of views, although being aware of the fact that one is not able to please every person in society. This would be an impossible task. It seems that one should adopt a moderate view rather than the proposed extreme views. This is not because the moderate view is "correct" but because one needs a broad consensus for a sound policy. The hardliners in the public debate on the conflict of abortion, be they proponents or opponents, may not be aware of the fact that neither view is sustainable for most people.

A sound way for governments with regard to a reasonable policy could be the acceptance of a more or less neutral stance that may function as a proper guide for law. But, in fact, the decisive claim of a "neutral stance" is, in turn, questionable. All ethical theories try to present a proper account of a so-called neutral stance but there is hardly any theory that could claim to be sustainable with regard to other approaches. However, the key seems to be, again, to accept a middle way to cover most points of views. In the end, a formation of a policy seeks a sound compromise people could live with. But this is not the end of the story. One should always try to find better ways to cope with hard ethical problems. The conflict of abortion is of that kind and there is no evidence to assume otherwise.

Clinical Ethics Consultation and Abortion

The vital issue of how one chooses whether or not to have an abortion is of utmost importance since people, in particular women, want to have a proper "guideline" that can support them in their process of ethical decision-making. According to pregnant women, the most crucial point seems not to be whether abortion is morally legitimate or not but, rather, how one should deliberate in the particular case. In fact, observations regularly show that women will nearly have the same number of abortions in contexts in which it is legal or not.

Gert is right in claiming that "the law can allow behavior that some people regard as morally unacceptable, such as early abortion, and it can prohibit behavior that some people regard as morally acceptable, such as late abortion. No one thinks that what the law decides about abortion settles the moral issue" (Gert 2004, 138). But what follows from that? What aspects should one consider and how should one decide in a particular case?

It would be best to consult a neutral person who has special knowledge and experiences in medicine and medical ethics (for example, clinical ethics consultation). Most people are usually not faced with hard conflicts of abortion in their daily lives and get simply swamped by it; they are unable to determine and evaluate all moral aspects of the given case and to foresee the relevant consequences of the possible actions (for example, especially with regard to very young women who get pregnant by mistake). They need professional help without being dominated by the person in order to clarify their own (ethical) stance.

However, the conflict of abortion as such may not be solvable, in the end, but the experienced professional is able to provide persons with feasible solutions for the particular case.

Euthanasia

Euthanasia, also called 'Mercy Killing' and 'Physician Assisted Suicide; is a term in medical ethics for the practice of interfering or intervening in a natural process towards death. In other words it is accelerating the natural course of death in terminally ill patients, when all treatments become ineffective or much too painful for the patient to bear. In short Euthanasia is ending a human life with the intention of relieving the person from an unbearable pain. Haris (2001) precisely defines Euthanasia as 'a deliberate intervention undertaken with the express intention of ending a life to relieve intractable suffering'.

The issue of Euthanasia has always remained controversial and still has failed to carry legal and constitutional support in most parts of the world. Suicide in any form and by any means is either punished or at least disapproved in human history. There is no permissibility of such a killing/suicide in Islam so Euthanasia can never be the part of Muslim law in Islamic world. Therefore the origin and development of this concept can be historically located in the non Muslim countries especially of the west. Back in 400 BC when the father of medicine Hippocrates formulated the oath still taken by the fresh medical graduates dictates 'I will give no deadly medicine to any one if asked, nor suggest any such counsel"., speaks against physician assisted suicide. Even in the 19th century, the US legislation proclaimed that if a suicide is committed on the advice of another person, the adviser would be guilty of a murder. In the early 20th century, the Supreme Court reevaluated its judgments concerning 'living will' and focusing how best to ensure the dignity and the independence for the 'end of life' with considerable changes in the health laws. In 1920 the book "Permitting the Destruction of Life not Worthy of Life" was published, in which the author Hoche advocated the death assistance be given under very controlled conditions. In 1935 Euthanasia society was formed in England to support mercy killing. 1939's Nazi's Euthanasia became very popular when Hitler ordered mercy killing of the sick and disabled. From 1995 to 2008, Euthanasia has been legalized in countries like parts of Australia, Netherland, Belgium and few states of the United States of America. [2]

There are several forms or kinds of Euthanasia; each form has its own ethical issues. Active Euthanasia: is the one which causes immediate death of the patient, by the direct and deliberate action of the physician. For example when a lethal injection is given to the patient or an overdose of a pain killer when the physician knows the after effects of such a dose.

Passive Euthanasia involves an indirect action by the physician for the death of the patient. This may include withdrawing or withholding the required treatment. For example switching off the life supporting machine like ventilator or not doing the required surgical procedures that can keep the person alive though for a shorttime. Voluntary Euthanasia:- takes place with the will of the patient, usually on his request to the physician.

Non-Voluntary Euthanasia occurs when the patient is unconscious or in comma for a long time, or unable to make decision for example a very young child, or a mentally retarded person. Therefore someone else related to the patient makes the decision of ending the patient's life.

Involuntary Euthanasia:- is oftentimes equated to murder because in this case thepatient does not opt for death but he is killed as the doctor thinks it to be in his benefit.

Indirect Euthanasia: – does not involve the intentional killing by the physician, butthe side effects of the treatment, usually given to reduce the pain accelerate the death of the patient.

Assisted Suicide:- includes cases when the patient seeks help from his physician todie. This can include making the lethal drugs available for the patients.

The most common argument given by the proponents of Euthanasia is its effective way of relieving excruciating pain. To this one argument there can be two counter arguments. Firstly the advancements made today in the field of medicine, especially in pain management weakens the justification for Euthanasia. Secondly research shows that terminally ill patients choose suicide not because of the physical pain but because of depression. A study of terminally ill patients published in The American Journal of Psychiatry in 1986 concluded:

'The striking feature of [our] results is that all of the patients who had either desired premature death or contemplated suicide were judged to be suffering from clinical depressive illness; that is, none of those patients who did not have clinical depression had thoughts of suicide or wished that death would come early'.

Researchers believe that a person diagnosed with terminal illness should be given time and support to pass through the five stages of the process – denial, anger, bargaining, depression and acceptance, and killing them before they come to terms with the situation is nothing less than a murder.

Find out how UKEssays.com can help you! Our academic experts are ready and waiting to assist with any writing project you may have. From simple essay plans, through to full dissertations, you can guarantee we have a service perfectly matched to your needs.

View our services
Boston Globe survey of 1991 shows that patients with incurable illnesses who see suicide as an option are mostly those who are neither tired of pain or of restrictedlife style, nor the fear of machine dependency but rather the feeling of being a burden on their family. Sometimes it's the family who advocate Euthanasia for the terminally ill patient, considering his life unworthy, and therefore a burden; which in turn throws the patient in the abbeys of depression. One should be afraid of the day when legalization of the right to die will become duty to die, pressurizing the already tormented patients to select Euthanasia as an only option. [3]

If we look at Euthanasia from another angle it is not a right to die but gives someone a right to kill. A right given to doctors and the relatives of a person to intentionally end his life. There is a need to differentiate between suicide and killing. Suicide is an individual act, whereas Euthanasia is not a private act. It involves the will of the person or the relatives and action of the physician, and known by everyone around. It is therefore more close to public killing than suicide. Such a power to kill can be abused for the most vulnerable people in the population.

There should be a public realization that if all forms of treatments fail or become ineffective or continuation of any medical or surgical procedure would increase the pain rather than alleviating it, the suffering soul should be given support in all possible ways and all efforts should be directed toward minimizing his agony and making whatever little time he has, comfortable.

As followers of Islam such an option as Euthanasia can never cross our minds for ourselves or for our dear ones. I have a personal experience of accompanying a close kin of mine to the dialysis sessions, where patients were not only dependent on machines for their lives but were not even allowed to drink water during the warmest summers, but never did I once heard a patient or any of his relative praying for a quick demise. They would seek Allah's blessings during the hardest of times and a kind of hope would get them going. I saw doctors trying to look for options to improve the quality of life of such patients but any thought of eliminating the patient's pain through killing them was out of question and option.

As Muslims it is our firm belief that every life is sacred and Allah never creates and sustains anyone without purpose. In the holy Quran He says 'And if anyone saved a life, it would be as if he has saved the life of whole people'. (Quran 5:32). Allah further commands 'take not the life which Allah made sacred otherwise in the course of justice'.

If we equate voluntary Euthanasia with suicide, then again none of us has a right to take his own life. How can we have this right when we have not created ourselves, in fact how can we destroy something of which we are not the owners. Our bodies and souls belong to the Almighty and have been entrusted to us to be taken care of in the best ways possible. Suicide is a crime which is not only punishable in this world but also unforgivable sin in the hereafter. Prophet Mohammad warned the people against suicide by saying '"Whoever kills himself with an iron instrument will be carrying it forever in hell. Whoever takes poison and kills himself will forever keep sipping that poison in hell. Whoever jumps off a mountain and kills himself will forever keep falling down in the depths of hell'. [4]

Our religion Islam not only emphasize on seeking all possible medical help during illness but further consoles the patients in pain by giving him the happy tiding for reward if he endures the pain with patience. In one of the hadith it is mentioned that when a true believer is afflicted with pain, even a prick of a thorn and he bears it with patience, then his sins will be forgiven and his wrongdoings will be discarded as the tree sheds off its leaves. Such words by the Holy Prophet can be a huge support for a sufferer of a terminal illness or of incurable and painful disease. Euthanasia cannot therefore be a part of the dictionary of a true believer.

The weak value system of the west has come up with the idea of deserting the old, weak and the sick by leaving them in the old houses and hospitals. These so called facilities also sometimes cost them huge amounts, which make them claim that people who become unproductive for the society and a burden on the productive fellows should die for the good of the people around and for their own ease. But the east has still kept its value system strong. Our religious and social values dictate us to take care with respect and dignity of the old, weak, sick and the helpless. Allah has specially stressed upon respecting and serving the parents specially when they become old. "and that you be kind to your parents. Whether one or both of them attain old age in your life, say not to them a word of contempt but address them in terms of honor. And lower to them the wing of humility out of compassion, and say: my Lord, bestow on them your mercy even as they cherished me in childhood" (Qur'an 17:25-25). As far as the issue of heavy cost is concerned to keep a terminally ill patient alive, Islam makes it a responsibility of the state and the society as a whole to cover the health care needed.

Euthanasia might be categorized into several kinds but Islam emphasizes the intentions involved in the act. If for example physician intents to alleviate the pain of the patients but the dose somehow kill him, the doctor cannot be accused of murder, or cannot be said to have practiced Euthanasia. The doctor is expected to help the patient in the process of life and not in process of death.

Important enough is to consider the relative nature of the terms like pain, suffering and agony. It really depends on the patience and tolerance level of each individual, which of course varies. What is suffering for one person might not be the same for the other, similarly excruciating pain for one can be bearable for someone else.

Conclusion: – Humans might be the wisest form of God's creation but still not wise enough to be given a right to decide for their own death or for the death of another of their own kind. All lives are precious and sacred and only such value system can be the basis of a human society, where the sanctity of life is maintained. Euthanasia in any of its forms, involves the intention of killing or finishing a still living human weakens the fabric of the society and gives an altogether a different lens to the members to see death as the only solution for all pains and torments, which blurs the vision to see other possibilities to fight the situation. Euthanasia should therefore be discouraged in all its forms and in all parts of the world.

Euthanasia, also called 'Mercy Killing' and 'Physician Assisted Suicide; is a term in medical ethics for the practice of interfering or intervening in a natural process towards death. In other words it is accelerating the natural course of death in terminally ill patients, when all treatments become ineffective or much too painful for the patient to bear. In short Euthanasia is ending a human life with the intention of relieving the person from an unbearable pain. Haris (2001) precisely defines Euthanasia as 'a deliberate intervention undertaken with the express intention of ending a life to relieve intractable suffering'. [1]

The issue of Euthanasia has always remained controversial and still has failed to carry legal and constitutional support in most parts of the world. Suicide in any form and by any means is either punished or at least disapproved in human history. There is no permissibility of such a killing/suicide in Islam so Euthanasia can never be the part of Muslim law in Islamic world. Therefore the origin and development of this concept can be historically located in the non Muslim countries especially of the west.

Back in 400 BC when the father of medicine Hippocrates formulated the oath still taken by the fresh medical graduates dictates 'I will give no deadly medicine to any one if asked, nor suggest any such counsel"., speaks against physician assisted suicide. Even in the 19th century, the US legislation proclaimed that if a suicide is committed on the advice of another person, the adviser would be guilty of a murder. In the early 20th century, the Supreme Court reevaluated its judgments concerning 'living will' and focusing how best to ensure the dignity and the independence for the 'end of life' with considerable changes in the health laws. In 1920 the book "Permitting the Destruction of Life not Worthy of Life" was published, in which the author Hoche advocated the death assistance be given under very controlled conditions. In 1935 Euthanasia society was formed in England to support mercy killing. 1939's Nazi's Euthanasia became very popular when Hitler ordered mercy killing of the sick and disabled. From 1995 to 2008, Euthanasia has been legalized in countries like parts of Australia, Netherland, Belgium and few states of the United States of America.

There are several forms or kinds of Euthanasia; each form has its own ethical issues.
Active Euthanasia: is the one which causes immediate death of the patient, by the direct and deliberate action of the physician. For example when a lethal injection is given to the patient or an overdose of a pain killer when the physician knows the after effects of such a dose.

Passive Euthanasia involves an indirect action by the physician for the death of the patient. This may include withdrawing or withholding the required treatment. For example switching off the life supporting machine like ventilator or not doing the required surgical procedures that can keep the person alive though for a shorttime.

Voluntary Euthanasia:- takes place with the will of the patient, usually on his request to the physician.

Non-Voluntary Euthanasia occurs when the patient is unconscious or in comma for a long time, or unable to make decision for example a very young child, or a mentally retarded person. Therefore someone else related to the patient makes the decision of ending the patient's life.

Involuntary Euthanasia:- is oftentimes equated to murder because in this case the patient does not opt for death but he is killed as the doctor thinks it to be in his benefit.

Indirect Euthanasia: – does not involve the intentional killing by the physician, but the side effects of the treatment, usually given to reduce the pain accelerate the death of the patient.

Assisted Suicide:- includes cases when the patient seeks help from his physician to die. This can include making the lethal drugs available for the patients.

The most common argument given by the proponents of Euthanasia is its effective way of relieving excruciating pain. To this one argument there can be two counter arguments. Firstly the advancements made today in the field of medicine, especially in pain management weakens the justification for Euthanasia. Secondly research shows that terminally ill patients choose suicide not because of the physical pain but because of depression. A study of terminally ill patients published in The American Journal of Psychiatry in 1986 concluded: 'The striking feature of [our] results is that all of the patients who had either desired premature death or contemplated suicide were judged to be suffering from clinical depressive illness; that is, none of those patients who did not have clinical depression had thoughts of suicide or wished that death would come early'.

Researchers believe that a person diagnosed with terminal illness should be given time and support to pass through the five stages of the process – denial, anger, bargaining, depression and acceptance, and killing them before they come to terms with the situation is nothing less than a murder.

Boston Globe survey of 1991 shows that patients with incurable illnesses who see suicide as an option are mostly those who are neither tired of pain or of restricted life style, nor the fear of machine dependency but rather the feeling of being a burden on their family. Sometimes it's the family who advocate Euthanasia for the terminally ill patient, considering his life unworthy, and therefore a burden; which in turn throws the patient in the abbeys of depression. One should be afraid of the day when legalization of the right to die will become duty to die, pressurizing the already tormented patients to select Euthanasia as an only option.

If we look at Euthanasia from another angle it is not a right to die but gives someone a right to kill. A right given to doctors and the relatives of a person to intentionally end his life. There is a need to differentiate between suicide and killing. Suicide is an individual act, whereas Euthanasia is not a private act. It involves the will of the person or the relatives and action of the physician, and known by everyone around. It is therefore more close to public killing than suicide. Such a power to kill can be abused for the most vulnerable people in the population.

There should be a public realization that if all forms of treatments fail or become ineffective or continuation of any medical or surgical procedure would increase the pain rather than alleviating it, the suffering soul should be given support in all possible ways and all efforts should be directed toward minimizing his agony and making whatever little time he has, comfortable.

As followers of Islam such an option as Euthanasia can never cross our minds for ourselves or for our dear ones. I have a personal experience of accompanying a close kin of mine to the dialysis sessions, where patients were not only dependent on machines for their lives but were not even allowed to drink water during the warmest summers, but never did I once heard a patient or any of his relative praying for a quick demise. They would seek Allah's blessings during the hardest of times and a kind of hope would get them going. I saw doctors trying to look for options to improve the quality of life of such patients but any thought of eliminating the patient's pain through killing them was out of question and option.

As Muslims it is our firm belief that every life is sacred and Allah never creates andsustains anyone without purpose. In the holy Quran He says 'And if anyone saved a life, it would be as if he has saved the life of whole people'. (Quran 5:32). Allah further commands 'take not the life which Allah made sacred otherwise in the course of justice'.

If we equate voluntary Euthanasia with suicide, then again none of us has a right to take his own life. How can we have this right when we have not created ourselves, in fact how can we destroy something of which we are not the owners. Our bodies and souls belong to the Almighty and have been entrusted to us to be taken care of in the best ways possible. Suicide is a crime which is not only punishable in this world but also unforgivable sin in the hereafter. Prophet Mohammad warned the people against suicide by saying '"Whoever kills himself with an iron instrument will be carrying it forever in hell. Whoever takes poison and kills himself will forever keep sipping that poison in hell. Whoever jumps off amountain and kills himself will forever keep falling down in the depths of hell'.

Our religion Islam not only emphasize on seeking all possible medical help during illness but further consoles the patients in pain by giving him the happy tiding for reward if he endures the pain with patience. In one of the hadith it is mentioned that when a true believer is afflicted with pain, even a prick of a thorn and he bears it with patience, then his sins will be forgiven and his wrongdoings will be discarded as the tree sheds off its leaves. Such words by the Holy Prophet can bea huge support for a sufferer of a terminal illness or of incurable and painful disease. Euthanasia cannot therefore be a part of the dictionary of a true believer.

The weak value system of the west has come up with the idea of deserting theold, weak and the sick by leaving them in the old houses and hospitals. These so called facilities also sometimes cost them huge amounts, which make them claim that people who become unproductive for the society and a burden on the productive fellows should die for the good of the people around and for their ownease. But the east has still kept its value system strong. Our religious and social values dictate us to take care with respect and dignity of the old, weak, sick and the helpless. Allah has specially stressed upon respecting and serving the parents specially when they become old. "and that you be kind to your parents. Whether one or both of them attain old age in your life, say not to them a word of contempt but address them in terms of honor. And lower to them the wing of humility out of compassion, and say: my Lord, bestow on them your mercy even as they cherished me in childhood" (Qur'an 17:25- 25). As far as the issue of heavycost is concerned to keep a terminally ill patient alive, Islam makes it a responsibility of the state and the society as a whole to cover the health care needed.

Euthanasia might be categorized into several kinds but Islam emphasizes the intentions involved in the act. If for example physician intents to alleviate the painof the patients but the dose somehow kill him, the doctor cannot be accused of murder, or cannot be said to have practiced Euthanasia. The doctor is expected tohelp the patient in the process of life and not in process of death.

Important enough is to consider the relative nature of the terms like pain, suffering and agony. It really depends on the patience and tolerance level of each individual, which of course varies. What is suffering for one person might not be the same for the other, similarly excruciating pain for one can be bearable for someone else.

Conclusion: – Humans might be the wisest form of God's creation but still not wise enough to be given a right to decide for their own death or for the death of another of their own kind. All lives are precious and sacred and only such value system can be the basis of a human society, where the sanctity of life is maintained. Euthanasia in any of its forms, involves the intention of killing or finishing a still living human weakens the fabric of the society and gives an altogether a different lens to the members to see death as the only solution for allpains and torments, which blurs the vision to see other possibilities to fight the situation. Euthanasia should therefore be discouraged in all its forms and in all parts of the world.

Female-infanticide What is infanticide?
Infanticide is the unlawful killing of very young children. It is found in bothindigenous and sophisticated cultures around the world.

Female infanticide
Female infanticide is the deliberate killing of girl babies. It is also described as gender-selective killing or "gendercide". (Similar words like 'gynocide' and 'femicide' are used to describe the killing of females of any age.) Female infanticide is more common than male infanticide, and in some countries, particularly India and China, is likely to have serious consequences on the balance of the sexes in the population. The reasons behind it are almost always cultural, rather than directly religious.The causes:

Anti-female bias
Societies that practise female infanticide always show many other signs of bias against females. Women are perceived as subservient because of their role as carers and homemakers, whilst men predominantly ensure the family's social and economic stability.

Family economics
Girl babies are often killed for financial reasons.

- **Earning power:** Men are usually the main income-earners, either because they are more employable or earn higher wages for the same work, or because they are able to do more agricultural work in subsistence economies. Since male babies have a greater income potential, they areless likely to be killed.
- **Potential pensions:** In many societies, parents depend on their children to look after them in old age. But in many of these cultures a girl leaves her parental family and joins her husband's family when she marries. The resultis that parents with sons gain extra resources for their old age, when their sons marry, while parents with daughters lose their 'potential pensions' when they marry and move away. This gives parents a strong reason to prefer male children. Some parents (particularly poor ones) who can't afford to support a large family, will kill female babies. Girls are considered a drain on family resources during their childhood without bringing economic benefits later on.
- **Dowry:** Some girl babies are killed so that the family doesn't have to pay a dowry when they get married. In Indian society it is tradition for the parents of the bride to give a dowry to the groom and his family. The dowry consists of large amounts of money and valuable goods. For families withseveral daughters this can be a serious financial burden.

Government policy
Governmental policies have also increased female infanticide as an unpredicted side-effect. For example, when the Chinese Government introduced a One Child per Family Policy there was a surge in female infanticide. Families needed to have a son because of their higher earning potential, so a girl baby was an economic disaster for them, and there was a strong motive to ensure that girl babies did notsurvive.

Caste
Some female infants are killed because they are regarded as being lower in the **caste** hierarchy than males.

Where does female infanticide occur?
Female infanticide is a significant problem in parts of Asia - infanticide does occur in the West, but usually as isolated family tragedies with no underlying pattern or gender bias.
India
Female infanticide and **female foeticide** (the selective abortion of girls in the womb) are significant issues in India.

Female infanticide has been a problem for centuries, partly as a result of the patriarchal nature of Indian society.

Tackling the issue
Modern India has tried several ways to tackle the issue. One initiative in the state of Tamil Nadu was taken to attack the underlying economic problems.

Where parents had one or two daughters but no son, and either of the parents was willing to be sterilised, the government offered the parents money to help look after the children. This money was to be paid annually throughout the daughter's education, followed by a lump sum on her twentieth birthday, either for use as a dowry or to fund further education.

China
Female infanticide has existed in China for a long time, and although the One Child per Family policy has added to the problem, it didn't cause it.

The One Child Policy was introduced by the Chinese Government in 1979 with the intention of keeping the population within sustainable limits even in the face of natural disasters and poor harvests, and improving the quality of life for the Chinese population as a whole.

Under the policy, parents who have more than one child may have their wages reduced and be denied some social services. Despite the egalitarian nature of Chinese society, many parents believe that having a son is a vital element of providing for their old age. Therefore in extreme cases, a baby is killed if it is not of the preferred sex, because of the pressure not to have more than one child.

Tackling the issue
The Chinese Government have acknowledged the problem and introduced laws todeal with it:

- Marriage law prohibits female infanticide.
- Women's Protection Law prohibits infanticide and bans discrimination against women who choose to keep female babies.
- Maternal Health Care Law forbids the use of technological advances, such as ultra-sound machines, to establish the sex of foetuses, so as not to pre- determine the fate of female infants or encourage selective abortion.

Origins of infanticide
Infanticide occurs in most cases as a way of restricting poverty and population. Throughout history infanticide has been regarded as a productive and efficient way to control starvation and poor standards of living caused by over population.

Confucianism
The male bias in China is deeply rooted in Chinese traditions which leads parents to want their first child to be a boy. Confucianism regards male children as more desirable since they provide security for the elderly, work and are important for the performance of ancestral rites.

Hinduism
Hindu authorities condemn infanticide. Son-preference in Hindu cultures is largely based on the fact that men are better providers, and that sons are required for the proper performance of funeral rites. Some writers argue that Hindu culture has long had a patriarchal bias against women.

Sikhism
Sikh authorities condemn infanticide. The Sikh religion is one of the most gender-neutral, and explicitly proclaims the equality of men and women. This makes it more surprising that censuses in India show there are far more male children than female children in the Sikh community.

In practice there does appear to be a strong preference for boys in the Sikh heartland. The community appears to give greater respect to the parents of boys, and boys themselves.

In response the Sikh religious organisation Akal Takht has re-emphasised that women are equal to men. It has banned neo-natal sex identification, selective abortion and the killing of female babies.

Islam
Islam has always condemned infanticide. Female infanticide was common in pre-Islamic Arabia. However, by the time of Muhammad, and the revelation of the Qur'an female infanticide was strictly forbidden, and regarded as seriously as adult murder.

The Qur'an on female infanticide:
When the infant girl, is buried alive, is questioned, for what crime she waskilled.

Surah 81 v 8 - 9
You shall not kill your children for fear of want. We will provide for themand for you. To kill them is a grievous sin.

Surah 17 v 31
Christianity
Christianity has always condemned infanticide.

Judaism
Judaism has always condemned infanticide. **Professional Ethics: Corporate Governance The ends and means of corporate governance**
There is significant debate about the ends and means of corporate governance, i.e., about who firms should be managed for, and who should (ultimately) managethem. Much of this debate is carried on with the large publicly-traded corporationin view.

Ends: shareholder primacy or stakeholder balance?
There are two main views about the proper ends of corporate governance. According to one view, firms should be managed in the best interests of shareholders. It is typically assumed that managing firms in shareholders' best interests requires maximizing their wealth. This view is often called "shareholder primacy" (Stout 2002) or—in order to contrast it more directly with its main rival (to be discussed below) "shareholder theory". (Confusingly, the label 'shareholderprimacy' is sometimes used—e.g., by Bainbridge [2008]—to refer to the view that shareholders should have ultimate control over the firm.) Shareholder primacy is the dominant view about the ends of corporate governance among financialprofessionals and in business schools.

A few writers argue for shareholder primacy on deontological grounds. On this argument, shareholders own the firm, and hire managers to run it for them on the condition that the firm is managed in their interests. Shareholder primacy is thus based on a promise that managers make to shareholders (Friedman 1970; Hasnas 1998). In response, some argue that shareholders do not own the firm. They own stock, a type of corporate security (Bainbridge 2008; Stout 2002); the firm itself may be unowned (Strudler 2017). Others argue that managers do not make, explicitly or implicitly, any promises to shareholders to manage the firm ina certain way (Boatright 1994). More writers argue for shareholder primacy on consequentialist grounds. On this argument, managing firms in the interests of shareholders is more efficient than managing them in any other way (Hansmann & Kraakman 2001; Jensen 2002). In support of this, some argue that, if managers are not given a single objective that is clear and measurable—viz., maximizing shareholder value—then they will have an enhanced opportunity for self-dealing (Stout 2002). Consequentialist arguments for shareholder primacy run into problems that afflict many versions of consequentialism: in requiring all firms to be managed in a certain way, it does not allow sufficient scope for personal choice (Hussain 2012). Most think that people should be able to pursue projects, including economic projects, that matter to them, even if those projects do not maximize welfare.

The second main view about the proper ends of corporate governance is given by stakeholder theory. This theory was first put forward by Freeman in the 1980s (Freeman 1984; Freeman & Reed 1983), and then refined by Freeman and variouscollaborators over the next 30 years (see, e.g., Freeman et al. 2010; Jones, Wicks, & Freeman 2002). According to stakeholder theory—or at least, early formulations of the theory—instead of managing the firm in the best interests of shareholders only, managers should seek to "balance" the interests of all stakeholders, where a stakeholder is anyone who has a "stake", or interest (including a financial interest), in the firm.

To its critics, stakeholder theory has seemed both insufficiently articulated and weakly defended. With respect to articulation, one question that has been pressed is: Who are the stakeholders (Orts & Strudler 2002, 2009)? The groups most commonly identified are shareholders, employees, the community, suppliers, and customers. But other groups have stakes in the firm, including creditors, the government, and competitors. It makes a great deal of difference where the line is drawn, but stakeholder theorists have not provided a clear rationale for drawing a line in one place rather than another. Another question is: What does it mean to "balance" the interests of all stakeholders—other than not always giving precedence to shareholders' interests (Orts & Strudler 2009)? With respect to defense, critics have wondered what the rationale for managing firmsin the interests of all stakeholders is. In one place, Freeman (1984) offers an instrumental argument for his view, claiming that balancing stakeholders' interests is better for the firm strategically than maximizing shareholder wealth. (This is precisely what defenders of shareholder primacy say about that view.) In another, he gives an argument that appeals to Rawls's justice as fairness.

In recent years, questions have been raised about whether stakeholder theory is appropriately seen as a genuine competitor to shareholder primacy, or is even appropriately called a "theory". In one article, Freeman and collaborators say thatstakeholder theory is simply "the body of research ... in which the idea of 'stakeholders' plays a crucial role" (Jones et al. 2002). In another, Freeman describes stakeholder theory as "a genre of stories about how we could live"

(1994: 413). It may be, as Norman (2013) says, that stakeholder is now best regarded as "mindset", i.e., a way of looking at the firm that emphasizes its embeddedness in a network of relationships.

It is important to realize that a resolution of the debate between shareholder and stakeholder theorists (however we conceive of the latter) will not resolve all or even most of the ethical questions in business. This is because this is a debate about the ends of corporate governance; it cannot answer all of the questions about the moral constraints that must be observed in pursuit of those ends (Goodpaster 1991; Norman 2013). Neither shareholder primacy nor stakeholder theory is plausibly interpreted as the view that corporate managers should do whatever is possible to maximize shareholder wealth and balance all stakeholders' interests, respectively. Rather, these views should be interpreted as views that managers should do whatever is morally permissible to achieve these ends. A large part of business ethics is trying to determine what morality permits in this domain.

Means: control by shareholders or others too?
Answers to questions about the means of corporate governance often mirror answers to question about the ends of corporate governance. Often the best way to ensure that a firm is managed in the interests of a certain party P is to give P control over it. Conversely, justifications for why the firm should be managed in the interests of P sometimes appeal P's rights to control it. Thus Friedman (1970) thinks that shareholders' ownership of the firm gives them a right to control the firm (which they can use to ensure that the firm is run in their interests). We might see control rights for shareholders as following analytically from the concept of ownership. To own a thing is to have a bundle of rights with respect to that thing. One of the standard "incidents" of ownership is control.

As noted, in recent years the idea that the firm is something that can be owned has been challenged (Bainbridge 2008; Strudler 2017). But contractarian arguments for shareholder control of firms have been constructed which do not rely on the assumption of firm ownership. All that is assumed in these arguments is that some people own capital, and others own labor. Capital can "hire" labor (and other inputs of production), on terms that it draws up, or labor can "hire" capital, on terms that it draws up, with society setting limits on what the terms may be. It just so happens that, in most cases, capital hires labor. These points areemphasized especially by those who regard the firm as a "nexus of contracts" among various parties.

Many writers find this result troubling. Even if the governance structure in most firms is in some sense agreed to, they say that it is unjust in other ways. Anderson(2015) characterizes standard corporate governance regimes as oppressive and unaccountable private dictatorships. To address this injustice, these writers call for various forms of worker participation in managerial decision-making, including the ability by workers to reject arbitrary directives by managers (Hsieh 2005), worker co-determination of firms' policies and practices, and exclusive control of productive enterprises by workers.

Arguments for these governance structures take various forms. One type of argument appeals to the value of protecting workers' interests (Brenkert 1992a; Hsieh 2005). A second type of argument appeals to the value of autonomy, or a right to freely determine one's actions, including one's actions at work (McCall 2001). A third type of argument for worker participation in managerial decision- making is the "parallel case" argument. According to it, if states should be governed democratically, then so should firms, because firms are like states in therelevant respects (Dahl 1985; Walzer 1983). A fourth argument for worker participation in firm decision-making sees it as valuable or even necessary trainingfor participation in political processes in the broader society (Cohen 1989).

Space considerations prevent a detailed examination of these arguments. But criticisms generally fall into two categories. The first insists on the normative priority of agreements, of the sort described above. There are few legal restrictions on the types of governance structures that firms can have. And some firms are in fact controlled by workers (Dow 2003; Hansmann 1996). To insist thatother firms should be governed this way is to say, according to this argument, that people should not be allowed to arrange their economic lives as they see fit. Another criticism of worker participation appeals to efficiency. Allowing workers to participate in managerial decision-making may decrease the pace of decision- making, since it requires giving many workers a chance to make their voices heard(Hansmann 1996). It may also raise the cost of capital for firms, as investors may demand more favorable terms if they are not given control of the enterprise in return (McMahon 1994). Both sources of inefficiency may put the firm at a significant disadvantage in a competitive market. And it may not be just a matter of competitive disadvantage. If it were, the problem could be solved by making allfirms worker-controlled. The problem may be one of diminished productivitymore generally.

Corporate social responsibility

Corporate social responsibility is based on the premise that a business can only thrive if it operates within a thriving society. In that way, the business depends onthe community it operates within, and as such, has an ethical and moral responsibility towards that community. A business is perceived as legitimate when its activities are congruent with the goals and values of the society in which the business operates.

Consumers and other companies are likely to shun firms that develop unethical reputations. And arguably, companies that don't pay attention to their social and ethical responsibilities are more likely to stumble into legal troubles, such as mass corruption or accounting fraud scandals – threatening the sustainability of the business itself.

By promoting respect for the company in the marketplace, CSR can result in higher sales, enhance employee loyalty and attract better personnel to the firm. Itis also a way to connect to the personal well-being of customers. In this way, the CSR can contribute towards higher profits for the company.

Therefore, by ensuring brand loyalty and consumer patronage, CSR can ensure that the business remains sustainable in the long-term and it stays profitable.

Ethical Responsibility

Responsibility is an ethical concept that refers to the fact that individuals and groups have morally based obligations and duties to others and to larger ethical and moral codes, standards and traditions.

Ethical Principles of Responsibility and Accountability

Responsibility in a business context refers to "a sphere of duty or obligation assigned to a person by the nature of that person's position, function or work."

The roles taken on by decision-makers imply a responsibility to perform certain functions associated with those roles. To be more specific, responsibility refers to more than just the primary function of a role; it refers to the multiple facets of that function, which includes both processes and outcomes, and the consequences of the acts performed as part of that set of obligations. A responsible actor may be seen as one whose job involves a predetermined set of obligations that need to be met in order for the job to be accomplished.

According to Aristotle, moral responsibility was viewed as originating with the moral agent as decision-maker, and grew out of an ability to reason, an awareness of action and consequences, and a willingness to act free from external compulsion.

Accountability is the readiness or preparedness to give an explanation orjustification to stakeholders for one's judgments, intentions and actions.

"It is a readiness to have one's actions judged by others and, where appropriate, accept responsibility for errors, misjudgments and negligence and recognition for competence, conscientiousness, excellence and wisdom." While responsibility is defined as a bundle of obligations associated with a role, accountability could be defined as "blaming or crediting someone for an action"— normally associated with a recognized responsibility. The accountable actor is "held to external oversight, regulation, and mechanisms of punishment aimed to externally motivate responsive adjustment in order to maintain adherence with appropriate moral standards of action."

In the professional context, accountability is about answering to   clients, colleagues and other relevant professionals. The demand to give an account of one's judgments, acts and omissions arises from the nature of the professional- client and the professional-professional relationships. For communication professionals, accountability has more specific implications. Recent years have seen more practical and concrete interpretation of the concept of accountability by communication specialists. It is associated with responsiveness to the views of all stakeholders, which includes a willingness to explain, defend, and justify actions.

While tracing the lines of responsibility and accountability can be difficult, in the end, if one is responsible in any way for an action, then one must accept some degree of accountability. On the other hand, if responsibility and accountability are not equitably shared and if the process by which they are assigned is not transparent, then problems will arise. In the corporate world, not every actor is blame-worthy, especially if the actor's autonomy is limited by structure, process, or circumstance. However, lack of autonomy is not an excuse for avoiding accountability entirely.

Media Ethics: ethical issues in PrivacyIntroduction

The use of social media is growing at a rapid pace and the twenty-first century could be described as the "boom" period for social networking. According to reports provided by Smart Insights, as at February 2019 there were over 3.484 billion social media users. The Smart Insight report indicates that the number of social media users is growing by 9% annually and this trend is estimated to continue. Presently the number of social media users represents 45% of the global population. The heaviest users of social media are "digital natives"; the group of persons who were born or who have grown up in the digital era and are intimate with the various technologies and systems, and the "Millennial Generation"; those who became adults at the turn of the twenty-first century. These groups of users utilize social media platforms for just about anything ranging from marketing, news acquisition, teaching, health care, civic engagement, and politicking to social engagement. The unethical use of social media has resulted in the breach of individual privacy and impacts both physical and information security. Reports in 2019, reveal that persons between the ages 8 and 11 years spend an average 13.5 hours weekly online and 18% of this age group are actively engaged on social media. Those between ages 12 and 15 spend on average 20.5 hours online and 69% of this group are active social media users. While children and teenagers represent the largest Internet user groups, for the most part they do not know how to protect their personal information on the Web and are the most vulnerable to cyber-crimes related to breaches of information privacy.

In today's IT-configured society data is one of, if not the most, valuable asset for most businesses/organizations. Organizations and governments collect information via several means including invisible data gathering, marketing platforms and search engines such as Google. Information can be attained from several sources, which can be fused using technology to develop complete profiles of individuals. The information on social media is very accessible and can be of great value to individuals and organizations for reasons such as marketing, etc.; hence, data is retained by most companies for future use.

Privacy

Privacy or the right to enjoy freedom from unauthorized intrusion is the negative right of all human beings. Privacy is defined as the right to be left alone, to be free from secret surveillance, or unwanted disclosure of personal data or information by government, corporation, or individual (dictionary.com). In this chapter we will define privacy loosely, as the right to control access to personal information. Supporters of privacy posit that it is a necessity for human dignity and individuality and a key element in the quest for happiness. According to Baase [5] in the book titled "A Gift of Fire: Social, Legal and Ethical Issues for Computing and the Internet," privacy is the ability to control information about one' s self as well as the freedom from surveillance from being followed, tracked, watched, and being eavesdropped on. In this regard, ignoring privacy rights often leads to encroachment on natural rights.

Privacy, or even the thought that one has this right, leads to peace of mind and can provide an environment of solitude. This solitude can allow people to breathe freely in a space that is free from interference and intrusion. According to Richards and Solove, Legal scholar William Prosser argued that privacy cases can be classified into four related "torts," namely:

1. Intrusion—this can be viewed as encroachment (physical or otherwise) on ones liberties/solitude in a highly offensive way.
2. Privacy facts—making public, private information about someone that is of no "legitimate concern" to anyone.
3. False light—making public false and "highly offensive" information about others.
4. Appropriation—stealing someone's identity (name, likeness) to gain advantage without the permission of the individual.

Technology, the digital age, the Internet and social media have redefined privacy however as surveillance is no longer limited to a certain pre-defined space and location. An understanding of the problems and dangers of privacy in the digital space is therefore the first step to privacy control. While there can be clear distinctions between informational privacy and physical privacy, as pointed out earlier, intrusion can be both physical and otherwise.

This chapter will focus on informational privacy which is the ability to control access to personal information. We examine privacy issues in the social media context focusing primarily on personal information and the ability to control external influences. We suggest that breach of informational privacy can impact: solitude (the right to be left alone), intimacy (the right not to be monitored), and anonymity (the right to have no public personal identity and by extension physical privacy impacted). The right to control access to facts or personal information in our view is a natural, inalienable right and everyone should have control over whosee their personal information and how it is disseminated.

In May 2019 the General Data Protection Regulation (GDPR) clearly outlined that it is unlawful to process personal data without the consent of the individual (subject). It is a legal requirement under the GDPR that privacy notices be given to individuals that outline how their personal data will be processed and the conditions that must be met that make the consent valid. These are:

- "Freely given—an individual must be given a genuine choice when providing consent and it should generally be unbundled from other terms and conditions (e.g., access to a service should not be conditional upon consent being given)."
- "Specific and informed—this means that data subjects should be provided with information as to the identity of the controller(s), the specific purposes, types of processing, as well as being informed of their right to withdraw consent at any time."
- "Explicit and unambiguous—the data subject must clearly express their consent (e.g., by actively ticking a box which confirms they are giving consent—pre-ticked boxes are insufficient)."
- "Under 13s—children under the age of 13 cannot provide consent and it is therefore necessary to obtain consent from

their parents."

Arguments can be made that privacy is a cultural, universal necessity for harmonious relationships among human beings and creates the boundaries for engagement and disengagement. Privacy can also be viewed as instrumental good because it is a requirement for the development of certain kinds of human relationships, intimacy and trust. However, achieving privacy is much more difficult in light of constant surveillance and the inability to determine the levels of interaction with various publics. Some critics argue that privacy provides protection against anti-social behaviors such as trickery, disinformation and fraud, and is thought to be a universal right. However, privacy can also be viewed as relative as privacy rules may differ based on several factors such as "climate, religion, technological advancement and political arrangements". The need for privacy is an objective reality though it can be viewed as "culturally rational" where the need for personal privacy is viewed as relative based on culture. One example is the push by the government, businesses and Singaporeans to make Singapore a smart nation. According to GovTech 2018 reports there is a push by the government in Singapore to harness the data "new gold" to develop systems that can make life easier for its people. The report points out that Singapore is using sensors robots Smart Water Assessment Network (SWAN) to monitor water quality in its reservoirs, seeking to build smart health system and to build a smart transportation system to name a few. In this example privacy can be describe as "culturally rational" and the rules in general could differ based on technological advancement and political arrangements.

In today's networked society it is naïve and ill-conceived to think that privacy is over-rated and there is no need to be concerned about privacy if you have done nothing wrong. The effects of information flow can be complex and may not be simply about protection for people who have something to hide. Inaccurate information flow can have adverse long-term implications for individuals and companies. Consider a scenario where someone's computer or tablet is stolen. The perpetrator uses identification information stored on the device to access their social media page which could lead to access to their contacts, friends and friends of their "friends" then participate in illegal activities and engage in anti- social activities such as hacking, spreading viruses, fraud and identity theft. The victim is now in danger of being accused of criminal intentions, or worse. These kinds of situations are possible because of technology and networked systems. Users of social media need to be aware of the risks that are associated with participation.

Social media
The concept of social networking pre-dates the Internet and mass communication as people are said to be social creatures who when working in groups can achieve results in a value greater than the sun of its parts. The explosive growth in the use of social media over the past decade has made it one of the most popular Internet services in the world, providing new avenues to "see and be seen". The use of social media has changed the communication landscape resulting in changes in ethical norms and behavior. The unprecedented level of growth in usage has resulted in the reduction in the use of other media and changes in areas including civic and political engagement, privacy and safety. Alexa, a company that keeps track of traffic on the Web, indicates that as of August, 2019 YouTube, Facebook and Twitter are among the top four (4) most visited sites with only Google, being the most popular search engine, surpassing these social media sites.

Social media sites can be described as online services that allow users to create profiles which are "public, semi-public" or both. Users may create individual profiles and/or become a part of a group of people with whom they may be acquainted offline. They also provide avenues to create virtual friendships. Through these virtual friendships, people may access details about their contacts ranging from personal background information and interests to location. Social networking sites provide various tools to facilitate communication. These include chat rooms, blogs, private messages, public comments, ways of uploading content external to the site and sharing videos and photographs. Social media is therefore drastically changing the way people communicate and form relationships.

Today social media has proven to be one of the most, if not the most effective medium for the dissemination of information to various audiences. The power of this medium is phenomenal and ranges from its ability to overturn governments (e.g., Moldova), to mobilize protests, assist with getting support for humanitarian aid, organize political campaigns, organize groups to delay the passing of legislation (as in the case with the copyright bill in Canada) to making social media billionaires and millionaires. The enabling nature and the structure of the media that social networking offers provide a wide range of opportunities that were nonexistent before technology. Facebook and YouTube marketers and trainers provide two examples. Today people can interact with and learn from people millions of miles away. The global reach of this medium has removed all former pre-defined boundaries including geographical, social and any other that existed previously. Technological advancements such as Web 2.0 and Web 4.0 which provide the framework for collaboration, have given new meaning to life from various perspectives: political, institutional and social.

Privacy and social media
Social medial and the information/digital era have "redefined" privacy. In today's Information Technology—configured societies, where there is continuous monitoring, privacy has taken on a new meaning. Technologies such as closed- circuit cameras (CCTV) are prevalent in public spaces or in some private spaces including our work and home. Personal computers and devices such as our smart phones enabled with Global Positioning System (GPS), Geo locations and Geo maps connected to these devices make privacy as we know it, a thing of the past. Recent reports indicate that some of the largest companies such as Amazon, Microsoft and Facebook as well as various government agencies are collecting information without consent and storing it in databases for future use. It is almost impossible to say privacy exists in this digital world (@nowthisnews).

The open nature of the social networking sites and the avenues they provide for sharing information in a "public or semi-public" space create privacy concerns by their very construct. Information that is inappropriate for some audiences are many times inadvertently made visible to groups other than those intended and can sometimes result in future negative outcomes. One such example is a well- known case recorded in an article entitled "The Web Means the End of Forgetting" that involved a young woman who was denied her college license because of backlash from photographs posted on social media in her private engagement.

Technology has reduced the gap between professional and personal spaces and often results in information exposure to the wrong audience. The reduction in theseparation of professional and personal spaces can affect image management especially in a professional setting resulting in the erosion of traditional professional image and impression management. Determining the secondary use of personal information and those who have access to this information should be the prerogative of the individual or group to whom the information belongs. However, engaging in social media activities has removed this control.
Privacy on social networking sites (SNSs) is heavily dependent on the users of these networks because sharing information is the primary way of participating in social communities. Privacy in SNSs is "multifaceted." Users of these platforms areresponsible for protecting their information from third-party data collection and managing their personal profiles. However, participants are usually more willingto give personal and more private information in SNSs than anywhere else on the Internet. This can be attributed to the feeling of community, comfort and family that these media provide for the most part. Privacy controls are not the priority ofsocial networking site designers and only a small number of the young adolescent users change the default privacy settings of their accounts. This opens the door for breaches especially among the most vulnerable user groups, namely young children, teenagers and the elderly. The nature of social networking sites such as Facebook and Twitter and other social media platforms cause users to re-evaluateand often change their personal privacy standards in order to participate in these social networked communitie.

While there are tremendous benefits that can be derived from the effective use of social media there are some unavoidable risks that are involved in its use. Much attention should therefore be given to what is shared in these forums. Social platforms such as Facebook, Twitter and YouTube are said to be the most effective media to communicate to Generation Y's (Gen Y's), as teens and young adults are the largest user groups on these platforms. However, according to Bolton et al. Gen Y's use of social media, if left unabated and unmonitored will have long-term implications for privacy and engagement in civic activities as this continuous use is resulting in changes in behavior and social norms as well as increased levels of cyber-crime.
Today social networks are becoming the platform of choice for hackers and other perpetrators of antisocial behavior. These media offer large volumes of data/information ranging from an individual's date of birth, place of residence, place of work/business, to information about family and other personal activities.

In many cases users unintentionally disclose information that can be both dangerous and inappropriate. Information regarding activities on social media canhave far reaching negative implications for one's future. A few examples of situations which can, and have been affected are employment, visa acquisition, and college acceptance. Indiscriminate participation has also resulted in situationssuch identity theft and bank fraud just to list a few. Protecting privacy in today's networked society can be a great challenge. The digital revolution has indeed distorted our views of privacy, however, there should be clear distinctions between what should be seen by the general public and what should be limited toa selected group. One school of thought is that the only way to have privacy todayis not to share information in these networked communities. However, achieving privacy and control over information flows and disclosure in networked communities is an ongoing process in an environment where contexts change quickly and are sometimes blurred. This requires intentional construction of systems that are designed to mitigate privacy issues.

Ethics and social media
Ethics can be loosely defined as "the right thing to do" or it can be described as the moral philosophy of an individual or group and usually reflects what the individual or group views as good or bad. It is how they classify particular situations by categorizing them as right or wrong. Ethics can also be used to refer to any classification or philosophy of moral values or principles that guides the actions of an individual or group. Ethical values are intended to be guiding principles that if followed, could yield harmonious results and relationships. They seek to give answers to questions such as "How should I be living? How do I achieve the things that are deemed important such as knowledge and happiness or the acquisition of attractive things?" If one chooses happiness, the next question that needs to be answered is "Whose happiness should it be; my own happiness or the happiness of others?" In the domain of social media, some of the ethical questions that must be contemplated and ultimately answered are:

- Can this post be regarded as oversharing?
- Has the information in this post been distorted in anyway?
- What impact will this post have on others?

As previously mentioned, users within the ages 8–15 represent one of the largest social media user groups. These young persons within the 8–15 age range are still learning how to interact with the people around them and are deciding on the moral values that they will embrace. These moral values will help to dictate how they will interact with the world around them. The ethical values that guide our interactions are usually formulated from some moral principle taught to us by someone or a group of individuals including parents, guardians, religious groups, and teachers just to name a few. Many of the Gen Y's/"Digital Babies" are "newbies" yet are required to determine for themselves the level of responsibilitythey will display when using the varying social media platforms. This includes considering the impact a post will have on their lives and/or the lives of other persons. They must also understand that when they join a social media network, they are joining a community in which certain behavior must be exhibited. Such responsibility requires a much greater level of maturity than can be expected from them at that age.

It is not uncommon for individuals to post even the smallest details of their lives from the moment they wake up to when they go to bed. They will openly share their location, what they eat at every meal or details about activities typically considered private and personal. They will also share likes and dislikes, thoughts and emotional states and for the most part this has become an accepted norm. Often times however, these shares do not only contain information about the person sharing but information about others as well. Many times, these details are shared on several social media platforms as individuals attempt to ensure thatall persons within their social circle are kept updated on their activities. With this openness of sharing risks and challenges arise that are often not considered but can have serious impacts. The speed and scale with which social media creates information and makes it available—almost instantaneously—on a global scale, added to the fact that once something is posted there is really no way of truly removing it, should prompt individuals to think of the possible impact a post can have. Unfortunately, more often than not, posts are made without any thought of the far-reaching impact they can have on the lives of the person posting or othersthat may be implicated by the post.

Why do people share?
According to Berger and Milkman there are five (5) main reasons why users are compelled to share content online, whether it is every detail or what they deem as highlights of their lives. These are:

* cause related
* personal connection to content
* to feel more involved in the world
* to define who they are
* to inform and entertain

People generally share because they believe that what they are sharing is important. It is hoped that the shared content will be deemed important to others which will ultimately result in more shares, likes and followers.

Figure below sums up the findings of Berger and Milkman which shows that the main reason people feel the need to share content on the varying social media platform is that the content relates to what is deemed as worthy cause. 84% of respondents highlighted this as the primary motivation for sharing. Seventy-eight percent said that they share because they feel a personal connection to the content while 69 and 68%, respectively said the content either made them feel more involved with the world or helped them to define who they were. Forty- nine percent share because of the entertainment or information value of the content. A more in depth look at each reason for sharing follows.

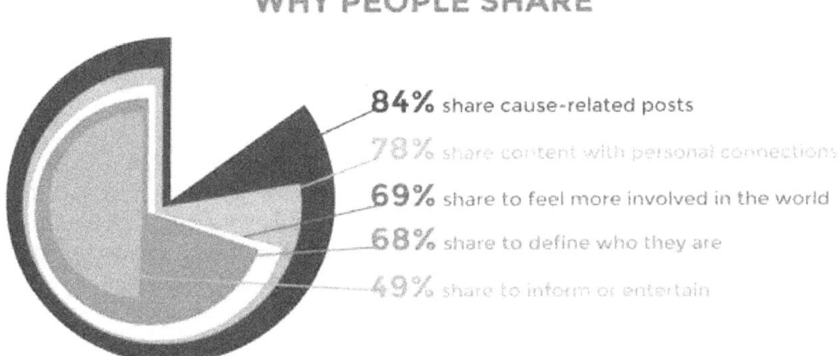

Figure Why people share source: Global Social Media Research.

Content related to a cause
Social media has provided a platform for people to share their thoughts and express concerns with others for what they regard as a worthy cause. Cause related posts are dependent on the interest of the individual. Some persons mightshare posts related to causes and issues happening in society. In one example, theparents of a baby with an aggressive form of leukemia, who having been told that their child had only 3 months to live unless a suitable donor for a blood stem cell transplant could be found, made an appeal on social media. The appeal was quickly shared and a suitable donor was soon found. While that was for a good cause, many view social media merely as platforms for freedom of speech because anyone can post any content one creates. People think the expression of their thoughts on social media regarding any topic is permissible. The problem with this is that the content may not be accepted by law or it could violate the rights of someone thus giving rise to ethical questions.

Content with a personal connection
When social media users feel a personal connection to their content, they are more inclined to share the content within their social circles. This is true of information regarding family and personal activities. Content created by users also invokes a deep feeling of connection as it allows the users to tell their stories and it is natural to want the world or at least friends to know of the achievement. This natural need to share content is not new as humans have been doing this in some form or the other, starting with oral history to the media of the day; social media. Sharing the self-created content gives the user the oppor-

tunity of satisfying some fundamental needs of humans to be heard, to matter, to be understood and emancipated. The problem with this however is that in an effort to gratify the fundamental needs, borders are crossed because the content may not be sharable (can this content be shared within the share network?), it may not be share-worthy (who is the audience that would appreciate this content?) or it may be out of context (does the content fit the situation?).

Content that makes them feel more involved in the world
One of the driving factors that pushes users to share content is the need to feel more in tune with the world around them. This desire is many times fueled by jealousy. Many social media users are jealous when their friends' content gets more attention than their own and so there is a lot of pressure to maintain one's persona in social circles, even when the information is unrealistic, as long as it gets as much attention as possible. Everything has to be perfect. In the case of a photo, for example, there is lighting, camera angle and background to consider. This need for perfection puts a tremendous amount of pressure on individuals to ensure that posted content is "liked" by friends. They often give very little thought to the amount of their friend's work that may have gone on behind the scenes to achieve that perfect social post.

Social media platforms have provided everyone with a forum to express views, but, as a whole, conversations are more polarized, tribal and hostile. With Facebook for instance, there has been a huge uptick in fake news, altered images, dangerous health claims and cures, and the proliferation of anti-science information. This is very distressing and disturbing because people are too willing to share and to believe without doing their due diligence and fact-checking first.

Content that defines who they are
Establishing one's individuality in society can be challenging for some persons because not everyone wants to fit in. Some individuals will do all they can to stand out and be noticed. Social media provides the avenue for exposure and many individuals will seek to leverage the media to stand out of the crowd and not just be a fish in the school. Today many young people are currently being brought up in a culture that defines people by their presence on social media where in previous generations, persons were taught to define themselves by their career choices. These lessons would start from childhood by asking children what they wanted to be when they grew up and then rewarding them based on the answers they give. In today's digital era, however, social media postings and the number of "likes" or "dislikes" they attract, signal what is appealing to others. Therefore, post that are similar to those that receive a large number of likes but which are largely unrealistic are usually made for self-gratification.

Content that informs and entertains
The acquisition of knowledge and skills is a vital part of human survival and social media has made this process much easier. It is not uncommon to hear persons realizing that they need a particular knowledge set that they do not possess say "I need to lean to do this. I'll just YouTube it." Learning and adapting to change in as short as possible time is vital in today's society and social media coupled with the Internet put it all at the finger tips. Entertainment has the ability to bring people together and is a good way for people to bond. It provides a diversion from the demands of life and fills leisure time with amusement. Social media is an outlet for fun, pleasurable and enjoyable activities that are so vital to human survival. It is now common place to see persons watching a video, viewing images and reading text that is amusing on any of the available social media platforms. Quite often these videos, images and texts can be both informative and entertaining, but there can be problems however as at times they can cross ethical lines that can lead to conflict.

Ethical challenges with social media use
The use of modern-day technology has brought several benefits. Social media is no different and chief amongst its benefit is the ability to stay connected easily and quickly as well as build relationships with people with similar interests. As with all technology, there are several challenges that can make the use of social media off putting and unpleasant. Some of these challenges appear to be minor but they can have far reaching effects into the lives of the users of social media and it is therefore advised that care be taken to minimize the challenges associated with the use of social media.

A major challenge with the use of social media is oversharing because when persons share on social media, they tend to share as much as is possible which is often times too much. When persons are out and about doing exciting things, it is natural to want to share this with the world as many users will post a few times a day when they head to lunch, visit a museum, go out to dinner or other places of interest. While this all seems relatively harmless, by using location-based services which pinpoint users with surprising accuracy and in real time, users place themselves in danger of laying out a pattern of movement that can be easily traced. While this seems more like a security or privacy issue it stems from an ethical dilemma—"Am I sharing too much?" Oversharing can also lead to damage of user's reputation especially if the intent is to leverage the platform for business. Photos of drunken behavior, drug use, partying or other inappropriate content can change how you are viewed by others. Another ethical challenge users of social media often encounter is that they have no way of authenticating content before sharing, which becomes problematic when the content paints people or establishments negatively. Often times content is shared with them by friends, family and colleagues. The unauthenticated content is then reshared without any thought but sometimes this content may have been maliciously altered so the user unknowingly participates in maligning others. Even if the content is not altered the fact that the content paints someone or something in a bad light should send off warning bells as to whether or not it is right to share the content which is the underlying principle of ethical behavior.

Conflicting views
Some of the challenges experienced by social media posts are a result of a lack of understanding and sometimes a lack of respect for the varying ethical and moral standpoints of the people involved. We have established that it is typical for persons to

post to social media sites without any thought as to how it can affect other persons, but many times these posts are a cause of conflict because of a difference of opinion that may exist and the effect the post may have. Each individual will have his or her own ethical values and if they differ then this can result in conflict. When an executive of a British company made an Instagram post with some racial connotations before boarding a plane to South Africa it started a frenzy that resulted in the executive's immediate dismissal. Although the executive said it was a joke and there was no prejudice intended, this difference in views as to the implications of the post, resulted in an out of work executive and a company scrambling to maintain its public image.

Impact on personal development
In this age of sharing, many young persons spend a vast amount of time on social media checking the activities of their "friends" as well as posting on their own activities so their "friends" are aware of what they are up to. Apart from interfering with their academic progress, time spent on these posts at can have long term repercussions. An example is provided by a student of a prominent university who posted pictures of herself having a good time at parties while in school. She was denied employment because of some of her social media posts. While the ethical challenge here is the question of the employee's right to privacy and whether the individual's social media profile should affect their ability to fulfill their responsibilities as an employee, the impact on the individual's long term personal growth is clear.

Conclusion
In today's information age, one's digital footprint can make or break someone; it can be the deciding factor on whether or not one achieves one's life-long ambitions. Unethical behavior and interactions on social media can have far reaching implications both professionally and socially. Posting on the Internet means the "end of forgetting," therefore, responsible use of this medium is critical. The unethical use of social media has implications for privacy and can result in security breaches both physically and virtually. The use of social media can also result in the loss of privacy as many users are required to provide information that they would not divulge otherwise. Social media use can reveal information that can result in privacy breaches if not managed properly by users. Therefore, educating users of the risks and dangers of the exposure of sensitive information in this space, and encouraging vigilance in the protection of individual privacy on these platforms is paramount. This could result in the reduction of unethical and irresponsible use of these media and facilitate a more secure social environment. The use of social media should be governed by moral and ethical principles that can be applied universally and result in harmonious relationships regardless of race, culture, religious persuasion and social status.

Analysis of the literature and the findings of this research suggest achieving acceptable levels of privacy is very difficult in a networked system and will require much effort on the part of individuals. The largest user groups of social media are unaware of the processes that are required to reduce the level of vulnerability of their personal data. Therefore, educating users of the risk of participating in social media is the social responsibility of these social network platforms. Adapting universally ethical behaviors can mitigate the rise in the number of privacy breaches in the social networking space. This recommendation coincides with philosopher Immanuel Kant's assertion that, the Biblical principle which states "Do unto others as you have them do unto you" can be applied universally and should guide human interactions. This principle, if adhered to by users of social media and owners of these platforms could raise the awareness of unsuspecting users, reduce unethical interactions and undesirable incidents that could negatively affect privacy, and by extension security in this domain.

Cyberspace
Cyberspace is a global domain within the information environment consisting of the interdependent network of information technology infrastructures (ITI) including the Internet, telecommunication networks, computer systems, and embedded processors and controllers. The term originates in science fiction, where it also includes various kinds of virtual reality (which is the experience of "being" in the alternate reality, or the simulated "being" in such a reality").

Cyberspace raises unique issues, especially regarding intellectual property and copyright infringement, and may call for new models of commerce. Furthermore, cyberspace has also become a unique area for developing human relationships and communities. While some argue that this universal ground for communication helps bring the world together, others point out that people will continue to associate narrowly with those of similar interests and economic and social status. Nevertheless, largely through the Internet, cyberspace has become a common ground for the rapid communication of ideas and values.

While cyberspace itself is a neutral space that allows for the rapid communication of ideas, the use of this space will determine its value and benefit for humankind. While the free use of this space is indeed valuable, especially as this cyberspace binds all humankind together in inseparable, interdependent relationships, the free use of this space also calls for its responsible use in order to ensure its value for humanity's overall pursuit of freedom and happiness. Thus, cyberspace mandates the responsible use of technology and reveals the need for a value- based perspective of the use of such technology.

Origins of the term
The word "cyberspace" (from cybernetics and space) was coined by science fiction author William Gibson in his 1982 story, "Burning Chrome," and popularized by his 1984 novel Neuromancer. The portion of Neuromancer cited in this respect is usually the following:

Cyberspace. A consensual hallucination experienced daily by billions of legitimate operators, in every nation, by children being taught mathematical concepts... A graphic representation of data abstracted from banks of every computer in the human system. Unthinkable complexity. Lines of light ranged in the nonspace of the mind, clusters and constellations of data. Like city lights, receding (69).

Gibson later commented on the origin of the term in the 2000 documentary No Maps for These Territories:

Note: The term "cyberspace" was coincd by science fiction writer William Gibson All I knew about the word "cyberspace" when I coined it, was that it seemed like an effective buzzword. It seemed evocative and essentially meaningless. It was suggestive of something, but had no real semantic meaning, even for me, as I sawit emerge on the page.

Metaphorical

The term Cyberspace started to become a de facto synonym for the Internet, and later the World Wide Web, during the 1990s. Author Bruce Sterling, who popularized this meaning, credits John Perry Barlow as the first to use it to refer to "the present-day nexus of computer and telecommunications networks."

Cyberspace as an internet metaphor

While cyberspace should not be confused with the real internet, the term is often used to refer to objects and identities that exist largely within the communication network itself, so that a web site, for example, might be metaphorically said to "exist in cyberspace." According to this interpretation, events taking place on the Internet are not, therefore, happening in the countries where the participants or the servers are physically located, but "in cyberspace."

The "space" in cyberspace has more in common with the abstract, mathematical meanings of the term than physical space. It does not have the duality of positive and negative volume (while in physical space for example a room has the negativevolume of usable space delineated by positive volume of walls, Internet users cannot enter the screen and explore the unknown part of the Net as an extension of the space they are in), but spatial meaning can be attributed to the relationshipbetween different pages (of books as well as webservers), considering the unturned pages to be somewhere "out there." The concept of cyberspace therefore refers not to the content being presented to the surfer, but rather to the possibility of surfing among different sites, with feedback loops between the user and the rest of the system creating the potential to always encounter something unknown or unexpected.

Videogames differ from text-based communication in that on-screen images are meant to be figures that actually occupy a space and the animation shows the movement of those figures. Images are supposed to form the positive volume that delineates the empty space. A game adopts the cyberspace metaphor by engaging more players in the game, and then figuratively representing them on the screen as avatars. Games do not have to stop at the avatar-player level, but current implementations aiming for more immersive playing space (such as in Laser tag) take the form of augmented reality rather than cyberspace, fully immersive virtual realities remaining impractical.

Although the more radical consequences of the global communication network predicted by some cyberspace proponents (that is, the diminishing of state influence envisioned by John Perry Barlow) failed to materialize and the word lostsome of its novelty appeal, the term continues to be used.

Some virtual communities explicitly refer to the concept of cyberspace, for example, Linden Lab calling their customers "Residents" of Second Life, while all such communities can be positioned "in cyberspace" for explanatory and comparative purposes (as Sterling did in The Hacker Crackdown and many journalists afterwards), integrating the metaphor into a wider cyberculture.

The metaphor has been useful in helping a new generation of thought leaders to reason through new military strategies around the world, led largely by the U.S. Department of Defense (DoD). The use of cyberspace as a metaphor has had its limits, however, especially in areas where the metaphor becomes confused with physical infrastructure.

Alternate realities in philosophy and artPredating computers

Before cyberspace became a technological possibility, many philosopherssuggested the possibility of a reality, or suggested that the reality in which we live in now is a reflection of some reality perhaps more pure than what we are aware of. In The Republic, Plato sets out his allegory of the cave, widely cited as one of the first conceptual realities. He suggests that we are already in a form of virtual reality which we are deceived into thinking is true. True reality for Plato is accessible only through mental training and is the reality of the forms. These ideas are central to Platonism and neoplatonism. Depending on how one views cyberspace in relation to physical reality, either people are living in a cyberspace- like reality in relation to a higher realm of ideas or cyberspace contains theabstract ideas that take form in the current, tangible reality. Another forerunner of the modern idea of cyberspace is Descartes' hypothetical that people might be deceived by an evil demon which feeds them a false reality, and so the only thing one can be certain of is that one thinks; in other words, one is a thinking thing. This argument is the direct predecessor of the modern ideas of brain in a vat and many popular conceptions of cyberspace take Descartes' ideas as their starting point.

Visual arts have a tradition, stretching back to antiquity, of artifacts meant to fool the eye and be mistaken for reality. This questioning of reality occasionally led some philosophers and especially theologians to distrust art as deceiving people into entering a world which was not real. The artistic challenge was resurrected with increasing ambition as art became more and more realistic with the invention of photography, film and finally, immersive computer simulations.

Influenced by computersPhilosophy

American counterculture exponents like William S. Burroughs (whose literary influence on Gibson and cyberpunk in general is widely acknowledged) wereamong the first to extol the potential of computers and computer networks for individual empowerment. Some contemporary philosophers and scientists (such as David Deutsch in The Fabric of Reality) use virtual reality in various thought experiments. Philip Zhai connects cyberspace to the platonic tradition:

Let us imagine a nation in which everyone is hooked up to a network of VR infrastructure. They have been so hooked up since they left their mother's wombs. Immersed in cyberspace and maintaining their life by teleoperation, they have never imagined that life could be any different from that. The first person that thinks of the possibility of an alternative world like ours would be ridiculed bythe majority of these citizens, just like the few enlightened ones in Plato's allegoryof the cave.

Cyberspace and virtual reality

Although cyberspace and virtual reality are often used interchangeably, these twoconcepts have a different orientation. While virtual reality refers to the simulated experience of reality, cyberspace refers to the plane of reality, or environment, within which this experience is made possible. Thus, experiences in cyberspace can entail aspects of virtual reality when a user is fully immersed in this alternate reality.

The difference between the two can be further described using an analogy of physical (space itself is not physical though) space and concepts of reality. On one hand, human beings presuppose a frame of reference called "space." Whether the space people live in is an empty container like a repository (Newtonnian concept) or people exist in space according to the relationship between things (Leibnizian concept) is debatable; likewise, human beings relate to reality through perception (Kantian concept of space as a form of intuition) or through a nexus of meanings (concept of "lived space" in Phenomenology). Either way, human beings presuppose a plane of experience called "space." Within this space, humans physically experience reality through their five senses.

By extension, this sense of reality can be applied to imagined objects. Cyberspace is a frame of reference within which people can have quasi-real experiences with such objects; virtual reality refers to the simulated experiences with these objects.
Human experience of reality is also extended to non-physical events orphenomena such as death and associated emotional feelings about it. Fear, anxiety, joy, and other emotional feelings are real without association with the physical senses. At the same time, virtual reality may suggest a false reality that can be virtually experienced. Thus, the whole question of reality poses a series of questions beyond current epistemological models in modern philosophy, which presuppose the primacy of sense perception.

Pornographic Ethics

"I can't define pornography," one judge once famously said, "but I know it when I see it." (Justice Stewart in Jacobellis v. Ohio 378 US 184 (1964).) Can we do better?

The word "pornography" comes from the Greek for writing about prostitutes. However, the etymology of the term is not much of a guide to its current usage, since many of the things commonly called "pornography" nowadays are neither literally written nor literally about prostitutes.

Here is a first, simple definition. Pornography is any material (either pictures or words) that is sexually explicit. This definition of pornography may pick out different types of material in different contexts, since what is viewed as sexually explicit can vary from culture to culture and over time. "Sexually explicit" functions as a kind of indexical term, picking out different features depending on what has certain effects or breaks certain taboos in different contexts and cultures. Displays of women's uncovered ankles count as sexually explicit in some cultures, but not in most western cultures nowadays (although they once did: the display of a female ankle in Victorian times was regarded as most risqué). There may be borderline cases too: do displays of bared breasts still count as sexually explicit in various contemporary western cultures? However, some material seems clearly to count as sexually explicit in many contexts today: in particular, audio, written or visual representations of sexual acts (e.g., sexual intercourse, oral sex) and exposed body parts (e.g., the vagina, anus and penis-especially the erect penis).

Within the general class of sexually explicit material, there is great variety in content. For example, some sexually explicit material depicts women, and sometimes men, in postures of sexual display (e.g., Playboy centrefolds). Some depicts non-violent sexual acts (both homosexual and heterosexual) betweenadults who are portrayed as equal and consenting participants. Other sexually explicit representations depict acts of violent coercion: people being whipped, beaten, bound, tortured, mutilated, raped and even killed. Some sexually explicit material may be degrading, without necessarily being overtly violent. This material depicts people (most often women) in positions of servility and subordination in their sexual relations with others, or engaged in sexual acts that many people would regard as humiliating. Some sexually explicit material involvesor depicts children. Some portrays bestiality and necrophilia; and so on.

On the first definition of pornography as sexually explicit material, all such material would count as pornography, insofar as it is sexually explicit. But this simple definition is not quite right. Anatomy textbooks for medical students are sexually explicit-they depict exposed genitalia, for example-but are rarely, if ever, viewed as pornography. Sexual explicitness may be a necessary condition for material to count as pornographic, but it does not seem to be sufficient. So something needs to be added to the simple definition. What else might be required?

Here is a second definition. Pornography is sexually explicit material (verbal or pictorial) that is primarily designed to produce sexual arousal in viewers. This definition is better: it deals with the problem of anatomy textbooks and the like. Indeed, this definition is one that is frequently employed (or presupposed) in discussions of pornography and censorship. Of course, it is important to distinguish here between sexually explicit material thatis wholly or primarily designed to produce sexual arousal (i.e., whose only or overriding aim is to produce sexual arousal) and material whose aim is to do thisin order to make some other artistic or political point. The film, Last Tango in Paris arguably aims to arouse audiences, but this is not its primary aim. It does so in order to make a broader political point.

It is sometimes assumed that pornography, in this second sense, is published and consumed by a small and marginalized minority. But, while exact estimates of the size and profitability of the international trade in pornography vary somewhat, itis generally agreed that the pornography industry is a massive international enterprise, with a multi-billion dollar annual turnover. In 2003, the pornography industry (taken to include adult videos, magazines, Cable/Pay per view, Internet and CD-Rom) is estimated to have grossed US$34 billion world-wide; and in excess of $8 billion in the U.S. alone, greater than the combined revenue of ABC, CBS, and NBC ($6.2. billion). Pornography is much more widely consumed than is sometimes supposed, and is a large and extremely profitable international industry.

However, the term "pornography" is often used with an additional normative force that the first and second definitions leave out. When many people describe something (e.g., a book such as Tropic of Capricorn or a filmsuch as Baise Moi)as "pornographic", they seem to be doing more than simply dispassionately describing its sexually explicit content or the intentions of itsproducers-indeed, in these debates, the intentions of producers are sometimes treated as irrelevant to the work's status as pornography. They seem to be saying, in addition, that it is bad-and perhaps also that its badness is not redeemed by other artistic, literary, or political merit the work may possess. (Consider, for example, how people use the term "visual pornography" to condemn certain sorts of art or television, often when the material is not even sexually explicit).

This suggests a third definition: pornography is sexually explicit material designed to produce sexual arousal in consumers that is bad in a certain way. This definition of pornography makes it analytically true that pornography is bad: by definition, material that is not bad in the relevant way is not pornography. It might be that all and only sexually explicit material is bad in a certain way (e.g., obscene): in which case, "pornography" will refer to all and only the class of sexually explicit materials. But it might be that only some sexually explicit material is objectionable (e.g., degrading to women), in which case only the bad subset of sexually explicit material will count as pornography. And, of course, it is possible that no sexually explicit material is bad in the relevant way (e.g., harmful to women), in which case we would have an error theory about pornography: there would be no pornography, so defined, merely harmless, sexually explicit "erotica".

A number of approaches define pornography as sexually explicit material that is bad—although they disagree as to the relevant source of its badness, and consequently about what material is pornographic. A particularly dominant approach has been to define pornography in terms of obscenity. (For critical discussions of this approach see Schauer 1982, Feinberg 1987, MacKinnon 1987.) The obscenity might be taken to be intrinsic to the content of the material itself (for example, that it depicts deviant sexual acts that are immoral in themselves) or it may lie in contingent effects that the material has (for example, that it tends to offend "reasonable" people, or to deprave and corrupt viewers, or to erode traditional family and religious values). If all sexually explicit material is obsceneby whichever of these standards is chosen, then all sexually explicit material will be pornography on this definition. This is the definition of pornography that moralconservatives typically favour.

But the badness of pornography need not reside in obscenity. Pornography might be defined, not as sexually explicit material that is obscene, but as that sexually explicit material that harms women. Thus many contemporary feminist definitions define "pornography" as sexually explicit material that depicts women's subordination in such a way as to endorse that subordination. (See Longino 1980, MacKinnon 1987.) This definition of pornography leaves it open in principle that there might be sexually explicit material that is not pornography: sexually explicit material that does not subordinate women will count as harmless "erotica".

Of course, women may not be the only people harmed by the production or consumption of certain sorts of sexually explicit material. The consumption of sexually explicit material has often been thought to be harmful to its (mostly male) consumers: for example, by corrupting their morals or by making them less likely to have loving, long-term sexual relationships. Many people strongly object to "child pornography": that subset of sexually explicit material that involves depictions of actual children engaged in sexual activity. This class of sexually explicit material is widely regarded as objectionable because it involves the actualsexual exploitation of children, together with a permanent record of that abuse which may further harm their interests.

I have discussed how, on this third approach to defining "pornography" as sexually explicit material that is bad or harmful in a certain way, there are three possibilities: "pornography" might name all, some or even no sexually explicit material, depending on what (if any) class of sexually explicit material is in fact bad in the relevant way. But it is worth noting that there is an interesting fourth possibility. It is possible that some non-sexually explicit material might also turn out to be bad in the relevant way. It might be that some non-sexually explicit material is obscene in the relevant sense (e.g., Andres Serrano's famously controversial artwork entitled "Piss Christ", which displays a plastic crucifix in urine with cow's blood). Or it might turn out that non-sexually explicit advertising that depicts women in positions of sexual servility in such a way as to endorse that subordination is also bad in the relevant way. (As many philosophers might be inclined to put the point, the sexually explicit materials that subordinate women via their depiction of women as subordinate may turn out not to form a natural kind.) In this case, there are two options. "Pornography" might be taken to name only the sexually explicit subset of material that is bad in the relevant sense (e.g., that depicts women as men's sexual subordinates in such a way as to endorse their subordination); or "pornography" might be taken to refer to all the material that is bad in that way, whether that material is sexually explicit or not. The former option would clearly stick more closely to the everyday conception of pornography as involving the sexually explicit. But it might be that this ordinary conception, on reflection, turns out not to capture what is of moral and political interest and importance. There may thus be a theoretical reason to conceive of pornography more broadly than simply sexually explicit material that is bad in a certain way, or perhaps simply to invent a new term that captures the theoretically interesting kind. Some feminists seem inclined to this broader approach, suggesting that material that explicitly depicts women in postures of sexual submission, servility or display in such a way as to endorse it counts as pornography. This may include some non-sexually explicit material that would notordinarily be thought of as pornography: for example, photographs in artwork, advertising or fashion spreads that depict women bound, chained or bruised in such a way as to glamorise these things.

The term "pornography" is used in all of these different ways in everyday discourse and debate, as well as in philosophical discussions: sometimes it is used to mean merely material which is sexually explicit; sometimes it is used to mean material which is sexually explicit and objectionable in some particular way; and so on. It seems to me that we do not need to choose between these different definitions, for all of them capture something of the term's everyday use. What matters crucially is that we know which definition is being used in a particular case. For the fact that "pornography" has different senses can have two very unfortunate consequences if these differences are not clearly noted and kept in mind: it can make it seem that there is disagreement when there is not; and it canobscure the real nature of the disagreement when there is. Here is one topical example of how this might happen. Some feminists object to pornography on the grounds that it harms women. Other feminists claim that pornography may not always be harmful to women, and may even sometimes be beneficial. It seems that there is genuine disagreement here. But is there? Not necessarily. For the two sides might mean different things by "pornography". Suppose that feminists who object to pornography are defining "pornography" as sexually explicit material that subordinates women. So pornography, for them, is that subset of sexually explicit material that in fact harms women. This definition makes it an analytic truth that pornography, wherever it exists, is bad from a feminist point of view. Feminists who defend pornography, however, may be using "pornography" to mean simply sexually explicit material (regardless of whether it is harmful to women). There may thus be no genuine disagreement here. For both sides might agree that sexually explicit material that harms women is objectionable. They might also agree that there is nothing objectionable about sexually explicit material that does not harm women (or anyone else). If protagonists in the debate are using "pornography" in different senses in this way, they may simply be talking past each other.

Two really substantive issues at stake in the feminist debate over pornography are 1) whether any sexually explicit material is in fact harmful to women; and, if so, what should be done about it?; and 2) whether all sexually explicit material is in fact harmful to women; and, if so, what should be done about it? (We can thus phrase two of the important issues, if we like, without mentioning "pornography" at all.) If we define "pornography" simply as sexually explicit material (regardless of whether it is harmful to women), then the first substantive issue must be posed in this way: "is there any pornography that is harmful to women; and, if so, what should be done about it?" However, if "pornography" is defined as that sexually explicit material that subordinates women then, while we can ask this question, we must pose it differently: we must ask "which pieces of sexually explicit material, if any, are pornographic; and what should be done about any pornography that exists?" A second substantive issue at stake in the debate is whether all sexually explicit material, either in principle or under current social conditions, is or would be harmful to women. Again, it should be noted that this question can be asked using either conception of "pornography", but it must be posed differently. If we define "pornography" simply as sexually explicit material (regardless of whether it is harmful), the question must be posed like this: "is all pornography as a matter of fact harmful?" On the other hand, if we define "pornography" as sexually explicit material that harms women, we must ask: "is all sexually explicit material as a matter of fact pornographic?" These are just terminological variants of the same substantive question: but when differentterminology is used by different participants in the debate, the exact questions at issue, which are actually very simple to state, can be obscured.

The shape of the traditional pornography debate

- **Conservative arguments for censorship**

Until comparatively recently, the main opposition to pornography came from moral and religious conservatives, who argue that pornography should be bannedbecause its sexually explicit content is obscene and morally corrupting. By "pornography", conservatives usually mean simply sexually explicit material (either pictures or words), since conservatives typically view all such material as obscene.

According to conservatives, the sexually explicit content of pornography is an affront to decent family and religious values and deeply offensive to a significant portion of citizens who hold these values. The consumption of pornography is badfor society. It undermines and destabilizes the moral fabric of a decent and stable society, by encouraging sexual promiscuity, deviant sexual practices and other attitudes and behaviour that threaten traditional family and religious institutions, and which conservatives regard as intrinsically morally wrong. Furthermore, pornography is bad for those who consume it, corrupting their character and preventing them from leading a good and worthwhile life in accordance with family and religious values.

According to conservatives, the state is justified in using its coercive power to uphold and enforce a community's moral convictions and to prevent citizens fromengaging in activities that offend prevailing community standards of morality and decency.

(See e.g., Devlin 1968, Sandel 1984.) This position is sometimes called 'legal moralism'. Governments also have a responsibility to prevent citizens from harming themselves. This is true, even where the citizen is not a child (who may not yet be competent to make responsible judgements for themselves about what is in their own best interests), but a mature adult who is voluntary engaged in an activity which they judge to be desirable and which causes no harm to others. The view that the state is entitled to interfere with the freedom of mentally competent adults against their will for their own good is often called 'legal paternalism'.

Conservatives therefore think that it is entirely legitimate for the state to prohibit consenting adults from publishing and viewing pornography, even in private, in order to protect the moral health of would-be consumers and of society as a whole.

The traditional liberal defence of a right to pornography

Traditional liberal defenders of pornography famously disagree, rejecting both the principle of legal moralism and the principle of legal paternalism, at least where consenting adults are concerned. This is not to say that liberal defenders of pornography necessarily approve of it. Indeed, they frequently personally find pornography-especially violent and degrading pornography-mindless and offensive. Many concede that pornography-by which they usually mean sexually explicit material whose primary function is to produce sexual arousal in viewers-is "low value" speech: speech that contributes little, if anything, of intellectual, artistic, literary or political merit to the moral and social environment. But this does not mean that it should not be protected-quite the opposite. A vital principle is at stake for liberals in the debate over pornography and censorship. The principle is that mentally competent adults must not be prevented from expressing their own convictions, or from indulging their own private tastes, simply on the grounds that, in the opinion of others, those convictions or tastes are mistaken, offensive or unworthy. Moral majorities must not be allowed to use the law to suppress dissenting minority opinions or to force their own moral convictions on others. The underlying liberal sentiment here is nicely captured in the famous adage (often attributed to the French philosopher, Voltaire): "I disapprove of what you say, but I will defend to the death your right to say it."

For liberals, there is a very strong presumption in favour of individual freedom, and against state regulation that interferes with that freedom. The only grounds that liberals typically regard as providing a legitimate reason for state restrictions on individual freedom is in order to prevent harm to others. Hence, in debates over censorship and other forms of state regulation that restrict the liberty of individuals against their will, the burden of proof is always firmly on those who argue for censorship to demonstrate that the speech or conduct in question causes significant harm to others. It must either be shown to directly cause actual physical violence to others (e.g., murder, rape, assault, battery), on a narrower understanding of "harm"; or to deliberately or negligently violate sufficiently important interests or rights of others, on a broader, interest-based conception of "harm".

Liberals have traditionally defended a right to pornography on three main grounds. (By the "right to pornography" here, and in what follows, I mean the negative right of consenting adults not to be prevented from making, publishing, exhibiting, distributing and consuming pornography in private). Firstly, on the grounds of freedom of speech or expression, which protects the freedom of individuals (in this case, pornographers) to express their opinions and to communicate those opinions to others, however mistaken, disagreeable or offensive others may find them. Liberals have tended to conceive of freedom, including freedom of expression, as negative freedom-as non-interference by others-rather than as positive freedom, which involves having the positive goods and facilities required to exercise the freedom. Freedom is thus something that individuals have just so long as there are no coercive external obstacles-notably, physical or legal restrictions-in their way.

Few liberals nowadays think that the (negative) right to freedom of speech is an absolute right: a freedom that can never legitimately be restricted by the state. If the speech causes sufficiently great harm to others then the state may have a legitimate interest in regulating or preventing it. There is no simple general formula or algorithm for determining when the harm caused to others is "sufficiently great" to justify legal restrictions in the case of speech and more generally. This will depend on the outcome of a complex process of carefully weighing and balancing the strength and nature of the harm and the competing interests at stake, and an analysis of the costs and benefits of alternative policies, that needs to be undertaken on a case by case basis.

However, when it comes to legislation that interferes with free speech, the liberal presumption against legislation is especially high. For liberals take freedom of expression to be an especially important right that takes precedence over most other rights and interests (including equality) should they ever conflict. Levels of harm that would normally be sufficient to justify regulating the conduct which causes them may be not be sufficiently great to justify restrictions in cases where the harm is caused by speech or expression. Hence, for liberals, justifying censorship of pornography requires that there is extremely reliable evidence to show that the publication or voluntary private consumption of pornography by consenting adults causes especially great and serious harm to others. The harm caused by expression must be very certain and very great before it is legitimate for a state to prohibit it. We would be justified in banning a certain type of pornography (e.g., bondage pictures) only when we are very sure that, on average, tokens of that type (i.e., most particular bondage pictures) cause very great harm.

Secondly, liberals have defended a right to pornography on the grounds of a right to privacy (or "moral independence", as one prominent liberal defender of pornography calls it), which protects a sphere of private activity within which individuals can explore and indulge their own personal tastes and convictions, free from the threat of coercive pressure or interference by the state and other individuals. The spectre of state intrusion into the private lives of individuals underpins much of the liberal discomfort about censorship of pornography.

Like the right to freedom of speech, the liberal commitment to privacy is not absolute. It can be overridden if the private activities of individuals are such as to cause significant harm to others. Thus, if there is reliable evidence to suggest that the voluntary private consumption of pornography causes sufficiently great harm to others then- providing this harm is sufficiently great and that state prohibitionsare the only effective way of preventing it-the state would have a legitimate interest in prohibiting it.

But-and this is the third prong of the traditional liberal defence-pornography is comparatively harmless. Neither the expression of pornographic opinions, nor theindulging of a private taste for pornography, causes significant harm to others, in the relevant sense of 'harm' (i.e., crimes of physical violence or other significant wrongful rights-violations). Hence, the publication and voluntary private consumption of pornography is none of the state's business.

The 'harm principle': when is the state justified in restricting individual liberty?
These three central ingredients in the liberal defence of pornography find their classic expression in a famous and influential passage from John Stuart Mill's On Liberty (1859). In this passage, Mill sets out the principle that underpins the prevailing liberal view about when it is justified for the state to coercively interfere with the liberty of its citizens. It is a principle that continues to provide the dominant liberal framework for the debate over pornography and censorship.Mill writes:

The only principle for which power can be rightfully exercised over any memberof a civilized community, against his will, is to prevent harm to others. His own good, either physical or moral, is not a sufficient warrant. He cannot rightfully be compelled to do or forbear because it will be better for him to do so, because it will make him happier, because, in the opinion of others, to do so would be wise or even right. These are good reasons for remonstrating with him, or reasoning with him, or persuading him, or entreating him, but not for compelling him, or visiting him with any evil in case he do otherwise. To justify that, the conduct from which it is desired to deter him, must be calculated to produce evil to someone else. The only part of the conduct of any one for which he is amenableto society, is that which concerns others. In the part which merely concerns himself, his independence is, of right, absolute. (Mill 1975: 15)

Mill's central claim is that society is justified in interfering with the freedom of mentally competent adults to say and do what they wish only when their conduct will cause harm to others. This has come to be known as the 'liberty principle' or 'harm principle'; and it forms the cornerstone of the traditional liberal defence of individual liberty. It protects the freedom of all mentally competent individuals to live and shape their own lives in accordance with their own preferences and beliefs, so long as they do not harm others in the process.

Mill goes on to stress that the harm principle is meant to apply "only to human beings in the maturity of their faculties"(Mill 1975:15). So the principle permits paternalistic intervention in the case of those who are not competent to make an informed decision about what is in their best interests for themselves, and so who"must be protected against their own actions as well as external injury": for example, young children or those adults whose decision-making abilities are temporarily or permanently impaired.

It is generally thought to follow that child pornography, which is taken to involve the actual sexual abuse or exploitation of children (with or without their apparentconsent), can legitimately be banned in order to protect the interests of children, who are not yet competent to fully understand the nature of the choice they are making or to grasp the impact of their decisions on their present and future interests. (This is not entirely uncontroversial, however: for it might be denied that children are harmed by participating in pornography. The North American Man Boy Love Association (NAMBLA), for example, denies that having sex with adults is harmful for children.) For the same reason, liberals think that children can quite rightly be prevented by parents or by the state from purchasing or viewing pornography, if this is thought likely to harm them. That child pornography should be banned is common ground between liberals and conservatives. However, pornography that involves the simulated abuse of children (for example, consenting adult actors dressed up as schoolgirls) cannot legitimately be prohibited under the harm principle, unless there is good evidence to suggest that consumption of this material causes significant harm to people other than those who consume it: by, for example, causing those who consume it to abuse children.

We are now in a better position both to see what it would take for liberals to think that censorship of pornography is justified and why liberals have been so unsympathetic to the sort of argument against pornography that conservatives make. Conservatives wish to prevent mentally competent adults from publishing and consuming pornography on the grounds that the choice to consume pornography is deeply morally misguided. But, as Mill insists, this is "not a sufficient warrant" for coercive interference with individual liberty. Neither the state nor moral majorities are entitled to restrict the private choices and activities of individuals against their will simply because, in the opinion of state officials or the social majority, that way of life is unworthy or unrewarding. Mill thinks that this sort of legal moralism will lead inevitably to a terrible "tyranny of the majority", crushing individual diversity and blocking human progress and flourishing.

However, following Mill, liberals are generally happy to allow that considerations of the individual or common good may entitle the state to use other, so- called non-coercive means to persuade citizens to make wise or better choices. Thus public education campaigns designed to inform citizens of the dangers of smoking or excessive alcohol consumption, or to persuade them to make "wise" choices (for example, to eat more fruit and vegetables) may be justified. While others cannot force an individual to do something (or to forbear from doing it) when they are not harming others, it is entirely legitimate to seek to advise, instruct or persuade them. So, if there are reasons to think that pornography is not good for the individual who consumes it (say, because it makes them less likely to be able to have successful loving or long-term relationships), public education campaigns to warn consumers of these dangers may be justified. Indeed this-education and debate-is precisely the solution that liberals typically recommend to counter any harm that pornography may cause. (See e.g., Feinberg 1985, Donnerstein et al. 1987, Dworkin 1985) This solution respects the freedom of rational agents to exercise their own rational capacities in deciding what to think and how to live.

However, liberals insist that if attempts at persuasion should fail, and where an individual's conduct poses no significant threat to the physical security or interests of others, the state may not use coercive legal mechanisms to enforce these "wise" choices. "The only freedom which deserves the name is that of pursuing our own good in our own way, so long as we do not attempt to deprive others of theirs, or impede their efforts to obtain it" (Mill 1975: 18). For Mill, the individual person is in the best position to judge what is in his or her own best interests; and, even if individuals may sometimes make bad choices, it is better in general that they be left free to make these mistakes. For no one's opinion about the good life is infallible; and, in any case, a life lived 'from the inside', in accordance with values that the individual endorses, is more likely to be a fulfilling one than a life where the individual is forced against their will to live as others as believe best.

In an influential liberal defence of pornography, Ronald Dworkin expresses this commitment in terms of a right to "moral independence". People, he says, "have the right not to suffer disadvantage in the distribution of social goods and opportunities, including disadvantages in the liberties permitted to them by the criminal law, just on the ground that their officials or fellow-citizens think that their opinions about the right way for them to lead their own lives are ignoble or wrong." (Dworkin 1985: 353.) The fact, if it is one, that the majority of people in a society prefer that pornography be banned because they regard it as immoral or offensive is not a legitimate reason for interfering with (pornographers') freedom of speech or for preventing consenting adults from consuming it in private. For allowing such illegitimate "external" preferences of a majority to dictate government policy would violate the right to moral independence of the producers and consumers of pornography. It would give moral majorities the power to dictate how members of minority or non-mainstream groups can live on the basis of the majority's opinions about what sort of people are most worthy and what sorts of lives are worth living, and this violates the basic right of all individuals to be treated with equal concern and respect.

Pornography and Offense: Justifying restrictions on the public display of pornography

However, Dworkin thinks, considerations of offence may provide some justification for preventing or restricting the public display of pornography so as to avoid its causing offense to non-consenting adults who might otherwise involuntarily or unwittingly be exposed to it. Joel Feinberg, another well-known liberal defender of pornography, agrees. But Feinberg thinks that such restrictions must be justified by a separate principle to the harm principle, for he thinks that certain sorts of unpleasant psychological states are not in themselves harms. Feinberg calls this additional principle the offense principle. The offense principle says that "It is always a good reason in support of a proposed criminal prohibition that it would probably be an effective way of preventing serious offense (as opposed to injury or harm) to persons other than the actor, and that it is probably a necessary means to that end (i.e., there is probably no other means that is equally effective at no greater cost to the other values)."

Like Dworkin, Feinberg thinks that the voluntary private consumption of pornography does not cause harm to others. Hence, wholesale criminal prohibitions on the publication and private voluntary consumption of pornography cannot be justified. But the public display of pornography may nonetheless constitute an "offensive nuisance" to non-consenting adults who are involuntarily exposed to it (just as neighbours who play bad music loudly into the wee hours of the morning may be an "offensive nuisance"). Since the harm-or rather, pseudo-harm-of pornography is the offense it may cause unwitting viewers involuntarily exposed to it, the solution is to restrict its exhibition to domains where such involuntary exposure will not occur, such as inside well sign- posted adult bookshops and cinemas where those who will be offended will know not to venture. Although this may prevent pornographers from distributing their opinions as widely as they might like, and may also cause some minor inconvenience to consumers (who may have to go further out of their way to find and view pornography, or suffer the embarrassment of having to sneak into known adult bookstores), these costs may be relatively small compared with the level of offense that involuntary exposure is likely to cause. Such restrictions on the public display of pornography would not amount to censorship, for pornographers are still free to publish and distribute their opinions. Nor would they violate consumers' right to privacy, for pornography would be freely available for willing consumers to view in private. The Williams Committee Report into Obscenity and Film Censorship in England made a similar recommendation, pointing to general considerations of public decency that prevent "offensive" public displays of conduct (e.g., nudity or sexual intercourse) that is appropriately seen or done only in private. Susan Wendell also agrees that the public display of certain sorts of pornography-visual, audio and written material that depicts and condones the unjustified physical coercion of women or other human beings- should be prohibited, although her particular concern is to remove the anxiety that involuntarily exposure to such coercive material is likely to cause women and the harm it is likely to do to their self-esteem (Wendell 1983).

Liberal defenders of the right to pornography may thus allow that restrictions on its public display may be justified. But only if pornography can reliably be shown to cause significant harm to people other than those who voluntarily consume it will there be a legitimate case for prohibiting its voluntary private consumption. When an individual's private activities cause harm to others then they become no longer merely a private matter, but of legitimate public interest; and the state may be justified in regulating them. Thus, Dworkin says, were excessive consumption of pornography shown to cause absenteeism from work, then the public and the state might have some legitimate interest in preventing it. But, Dworkin thinks, there is as yet no reliable evidence that firmly establishes that the voluntary private production or consumption of pornography by consenting adults causes this or any other sufficiently significant harm to others, in the relevant sense of 'harm'. Hence, pornography satisfies only harmless personal preferences for sexual gratification; and is therefore none of the state's business.

The dangers of censorship
Liberals also have technical concerns about how censorship laws might work in practice. Many liberal (and feminist) objections to censorship of pornography point to the practical costs and dangers of censorship, arguing that even if pornography does cause some harm to others, the risks involved in censoring it are too great. They point to the difficulties involved in formulating a legal definition of 'pornography' that will be sufficiently precise to minimize the danger that censorship laws targeting pornography will be used (intentionally or unintentionally) to censor other unpopular material, including valuable literary, artistic and political works. Censoring pornography may thus place us on a dangerous "slippery slope" to further censorship of other material; and may have a general "chilling effect" on expression, making people reluctant to say or publish things that might be construed as pornography and for which they could be prosecuted.

These are serious dangers; and they need to be carefully taken into account in weighing the costs and benefits of censorship as a solution to any harm that pornography might cause. But it is worth noting that they are inherent in many existing forms of legislation, and are not always taken to be insoluble or to constitute a decisive reason against censorship in themselves.

Recent liberal dissent
Although traditional defenders of a right to pornography have been liberals, it is important to note that not all contemporary liberals defend such a right. Indeed, the question of whether there might be good liberal grounds for prohibiting or otherwise regulating the voluntary private consumption of (some) pornography has become the subject of increasing and lively debate. Inspired by more recent feminist arguments against pornography, some scholars argue that the liberal commitment to protecting individual autonomy, equality, freedom of expression and other important liberal values may in fact support a policy that prohibits certain kinds of pornography, rather than the permissive stance that liberals have traditionally favoured. (See e.g., Dyzenhaus 1992, Easton 1994: 42–51, Langton 1990, Okin 1987, West 2003.) These theorists do not normally reject the harm principle, broadly understood: They generally agree that the crucial question in determining whether censorship of pornography is justified is whether there is reliable evidence to show that the publication or viewing of pornography by consenting adults causes sufficiently great harm to significant interests of others. Rather, they are open to the legitimacy of censorship because they think that the production and consumption of certain sorts of sexually explicit material—in particular, violent pornography and non-violent but degrading pornography—may in fact cause sufficiently significant harm to others, particularly women.
These theorists often follow social science researchers in drawing more fine-grained distinctions within the general category of pornography (i.e., the sexually explicit material whose primary function is to produce sexual arousal in those who view or read them). They often distinguish between

1. violent pornography;
2. non-violent but degrading pornography; and
3. non-violent and non-degrading pornography,

Since there is some evidence to suggest that some of these materials (e.g., in categories 1 and 2) may be harmful in ways that other material (e.g., category 3) is not. I will summarize some of this important evidence shortly.

One important dimension of the disagreement between those liberals who defend a right to pornography and those who think that liberals should be open to the legitimacy of censorship is empirical: they disagree about the crucial empirical issue of whether there is reliable evidence to show that the production and consumption of pornography by consenting adults in fact causes harm to others, particularly women. But frequently they also disagree about some important conceptual matters as well. In particular, they may disagree (albeit sometimes implicitly) about how three central elements of the harm principle should be understood: (i) exactly what counts as "harm" to others, in the relevant sense; (ii) when can we say that something is a "cause", or a sufficiently "direct cause", of a harm; and (iii) how much harm to others is "sufficiently great" to justify coercive sanctions against the speech or conduct that produces it. In other words, they disagree about how the harm principle should be interpreted and applied.

Many argue that more traditional liberal conceptions of the interests or rights that individuals have, and so of what activities can cause harm to them, is too narrow. It ignores the way in which threats to individuals' interests can come not just from the state, but also from other social practices and circumstances (e.g., substantive socio-economic disadvantage) that can prevent the meaningful exercise of freedom just as effectively. The state may thus have a legitimate role to play in promoting the social conditions that enable individuals to exercise their rights in meaningful ways, and in regulating such activities of non-governmental agents or groups as may serve significantly to infringe them.

Pornographic Ethics
A 2008 study on university campuses found that a whopping 87 percent of "emerging" adult men (aged 18-26), and 31 percent of emerging adult women report using porn at some level. Twenty percent of young men report using pornography daily or every other day, and almost half use it at least weekly. But the shock factor of pornography consumption statistics do not stop there: The sky is blue and men view porn—we've lost the shock value in our passive acceptance. Perhaps the more telling pornography statistic is that slightly over two thirds of young men, and nearly half of young women believe that porn consumption is morally acceptable.

This statistic of acceptance is particularly interesting because it is pulled from our generation, which often defines right and wrong in terms of consequences. Consequence-based morality maintains that if something doesn't hurt yourself or others, it's not wrong. The principle of "Thou shalt not hurt" thus becomes the backbone of discursive moral reasoning, as observed by the National Study of Youth and Religion. Removing an external moral standard from moral reasoning makes it difficult to condemn sex trafficking, exploitation, and violence, much less explicit sexual content and nudity. But even in terms of a "Thou shalt not hurt" moral code, passively accepting pornography overlooks the very realconsequences of porn consumption.

Healthy sexuality combines emotional, social, intellectual, and physical elements, but pornography separates the mechanized components of intercourse from real sexuality itself. It leads to decreased sensitivity toward women and increased aggression. It also leads to a decreased ability to build healthy relationships or experience sexual satisfaction; users are increasingly unable to properly link emotional involvement with sex. Indeed, porn fosters incredibly unhealthy views about sexuality and human beings. Most porn portrays women as sex-obsessed, mindless objects, promiscuous and subordinate. As feminist scholar Catharine MacKinnon might propose, the prevalence of pornography begs the question: Arewomen human? Though that question seems extreme, ask yourself if a good society can intentionally engage in a medium that portrays half of its members in such a derogatory manner.

There is much discussion on how the government should regulate the big business of pornography, seesawing between free-wheeling libertarianism and heavy-handed censorship.

Indeed, we are increasingly desensitized to discussion about porn use and regulation, even as research proves the effects of pornography are life altering, and stories of sex exploitation, psychological problems, and abuse dominate inspections into the porn industry. Many Americans embrace fair-trade coffee, concerned about the industries that produce their goods, but few consumers express concern about porn industry operations, and its employees and victims.

Even by the often-cited moral standards of individual choice and "Thou shalt not hurt," the porn discussion demands our moral attention. Recent work by neurologists illustrates the very real addictive properties of pornography. Porn addictions restrict real individual choice. University of Texas-San Antonio's Dr. Donald L. Hilton, Jr.'s research on porn addiction explains that pleasure chemicals in the brain are gradually overused when a person views pornography; the brain then limits dopamine production, causing the viewer to become starved for dopamine.

Despite the personal and social costs of pornography, health services are absurdlysilent on the issue of such an exploitative and harmful industry. Harvard's University Health Services and Office of Sexual Prevention and Response dance around the issue without offering services or information to students about porn consumption and addiction. OSAPR refused the requests of True Love Revolution officers to assist with the White Ribbon Against Pornography Week without citing any reasons. OSAPR should make a concerted effort to reach out to students who are struggling with porn and educate students on the harmful effects of pornography. University offices shy away from addressing the porn issue as a tangible part of students' personal lives; they instead turn it into a vague, elusive matter.

Perhaps the University avoids the porn issue in order to avoid moral or social controversy, but fear of stirring up debate does few favors for students who struggle with porn consumption. University of Chicago professor Jean Bethke Elshtain argues in The Social Costs of Pornography that we should not dismiss the "moral" in our avoidance of the "moralistic." Elshtain maintains that in order to be responsible citizens, we must ask ourselves, "What sort of community is this?

Is it reasonably decent and kind? Is it a fit place for human habitation, especially for the young? What happens to the most vulnerable among us? How do we ill- dignify the human body, and how do we forestall such affronts?" Such questions demand long-winded, nuanced answers, yet it is worth seeking these answers. They are pertinent to those who are involved in the porn industry, and they are pertinent to our own lives. We should all be asking ourselves whetherpornography is compatible with a respectful and good society.

Representation
Representation is simply the act of imitation or the act of identification, people identify themselves by means of their mimetic ability, when they see themselves in others and perceive a state of mutual equality. Representation of reality may refer to simile, similarity and symbolization of the world when we take it as a transformation of myth. The idea of representation at its simple level involves ourunderstanding for the action of representation and how we define that act. This essay details media representation of reality as outlined by key theorists and theirtheories in the classical age and it further explains representation as a substitute and also as ideology.

Classical age refers to the antique period before the birth of Jesus Christ (Auerbach, E, 1974). Key philosophers during this period included people such as Plato who is the ancient Greek philosopher; Aristotle who is also a Greek philosopher and he was Plato's student; Saint Thomas Aquinas who is a theologian from Italy; Galileo Galilei an Italian physician, astronomy andphilosopher and last but not least Francis Bacon who is an English philosopher and leader of scientific revolution. I will critically do an in-depth analysis/discuss representation as outlined by this philosophers and I will also distinguish representation as a substitute and ideology.

First of all let's consider Plato who takes 'representation' with several meanings and connotations in the dialogue and alters the term according to the context in which he uses it. Plato can perhaps be identified as the culprit behind the idea that representation are lacking in truth or 'real' quality. Plato view representation as imitation or ' mimesis. '(Annas, 1982).
For Plato, more than two thousand years ago, an image was the representation ofsomething and was not, could not, be an origi-

nal. It was always an imitation and always lacking in value when compared to the original since it was not an original it had to be a simulacrum, a false claim to being. (Annas, 1982).

Plato simulacrum calls into question, the entire relationship between the real objects and its copy, and also prioritises the two entities in terms of value. Plato discuss 'representation' as likening oneself to another in speech and bodily behaviour and as addressing the lower part of man's soul; he also refers to the epistemology and metaphysics of the concept. (Spring, 1985)
In contradicting this, Aristotle who is known to be Plato's student 'representation' does not refers to the imitation of idea and appearance, like that of Plato. Aristotle view representation as a sign and argues that each area of knowledge is imitated in the sense that as a human being we all learn through imitation (Annas,1982)

According to Angelo (1985) Aristotle is the first to deal with 'representation' as a theory of art. He dwell on the concept of representation as an aesthetic theory of art and considers imitation in terms of the form it is embodied. Aristotle states that all human action are mimetic and that men learn through imitation e.g. in thesocial learning theory of Albert Bandura it is said that we learn by imitating from an early age. In particular to him 'representation' is a distinguishing quality of an art.

For Plato, the artist was nothing but an imitator. This imitator while pretending to represent the real, did nothing more than give representation to an opinion aboutthe real. Plato's student Aristotle, perhaps more diplomatically than Plato, described the image of painted figure not as the likeness of a character but rather as a sign of the character. Aristotle view representation of reality as referent to someone or something but does not try to pose as that someone or something (Summers, 1996:6).

However, he carefully makes a distinction between difference kinds of knowledge e.g. he claims that art and philosophy deal with different kinds of truth; philosophy deals with concrete and absolute truth, whereas art deals with aesthetic and universal truth. Aristotle take's representation as an active aesthetic process. (Crane, R, S & Keats, W, R et al, 1996).

Plato and Aristotle attributed different meanings to the term representation. Plato considers representation as in ethical and political context whereas Aristotleuses representation as an aesthetic phenomenon and as an activity of the artist asI have explained in the above paragraph; they both agree that poetry is mimetic but they have different idea about poetry and representation. (Summers, 1996). Plato and Aristotle argue that artist (Demiurge) and poet imitate nature, thus, a work of art is a reflection of nature. However, they have different views on the functions of imitation in art and literature. Plato believes in the existence of the ideal world, where exists a real form of every object found in nature. A work of artwhich reflects nature and is twice far from the reality it represents. Aristotle, on the other hand, does not deal with the ideal world, instead he analyses nature. He argues that a work of art does not imitate nature as it is, but as it should be. In this sense, an artist does not violate the truth but reflects the reality.

Plato's main concern is with the public recitation of dramatic and epic poetry and in Plato there is emulation between philosophy and poetry. The poet influences the character of the young in every way and has corruptive impact upon the education of the young mind. In addition, poets don't have a true knowledge of the things. Plato suggests that the emotional appeal is a threat to reason, that mimetic art is remote from reality, that the poet is not serious and knows nothing about poetry and cannot give satisfactory information about his art.
It is obvious that he resists the concept of imitation in the case of poetic composition. Tragedy, in particular, and poetry, in general, is concerned with pleasure rather than instruction and since it is not possible to imitate a wise and quiet person in the play, since such a person does not fit the content of tragedy, 'representation' is ethically distracting. Therefore, the function of various discussions of representational art in the Republic is ethical; wherever he mentions art he discusses it in relation to education and ethics (Annas, 1982).

Although Aristotle agrees with Plato that poetry has the power to stimulate emotions, he does not pay much attention to the ethical and epistemological aspects of 'representation'. Yet he dwells on the pleasure that men take in learning and argues that tragedy discharges the feelings and spectators leave the play in a state of calm, free of passions.

Plato worries about the moral effect of poetry, while Aristotle strikes to psychology and returns repeatedly to shuddering terror and pity that the tragedy is creating in the spectator, who therefore repeats or imitates what has already taken place on stage. And that, in its turn, spectator repeats or imitates what has already taken place.(Phillip, 1996).

Plato argues that there is a duality between art (representation and narrative art) and ethics. This manner of representation (impersonation), according to Plato, leads to the loss-of-self or transformation of identity and becomes a matter of moral destruction. Aristotle also takes the same activity of impersonation, but in adifferent way. (Gerathy, 1996:275).

After few years a medieval catholic theologian Thomas Aquinas acknowledged thevertical nature that symbolic representation had now taken on; a lower verse which indicates points to represent the higher God. Although denying that the higher and the lower are equivalents, Aquinas admitted that the higher can be addressed through the lower. Aquinas view representation as a divine instrument.

According to Aquinas representation have, in the midst of the mysteries of the faith, become almost supernatural mediums between mankind and God. In fact Aquinas encouraged this practice; since we cannot directly be exposed to divine truth, the faith must be translated into something which is represented to be consumed by us through our lower or human sense.

Representation and differences-Marginalization

Media represent one of the most dynamically changing systems in society. The evolution of media has been determined by the progress in the area of information and communication technologies, their spread and mass usage, whereas it includes numerous and diverse political, economic, cultural, ethical, and social implications. The editor of the publication, Rachna Sharma, statedfollowing in the Introduction: "Today, while observing 'movements' on socialissues at an increased frequency, with increased participation of the public, the claimed media interventions and the changing role of governments in this triangular relationship, one is compelled to locate the issue of marginalised sections in society."

The present is, above all, the time of social media characterised by a high degree of civic activism and individual freedom in the creation and presentation of the content: on the other hand, the power and economic strength of international media conglomerates has been growing on a regional and global scale. It is often discussed the undeniable contribution of the media to building a democratic society, a healthy public environment and their ability to help to radical social transformations, however we may also see that media provide a diametrically different space for the presentations of certain groups. If they highlight specific social participants, others are out of focus of the mainstream media. This bipolarity in displaying marginalised groups in society is one of the paradoxes of the postmodern society and a significant feature of the contemporary mainstream mass media.

Relevant responding to numerous questions related to the establishment and clarification of relations between media, the state and marginalized groups has become the subject of an academic debate, the results of which have the potential to reach the broader social awareness and media practice. In March 2016, the National seminar on the topic Media, the State and the Marginalized: Tackling Challenges took place at the Department of Journalism, Kalindi College, University of Delhi in India. The reviewed publication consists of selected papers presented at the seminar, edited by Rachna Sharma, Assistant Professor in the Department of Journalism of Lady Shri Ram College for Women at Delhi University, India. The publication includes 21 chapters summarised in five major thematic areas, as follows: Part I: Media and Political Communication, Part II: Representation of the Marginalised and Media Ethics, Part III: New Media, Social Media and Digital Activism, Part IV: Alternative and Community Media: The Mediaof the Marginalised? and Part V: Critical Theory, Media Criticism and Media Reforms. A part of the proceedings is a brief dictionary, in which the reader can find definitions of key terms related to the solved issues and an index of concepts and names that will help them in orientation in the content. It consists of 331 pages.

As indicated by the structure of the publication, its ambition is to provide a variety of views on the dynamically changing relation between media, the state and marginalized groups in an effort to comprehensively understand current social-political and social-cultural processes, which the contributors managed to accomplish. Individual authors address selected areas in a comparative and interdisciplinary perspective. This is mainly due to the composition of the authors' team, which includes leading Indian experts from different areas, such as media studies, cultural studies, journalism, sociology, Public Relations, as well as long- standing experts from media practice. It is an interdisciplinary approach to exploring how media are in the digital age, who marginalised groups are in current social-political-economic structures and how they are reported by mainstream media that can be considered as a significant contribution of the publication to the wider debate on the subject. Despite the fact that the issue is dealt with by the authors from the domestic, Indian perspective, its overlap lies in a qualitative and quantitative solution. This approach expands the possibilities of publication's use. It can serve not only to academics and researchers, but also to the students of media studies, journalism, political science, and sociology. However, also workers in the media, especially in the news-service and others who are interested in the issue of marginalized groups in Indian society and its various stances can find a lot of inspirational information. Thus, notions presentedin individual contributions may serve as the basis for the theoretical and empiricalcomparative research of the allocated groups in other countries, as well. We should particularly appreciate the fact that the findings published in the book Media, the State and Marginalisation: Tackling Challenges may serve as the foundation for institutional debate aimed at addressing the problematic position of the marginalized groups in the Indian society heading towards formulating reforms. Thus, I consider the reviewed publication as an extraordinarily impressive contribution to the discussion on tackling the position of marginalized groups in modern society, with a significant overlap to the theory and the endeavour to practically apply the findings not only in media practice, but also in formulating measures at society-wide level.

Martin Slivka

'The Master of nine crafts', Professor Karol Plicka, was Martin Slivka's role model and inspiration. A few of his films and scholarly analyses published in several books were devoted to Plicka and his extraordinary artistic accomplishments. He was not only Slivka's inspiration but also the object of his profound research inquiries. Slivka's own creative path unfolded from his Master's work he admired so much. This creative path was extraordinarily rich and diverse – he was an excellent documentary filmmaker, screenwriter, playwright, director, as well as a prominent ethnologist, a scientist and, ultimately, a lecturer who inspired and provoked his students by creating a space for free search of connections through his lectures.

He considered education, creativity and ethics to be the basic values any artist should have possessed. He is one of the key personalities of our culture that need to be re-discovered, reflected on by returning to their messages, confronted with the world. Martin Slivka was the co-founder of modern Slovak documentary film; he made more than 140 remarkable film documents. His independent debut, Water and Work (1963), highlighted the fact that a gifted filmmaker possessing a precious artistic opinion has just entered the area. The motion picture, which focuses on technical landmarks such as mills, uses artworks of prominent Slovak artists, e.g. music of Ilja Zeljenka and images of Jozef Grussmann, yet without any explicit spoken comments.

In addition to many other Slivka's films worthy of our attention, the documentary from Bulgaria Man Is Leaving (1968) is truly exceptional. "He reconsidered the traditionally descriptive ethnographic film works, (...) talking about the place of death in human life, about things that are common in all cultures," The History of Slovak Cinematography (2016) claims. The same publication also states that "During the period of 1963 – 1969, the authors of various generations, e.g. Karol Skřipský (1908), Vlado Kubenko (1924), Martin Slivka (1929), Dušan Hanák (1938) and Dušan Trančík (1946) created their masterpieces, their opuses". However, it was no coincidence; the political situation of the 1960s in our country but also anywhere else in the world seemed to universally inspire the best creators of different generations active in different areas of artistic life. Martin Slivka used similar artistic approaches to creating films about art and film portraits of prominent Slovak artists.

Moreover, he remained faithful to ethnographic film, exploring folk culture in its essence (but through a modern film language), customs and folk theatre that he also reflected on in his academic publications. The publication The Slovak Folk Theatre (2002) is the result of his researching and seeking. His precise workpreparations necessarily involved searching for co-creators who, in his opinion, would provide their future collective work with the best possible quality. That is why Milan Rúfus, one of the most outstanding personalities of Slovak literature, wrote comments on some of his films. Moreover, world-famous music artists suchas Krzysztof Penderecki and Ilja Zeljenka were willing to link their music with Slivka's films. Martin Slivka's filmmaking skills were connected to his ethnological erudition, based on multidisciplinary approaches to the presented themes, as his unique studies on this topic clearly reflected.

He was a rebellious, stubborn debater; his former students, and there are many, are grateful not only for his professional supervision but also for the intellectual search they were lucky to experience while standing beside him. "It is difficult, if I may use his own words, to 'establish Martin Slivka in any structure'. He is a patriarchal tradition of the East and a Renaissance legacy of the West, all in one.

His whole being completely smells of humanity," writes one of his most successfulstudents, the film director Mário Homolka. While appreciating his work, it is impossible to omit the 13-part television series The Children of the Wind (1990) about the lives of Gypsies in many European countries. His son Ľubomír worked with him and despite many difficulties they experienced in many countries while making the series, they created a unique piece of art that is still unmatched in this area of creative expression and, as I daresay, it will remain unmatched for a long time. The film's value will definitely increase, since it offers a set of thorough, yet subtle expressions of the quickly vanishing Romani traditions. Martin Slivka is the winner of many prizes and awards, one of the most discussed Slovak filmmakers. Above all, he will be remembered as an inventive, wise and loving man, as a true renaissance person who knew how to understand human weaknesses and always tried to overcome these weaknesses through considerable doses of irony that was so typical for all his works.

Milan Stano

Painter, graphic designer, cartoonist. Publisher, editor, writer and connoisseur of everything connected with travelling around the world. His inspirations are tangible not only in images and writings he has created but also in endless considerations, comparisons and evaluations reflecting on his works. He is original, capable in each of the mentioned creative fields, unrepeatable. He is tough and hardworking. Most of his paintings are landscapes, images of rural environments and urban visions. Following his paintings, he travels across the country with his rack, sketchbook, colours and brushes. "In his paintings, a calm landscape emerges, radiating harmony, balance; through urban motives and folk architecture, he creates poetic compositions," wrote a critic. The humorous images of Slovak folklore and folk traditions also define the cartoons he has been publishing since 1966: "I love Slovak humour; the soul of the nation, the unbound joy of life, the sense of justice and the mockery of stupidity are all enchanted within it," wrote Milan Stano. That is why he also became the publisher, editor and later editor-in-chief of the independent satirical monthly magazine

Kocúrkovo, published by Štúdio humoru a satiry since 1990. That is where he started to publish books as well. His cartoons are kind, ironic and provocative at the same time, always able to reflect the problems Slovakia has to face – after all, the reader should become acquainted with various cultural or historical contexts –; however, they also point out the more general questions of being, joy and 'borderless' stupidity. They represent timelessness and a peculiar dialogue with the universe. His heroes are mostly sketched with a closed line, and that is the hallmark of his work: "I understand the caricature as a system of fine arts philosophy through which I can contribute to creating a certain atmosphere. For example, a humorous drawing allows me to create a sense of good mood, optimism, while a cartoon satire helps me create an atmosphere of criticism. The caricature is a good companion," wrote the author.

Legal Ethics: law and moralityEthics

Ethics is a branch of philosophy that aims to answer the basic question, "What should I do?" It's a process of reflection in which people's decisions are shaped bytheir values, principles, and purpose rather than unthinking habits, social conventions, or self-interest. Our values, principles, and purpose are what give us a sense of what's good, right,and meaningful in our lives. They serve as a reference point for all the possible courses of action we could choose. On this definition, an ethical decision is one made based on reflection about the things we think are important and that is consistent with those beliefs.

While each person is able to reflect and discover their own sense of what's good, right, and meaningful, the course of human history has seen different groups unify around different sets of values, purposes and principles. Christians, consequentialists, Buddhists, Stoics and the rest all provide different answers to that question, "What should I do?" Each of these answers is a 'morality'.

Morality

Many people find morality extremely useful. Not everyone has the time andtraining to reflect on the kind of life they want to live, considering all the different combinations of values, principles, and purposes. It's helpful for them to have a coherent, consistent account that has been refined through history and can be applied in their day to day lives.

Many people also inherit their morality from their family, community or culture – it's rare for somebody to 'shop around' for the morality that most closely fits their personal beliefs. Usually the process is unconscious. There's a challenge here: if we inherit a ready-made answer to the question of how we should live, it's possible to apply it to our lives without ever assessing whether the answer is satisfactory or not.

We might live our whole lives under a moral system which, if we'd had the chance to think about, we would have rejected in part or in full.

Law

The law is different. It's not a morality in the strict sense of the word because, at least in democratic nations, it tries to create a private space where individuals can live according to their own ethical beliefs or morality. Instead, the law tries to create a basic, enforceable standard of behaviour necessary in order for a community to succeed and in which all people are treated equally.

Because of this, the law is narrower in focus than ethics or morality. There are some matters the law will be agnostic on but which ethics and morality have a lot to say. For example, the law will be useless to you if you're trying to decide whether to tell your competitor their new client has a reputation for not paying their invoices, but our ideas about what's good and right will still guide our judgement here.

There is a temptation to see the law and ethics as the same – so long as we're fulfilling our legal obligations we can consider ourselves 'ethical'. This is mistaken on two fronts. First, the law outlines a basic standard of behaviour necessary for our social institutions to keep functioning. For example, it protects basic consumer rights. However, in certain situations the right thing to in solving a dispute with a customer might require us to go beyond our legal obligations.

Secondly, there may be times when obeying the law would require us to act against our ethics or morality. A doctor might be obligated to perform a procedure they believe is unethical or a public servant might believe it's their duty to leak classified information to the press. Some philosophers have argued that a person's conscience is more binding on them than any law, which suggests to the letter of the law won't be an adequate substitute for ethical reflection.

Law and Morality

Law and morality are too vague to understand. It must be added here that the notions of law and justice can't be captured and presented before us within a few sentences. These notions are too vast that even words are not sufficient to define them.

In general view morality is the quality of being in accord with standards of right or wrong conduct. Morality, speaks of a system of behavior in regards to standards of right or wrong. The word carries the concepts of: (1) moral standards, with regard to behavior; (2) moral responsibility, referring to our conscience; and (3) a moral identity, or one who is capable of right or wrong action. Morality has become a complicated issue in the multi-cultural world we live in today. Timeless wisdom explains that there cannot be a complete law unless there lays the effect and inclusion of morality. My Project explores what is Moore's concept of morality and how he explains its affects on our behavior, our conscience, our society, and our ultimate destiny.

Law and morality are too vague to understand. It must be added here that the notions of law and justice can't be captured and presented before us within a few sentences. These notions are too vast that even words are not sufficient to define them. Many jurists from the ancient Greek period to the modern and even the post-modern era have attempted numerously to define these concepts, but have failed. One of the reasons may be that the roots of these concepts lie somewhere within the human psyche, which is extremely random and versatile. Well it is required to describe the tenets of the two main schools of law.

Theory of Relationship between Law and Morality

Ever since the revival of the scientific study of jurisprudence the connection of law and morality has much discussed, but the question is not yet, and perhaps never will be settled. Every variety of opinion has been entertained, from the extreme doctrine held by Austin that for the purpose of the jurist, law is absolutely independent of morality, almost to the opposite positions, held by every Oriental cadi, that morality and law are one. The question is an important one, and upon the answer which is given to it depends upon the answer which is consequences. The problem is an intensely practical one.

The popular conception of the connection between law and morality is that in some way the law exists to promote morality, to preserve those conditions which make the moral life possible, and than to enable men to lead sober and industrious lives. The average man regards law as justice systematized, and justice itself as a somewhat chaotic mass of moral principles. On this view, the positive law is conceived of as a code of rules, corresponding to the code of moral laws, deriving its authority from the obligatory character of those moral laws, and being just or unjust according as it agrees with, or differs from them. This, like all other popular conceptions, is inadequate for scientific purposes, and the jurist, so for at least as he is also a scientist, is compelled to abandon it. For it is contradicted by the fact's. positive laws do not rest upon moral laws and common notions of justice furnish no court of appeal from the decrees of the State. The average man confounds law and morality, and identifies the rules of law with the principles of abstract justice.

No Distinction in Ancient Times

In the earlier stages of the society there was no distinction between law and morals. In Hindu law, the prime source of which are the Vedas and the Smritis, we do not find such distinction in the beginning. However, later on, Mimansa laid down certain principles to distinguish obligatory from recommendatory injunctions. In the West also the position was similar. The Greeks in the name of the doctrine of 'natural right' formulated a theoretical moral foundation of law. The roman jurist in the name of 'natural law' recognized certain moral principles as the basis of law. In the Middle Ages, the Church become dominant in Europe. The 'natural law' was given a theological basis and Christian morals were considered as the basis of law.

Moral as a part of law

There are some who assert that even if law and morals are distinguishable it remains true that morality is in some way an integral part of law or of legal development, that morality is "secreted in the interstices" of the legal system, and to that extent is inseparable from it.

Thus it has been said that law in action is not a mere system of rules, but involves the use of certain principles, such as that of the equitable and the good (aequum et bonum). By the skilled application of these principles to legal rules the judicial process distills a moral content out of the legal order, though it is admitted that this does not permit the rules themselves to be rejected on the general found of their immorality.

Another approach would go much further and confer upon the legal process an inherent power to reject immoral rules as essentially non-legal; this seems to resemble the classical natural law mode of thought, but it is urged, the difference is that according to the present doctrine it is a matter of the internal structure of the legal system, which treats immoral rules as inadmissible rather than as being annulled by an external law of nature.

If value judgments such as moral factors, form an inevitable feature of the climate of legal development, as in generally admitted, it is difficult to see the justification for this exclusive attitude. Value judgment which enter into law will require consideration of what would be a just rule or decision, even though not objective in the sense of being based on absolute truth, may, nevertheless, be relatively true, in the sense of corresponding to the existing moral standards of the community.

Whether it is convenient or not to define law without reference to subjective factors, when we come to observe the phenomena with which law is concerned and to analyze the meaning and use of legal rules in relation to such phenomena, it will be found impossible to disregard the role of value judgments in legal activity, and we cannot exercise this functional role by stigmatizing such judgments as merely subjective or unscientific.

The Problem about the Nature of Law J.Raz (1982)

The theory of knowledge attempts to clarify the nature of knowledge, the philosophy of logic examines the definition of logic, moral philosophy reflects on the nature and boundaries of morality and so on.

One finds philosophers who took the enquiry concerning the nature of law to be an attempt to define the meaning of the word "law". Traditionally those who adopted the linguistic approach concentrated on the word "law". However, it encountered the overwhelming problem that that word is used in a multiplicity of non-legal contexts. We have laws of nature and scientific laws, laws of God and thought, of logic and of language, etc. Clearly the explanation of "law" has to account for its use in all these contexts and equally clearly any explanation which is so wide and general can be of very little use to legal philosophers.

Only one assumption can the explanation of "law" hope to provide the answer to the legal philosopher's inquiry into the nature of law. That assumption is that the use of "law" in all its contexts but one is analogical or metaphorical or in some other way parasitical on its core meaning as displayed in its use in one type of context and that that core meaning is the one the legal philosopher has at the centre of his enquiry. Unfortunately, the assumption is mistaken. Its implausibility is best seen by examining the most thorough and systemic attempt to provide an analysis of "law" based on this assumption, that proposed by John Austin in The Province of Jurisprudence Determined.

The Lawyers' Perspective

Many legal philosophers start from an unstated basic intuition:

"The law has to do with those considerations which it is appropriate for the courts to rely upon in justifying their decisions."

Most theorists tend to be by education and profession lawyers and their audience often consists primarily of law students. Quite naturally and imperceptibly they adopted the lawyers' perspective on the law. Lawyers' activities are dominated by litigation in court, actual or potential. They not only conduct litigation in the courts. They draft documents, conclude legal transactions, advise clients, etc., always with an eye to the likely outcome of possible litigation in which the validity of the document or transaction or the legality of the client's action may be called into question. From the lawyer's point of view the law does indeed consist of nothing but considerations appropriate for courts to rely upon.

Hans Kelsen says he follows a combination of the linguistic approach and the institutional approach: "Any attempt to define a concept in question. In defining the concept of law we must begin by examining the following questions:

Do the social phenomena generally called law present a common characteristic distinguishing them from other social phenomena of a similar kind?

The clue to the methodological approach Kelsen was in fact pursuing is in his insistence that legal theory must be a pure theory. Kelsen regarded it as doubly pure. It is pure of all moral argument and it is pure of all sociological facts. Kelsen indicates his belief that the analysis of legal concepts and the determination of the content of any legal system depends in no way at all on the effects the law has on the society or the economy, nor does it involve examination of people's motivation in obeying the law or in breaking it.

For Kelsen, it is self-evident that legal theory is free of all moral considerations. The task of legal theory is clearly to study law. If law is such that it cannot be studied scientifically then surely the conclusion that if the law does involve moral considerations and therefore cannot be studied scientifically, then legal theory will study only those aspects of the law which can be studied scientifically. Since Kelsen has no good reason to insist that legal theory should be free from moral consideration, he has no good reason to delimit the law in the way he does.

The international Approach

It is the lawyer's perspective which delivers the verdict. Yet there is something inherently implausible in adopting the lawyer's perspective as one fundamental methodological stance. There is no doubting the importance of the legal profession and of the judicial system in society. It is however, unreasonable to study such institutions exclusively from the lawyer's perspective. Institutional approach seems much superior to its rivals. The institutional approach strives to present an analysis of a central political institution should be accepted as the analysis of law. From the institutional point of view, the basic intuition is the starting point for further critical reflection. It is entirely plausible to regard the notion of law as bound up with that of a judicial system but what are the essential characteristics of a court and why are they important to the political organization of society? Three features characterize courts of law:

1. They deal with disputes with the aim of resolving them.
2. They issue authoritative rulings which decides these disputes.
3. In their activities they are bound to be guided, at least partly, by positivist authoritative consideration.

At the highest level of philosophical abstraction the doctrine of the nature of law can and should be concerned with explaining law within the wider context of social and political institutions. It shows how the inclination to identify the theory of law with a theory of adjudication and legal considerations with all those appropriate for courts is based on a short sighted doctrine overlooking the connection of law with the distinction between executive and deliberative conclusion. Clearly, a theory of adjudication is a moral theory. It concerns all the considerations affecting reasoning in the courts, both legal and non-legal.

When the doctrine of the nature of law is identified with a theory of adjudication it becomes itself a moral theory. The doctrine of the nature of law yields a test for identifying law the use of which requires no resort to moral or any other evaluative argument. But it does not follow that one can defend the doctrine of the nature of law itself without using evaluative arguments. Its justification is tied to an evaluative judgment about the relative importance of various features of social organizations and these reflect our moral and intellectual interest and concerns.

Law and Morality

In the modern world, morality and law are almost universally held to be unrelated fields and, where the term "legal ethics" is used, it is taken to refer to the professional honesty of lawyers or judges, but has nothing to do with the possible "rightness" or "wrongness" of particular laws themselves.

This is a consequence of the loss of the sense of any "truth" about man, and of the banishment of the idea of the natural law. It undermines any sense of true human rights, leaves the individual defenseless against unjust laws, and opens the way to different forms of totalitarianism. This should be easy enough to see for a person open to the truth; but many people's minds have set into superficial ways of thinking, and they will not react unless they have been led on, step by step, to deeper reflection and awareness.

Relationship between Law and Morality or Ethics

Law is an enactment made by the state. It is backed by physical coercion. Its breach is punishable by the courts. It represents the will of the state and realizes its purpose.

Laws reflect the political, social and economic relationships in the society. It determines rights and duties of the citizens towards one another and towards the state.

It is through law that the government fulfils its promises to the people. It reflects the ociological need of society.

Law and morality are intimately related to each other. Laws are generally based on the moral principles of society. Both regulate the conduct of the individual in society.

They influence each other to a great extent. Laws, to be effective, must represent the moral ideas of the people. But good laws sometimes serve to rouse the moral conscience of the people and create and maintain such conditions as may encourage the growth of morality.

Laws regarding prohibition and spread of primary education are examples of this nature.Morality cannot, as a matter of fact, be divorced from politics. The ultimate end of a state is the promotion of general welfare and moral perfection of man.

It is the duty of the state to formulate such laws as will elevate the moral standard of the people. The laws of a state thus conform to the prevailing standard of morality. Earlier writers on Political Science never made any distinction between law and-morality.

Plato's Republic is as good a treatise on politics as on ethics. In ancient India, the term Dharma connoted both law and morality. Law, it is pointed out, is not merely the command of the sovereign, it represents the idea of right or wrong based on the prevalent morality of the people.

Moreover, obedience to law depends upon the active support of the moral sentiments of the people. Laws which are not supported by the moral conscience of the people are liable to become dead letters.

For example laws regarding Prohibition in India have not succeeded on account ofthe fact that full moral conscience of the people has not been aroused in favor of such laws.

As Green put it, "In attempting to enforce an unpopular law, a government may be doing more harm than good by creating and spreading the habit of disobedience to law. The total cost of such an attempt may well be greater than the social gain."

Although law and morality arc interdependent yet they differ from each other in their content, definiteness and sanction.

Some points of distinction between law and morality may be brought out asfollows:
Law: The Oxford English Dictionary defines the law as: 'the body of rules, whether proceeding from formal enactment or from custom, which a particular state or community recognizes as binding on its members or subjects.'

That this should be regarded as the definition of law for the English language is evidence of the influence legal positivism has upon the philosophy of law in our culture. The central themes of positivism are the contentions: firstly, that the existence of law rests upon identifiable social facts and, secondly, that it is necessary to maintain a conceptual distinction between law and morality. In this essay I will examine the positivist assertion that law is identifiable independently of morality, with a particular focus on the theory of H.L.AHart.

1. Law regulates and controls the external human conduct. It is not concerned with inner motives. A person may be having an evil intention in his or her mind but law does not   care for it.
2. Law will move into action only when this evil intention is translated into action and some harm is actually done to another person.
3. Law is universal in a particular society. All the individuals are equally subjected to it. It does not change from man to man.
4. Political laws are precise and definite as there is a regular organ in every state for the formulation of laws.
5. Law is framed and enforced by a determinate political authority. It enjoys the sanction of the state. Disobedience of law is generally followed by physical pun- islment.
6. The fear of punishment acts as a deterrent to the breach of political law.
7. Law   falls within the purview of a subject known as Jurisprudence.

Morality:

1. Morality regulates and controls both the inner motives and the external actions. It is concerned with the whole life of man.
   The province of law is thus limited as compared with that of morality because lawis simply concerned with external actions and docs not take into its fold the inner motives.
   Morality condemns a person if he or she has some evil intentions but laws are not applicable   unless these intentions are manifested externally.
2. Morality is variable. It changes from man to man and from age to age. Every man   has   his   own moral principles.
3. Moral   laws   lack   precision   and   definiteness   as   there   is   no   authority   to   make   and   enforce them.
4. Morality is neither framed nor enforced by any political authority. It does not enjoy the support of the state. Breach of moral principles is not accompanied by any physical punishment.
The only check against the breach of morality is social condemnation or individual conscience. 'Moral actions are a matter of choice of inner conscience of the individual, laws are a matter of compulsion'.

5. Morality is studied under a separate branch of knowledge known as Ethics.
   We may conclude the discussion in the words of Gilchrist, "The individual moral life manifests itself in manifold ways. The state is the supreme condition of the individual moral life, for without the state no moral life is possible.

The state, therefore, regulates other organizations in the common interest. The state, however, has a direct function in relation to morality."

Points to Remember
Laws may be defined as external rules of human conduct backed by the sovereign political authority. Law and morality are intimately related to each other.

Laws are generally based on the moral principles of a particular society. Some points of distinction may be brought out as follows:
(a)   Laws regulate external human conduct whereas morality mainly regulatesinternal conduct.
(b)   Laws are universal; morality is variable.
(c)   Laws are definite and precise while morality is variable.
(d)   Laws are upheld by the coercive power of the state; morality simply enjoys the support of public opinion or individual conscience.
(e)   Laws are studied under Jurisprudence but morality is studied under Ethics.\

Law and freedom
Both law and morality imply human freedom. Clearly, without freedom one cannot speak of morality. But the same holds for law, for if it were automatically and not freely obeyed, men would be mere robots. Law is not a simple indication of what happens, such as the law of physics; it is an admonition to free persons about what they are required to do if they wish to live freely and responsibly in society; and it normally carries with it a sanction or punishment to be imposed on whoever is shown to have acted against given norms of conduct. Just law, properly understood, appeals to freedom.

Nevertheless one of the most generalized liberal ideas is that law is by nature the enemy of freedom. Servais Pinckaers holds that Catholic moralists have gone through many centuries under the influence of this mentality which has led, by reaction, to the anti-law approach of much of contemporary moral theology. In this view, law and freedom were seen as "two opposed poles, law having the effect of limitation and imposing itself on freedom with the force of obligation. Freedom and law faced each other as two proprietors in dispute over the field of human actions. The moralists commonly said, "Law governs this act, freedom governs that one..." The moralists were traditionally the representatives of the moral law, and their mission was to show to conscience how to apply it in a particular situation, in a "case of conscience". Today we witness a strong tendency to invert the roles; the moralists now regard themselves as defenders offreedom and of personal conscience" [as against the law].

Law and justice
Law cannot attempt to regulate the purely interior sphere of personal conduct; morality can. Human or civil law is connected with external actions, precisely insofar and because they impinge on the rights or lawful actions of others. Hence the necessary connection of law with justice. For the regulation of interpersonal relations must work from the basic principle of justice: "to each his due". Hence arises the fundamental question of what is due to each one, and from this the further question of human rights.

To each his due. Something is due to each. This is the sense of equality before the law. "The possibility of giving his or her due not only to a relative, friend, citizen orfellow believer, but also to every human being simply because he is a person, simply because justice requires it, is the honor of law and of jurists. If there is an expression of the unity of the human race and of equality between all human beings, this expression is rightly given by the law, which can exclude no one from its   horizon under pain of altering its specific identity".

Even for those who see law and freedom in mutual opposition, the whole conceptof law is essentially connected with that of justice. The ancient principle lexiniusta non est lex (an unjust law is not a law), is at the basis of so many modern protests in the name of freedom. "This law is discriminatory, therefore it is not just". But justice is a moral concept; so these protests bear out the intrinsic connection between law and morality,"There is another crucial link between the virtues and law, for knowing how to apply the law is itself possible only for someone who possesses the virtue of justice".

'The law must respond to "living situations"...' Very good, but not in the sense that it must take the situation as its norm. Justice must remain the norm, and sometimes the law must regain ground for justice.

Influence of Morals on Law
Law and Morals act and react upon and mould each other. In the name of 'justice', 'equity', 'good faith', and 'conscience' morals have in-filtered into the fabrics of law. In judicial law making, in the interpretation of legal precepts, in exercising judicial discretion (as in awarding punishment) moral considerations play a very important role. Morals work as a restraint upon the power of the legislature because the legislature cannot venture to make a law which is completely against the morals of the society. Secondly, all human conduct and social relations cannot be regulated and governed by law alone. A considerable number of them are regulated by morals. A number of action and relations in the life of the community go on very smoothly without any intervention by law. Their observance is secured by morals. So far as the legal rules are concerned, it is not the legal sanction alone that ensure their obedience but morals also help in it. Thus, morals perfect the law. 'In marriage, so long as love persist, there is little need of law to rule the relations of the husband and wife – but the solicitor comesin through the door, as love flies out of the window.'
Growing Importance of Morals

Now, sociological approach has got its impact upon the modern age. This approach is more concerned with the ends that law has to pursue. Thus, recognized values, or, in other words, morals (of course the morals of the modernage) have become a very important subject of study for good law making. On international law also morals are exercising a great influence. The brutalities and inhuman acts in World Wars made the people to turn back to morals and efforts are being made to establish standards and values which the nations must follow. Perhaps there is no other so forceful ground to justify the Nuremberg Trials as morals. If the law is to remain closer to the life of the people and effective, it mustnot ignore morals.

Legal Obligation and Authority

Whatever else they do, all legal systems recognize, create, vary and enforceobligations. This is no accident: obligations are central to the social role of law andexplaining them is necessary to an understanding of law's authority and, therefore, its nature. Not only are there obligations in the law, there are also obligations to the law. Historically, most philosophers agreed that these include a moral obligation to obey, or what is usually called "political obligation." Voluntarists maintained that this requires something like a voluntary subjectionto law's rule, for example, through consent. Non-voluntarists denied this, insistingthat the value of a just and effective legal system is itself sufficient to validate law's claims. Both lines of argument have recently come under intense scrutiny, and some philosophers now deny that law is entitled to all the authority it claims for itself, even when the legal system is legitimate and reasonably just. On this view there are legal obligations that some of law's subjects have no moral obligation to perform.

Obligations In the Law

Every legal system contains obligation-imposing laws, but there is no decisive linguistic marker determining which these are. The term "obligation" need not be used, nor its near-synonym, "duty." One rarely finds the imperative mood. The Canadian Criminal Code imposes an obligation not to advocate genocide thus: "Every one who advocates or promotes genocide is guilty of an indictable offence and liable to imprisonment for a term not exceeding five years." The English Sale of Goods Act says that, "Where the seller sells goods in the course of a business, there is an implied condition that the goods supplied under the contract are of merchantable quality." That these laws create obligations follows from the way "offence" and "implied condition" function in their respective areas of law, not from the language in which they are expressed.

On the face of it, some laws have other functions. A requirement that "a will mustbe signed" generally imposes no duty—not a duty to make a will, and not even a duty to have it signed if you do—it sets conditions in the absence of which the document simply does not count as a valid will. Nonetheless, some philosophers, including Jeremy Bentham and Hans Kelsen, argue that the content of every legal system can and should be represented solely in terms of duty-imposing and duty- excepting laws. Bentham asks, "What is it that every article of law has in common with the rest? It commands and by doing so creates duties or, what is another word for the same thing, obligations". They think that analyzing laws this way reveals what legislators or subjects most need to know: under what conditions the coercive power of law will ultimately be met. Others argue that even if such a reduction were possible, it would be unwieldy, uninformative and unmotivated, concealing as it does the different social functions that laws fulfil (Hart 1994: 26– 49) and the different kinds of reasons for action that they create (Raz 1990). Others still, despairing of any principled way of knowing what a law is, have abandoned the problem entirely and tried to develop a theory of law that bypasses it. At a minimum, it does seem clear that whether or not all laws impose obligations, they can only be fully understood through their relations to those thatdo. Thus, a legal right is an interest that warrants holding others under an obligation to protect it, a legal power is the ability to create or modify obligations,and so forth.

What then are legal obligations? They are legal requirements with which law's subjects are bound to conform. An obligatory act or omission is something the lawrenders non-optional. Since people plainly can violate their legal obligations, "non-optional" does not mean that they are physically compelled to perform, nor even that law leaves them without any eligible alternative. On the contrary,people often calculate whether or not to perform their legal duties. Could it be then that obligations are simply weighty reasons to perform, even if sometimes neglected or outweighed? This cannot be a sufficient condition: high courts have important reasons not to reverse themselves too frequently, but no legal obligation to refrain. Nor is it necessary: one has an obligation, but only a trivial reason, not to tread on someone's lawn without his consent.

If their content does not account for the stringency of obligations, what does? An historically important, though now largely defunct, theory explained it in terms of penalty. Following Hobbes and Bentham, the English jurist John Austin says that to have a legal obligation is to be subject to a sovereign command to do or forbear, where a command requires an expression of will together with an attached risk, however small, of suffering an evil for non-compliance. "When I am talking directly of the chance of incurring the evil, or (changing the expression) of the liability or obnoxiousness to the evil, I employ the term duty, or the term obligation…" (Austin 1832, 18). Others conceived an indirect connectionbetween duty and sanction. Hans Kelsen holds that what is normally counted as the content of a legal duty is in reality only part of a triggering condition for the mandatory norm which commands or authorizes officials to impose a sanction: "[A] norm: 'You shall not murder' is superfluous, if a norm is valid: 'He who murders ought to be punished'"(Kelsen 1967, 55). And thus, "Legal obligation is not, or not immediately, the behavior that ought to be. Only the coercive act, functioning as a sanction, ought to be" (Kelsen 1967, 119).

None of these versions of the sanction theory survived H.L.A. Hart's criticisms (Hart 1994, 27–42; cf. Hacker 1973). First, they misleadingly represent a range of disparate legal consequences—including compensation and even invalidation—asif they all function as penalties. Second, they render unintelligible many familiar references to duties in the absence of sanctions, for example, the duty of the highest courts to apply the law. Third, they offer an inadequate explanation of non-optionality. "You have an obligation not to murder" cannot merely mean "If you murder you will be punished," for the law is not indifferent between people, on the one hand, murdering and being jailed, and on the other hand not murdering at all. "The right to disobey the law is not obtainable by the payment of a penalty or a licence fee". Such dicta are commonplace and reflect familiar judicial attitudes. Most important, the normal function of sanctions in the law is to reinforce duties, not to constitute them. It is true that one reason people are interested in knowing their legal duties is to avoid sanctions, but this is not the only reason nor is it, contrary to what Oliver Wendell Holmes supposed, a theoretically primary one. Subjects also want to be guided by their duties—whether in order to fulfil them or deliberately to infringe them—and officials invoke them as reasons for, and not merely consequences of, their decisions.

Sensitivity to such matters led Hart to defend a rule-based theory. He says that while sanctions might mark circumstances in which people are obliged to conform, they have an obligation only when subject to a practiced social rule requiring an act or omission. The fact that subjects use it as a rule marks it as normative. Three further features distinguish obligation-imposing rules: they must be reinforced by serious or insistent pressure to conform; they must be believed important to social life or to some valued aspect of it; and their requirements may conflict with the interests and goals of the subject (Hart 1994, 85–88). This account of the nature of obligations is not an account of their validity. Hart does not say that a legal duty is binding whenever there is a willingness to deploy serious pressure in its support, etc. He holds that a duty is legally valid if it is part of the legal system (i.e., if it is certified as such by the tests for law in that system), and a legal duty is morally valid only if there are sound moral reasons to comply with it. But, at least in his early work, he offers the practice theory as an explanation of duties generally—legal duties are the creatures of legal rules, moral duties of moral rules and so on.

The constitutive role of social pressure is sometimes considered an Austinian blemish on Hart's theory, but there are in any case more serious problems with it as a general account of obligations. People readily speak of obligations when they are well aware that there are no relevant social practices, as might a lone vegetarian in a meat eating society. And Hart's practice conditions may be satisfied in cases where there is no obligation but only generally applicable reasons, as when victims are regularly urged to yield their wallets to a mugger. At best, Hart's theory will apply only to a special class of obligations in which the existence of a conventional practice is an essential part of the reasons for conformity, though even here, the theory is open to doubt. A third account is reason-based. On this view, what constitutes obligations is neither the social resources with which they are enforced, nor the practices in which they may be expressed, but the kind of reasons for action that they offer. Legal obligations are content-independent reasons that are both categorical and pre-emptive in force. The mark of their content-independence is that their force does not depend on the nature or merits of the action they require: in most cases, law can impose an obligation to do X or to refrain from doing X. That they are pre-emptive means that they require the subject to set aside his own view of the merits and comply nonetheless. That they are categorical means that they do not condition their claims on the subject's own goals or interests.

This view is foreshadowed in both Hobbes and Locke, but its most influential contemporary version is due to Joseph Raz. He argues that obligations are categorical reasons for action that are also protected by exclusionary reasons not to act on some of the competing reasons to the contrary. Obligations exclude some contrary reasons—typically at least reasons of convenience and ordinary preference—but they do not normally exclude all: an exclusionary reason is not necessarily a conclusive reason. The stringency of an obligation is thus a consequence not of its weight or practice features, but of the fact that it supports the required action by special normative means, insulating it from the general competition of reasons. Or at any rate this is what obligations do when they have the force the claim, i.e., when they are binding. The theory does not assume that all legal obligations actually are binding from the moral point of view, but it does suppose that the legal system puts them forth as if they were—a consequence that some have doubted. (Hart 1982, 263–67; Himma 2001, 284–97) And while this account is invulnerable to the objections to sanction-based and practice-based theories, it does need to make good the general idea of an 'exclusionary reason', and some philosophers have expressed doubts on that score also (Perry 1989, Regan 1987): is it ever reasonable to exclude entirely from consideration an otherwise valid reason? The account has, nonetheless, been adopted by legal philosophers with otherwise starkly contrasting views of the nature of law.

Authority, Obligation, and Legitimacy
A competitive market is not a legal system, even though people adjust their behaviour in response to relative prices and the whole constitutes a form of social order. Neither was the system of mutual nuclear deterrence, though it guided behaviour and generated norms that regulated the Cold War. Many philosophers and social scientists agree that a social order is a legal system only if it has effective authority. An effective (or de facto) authority may not be justified, but it does stand in a special relation to justified (de jure) authority. Justified authority is what effective authorities claim, or what they are generally recognized to have.

What is legal authority, and how is it related to obligations? It is a kind of practical authority, i.e. authority over action. On one influential view, "To claim authority is to claim the right to be obeyed" (Wolff 1970, 5). There are, of course, authorities that make no such claim. Theoretical authorities, i.e., experts, are not characterized by claims to obedience—they need not even claim a right to be believed. And there are weaker forms of practical authority. To give someone authority to use your car is merely to permit him. But political authority, of which legal authority is one species, is normally seen as a right to rule, with a correlative duty to obey. On this account law claims the right to obedience wherever it sets out obligations. And to obey is not merely to comply with the law; it is to be guided by it. Max Weber says it is "as if the ruled had made the content of the command the maxim of their conduct for its very own sake" (Weber 1963, 946). Or, as Robert Paul Wolff somewhat more perspicuously puts it: "Obedience is not a matter of doing what someone tells you to do. It is a matter of doing what he tells you to do because he tells you to do it" (Wolff 1970, 9). This is not to say that one obeys only in treating the authority's say-so as an indefeasible reason for action; but one must treat as a binding content-independent reason. The question whether there is an obligation of obedience to law is a matter of whether we should act from the legal point of view and obey the law as it claims to be obeyed.

It is an interesting feature of this account that it supposes that one can tell what the authority requires independent of whether the requirement is justified on its merits. Richard Friedman argues: "[I]f there is no way of telling whether an utterance is authoritative, except by evaluating its contents to see whether it deserves to be accepted in its own right, then the distinction between an authoritative utterance and advice or rational persuasion will have collapsed" (Friedman 1973, 132). An idea of this sort is developed by Raz into one of the leading arguments for the "sources thesis", the idea that an adequate test for the existence and content of law must be based only on social facts, and not on moralarguments. Authority's subjects "can benefit by its decisions only if they can establish their existence and content in ways which do not depend on raising the very same issues which the authority is there to settle" (Raz 1994, 219). If law aims to settle disputes about moral issues, then law must be identifiable without resolving these same disputes. The law is therefore exhausted by its sources (such as legislative enactments, judicial decisions, and customs, together with localconventions of interpretation). This kind of argument has been generalized (see Shapiro 1998), but also subjected to criticism. It is uncertain what sort of constraint is posed by the idea that it should not involve "the very same issues"— perhaps if morality is a necessary condition only there could be moral tests for authority that leave the relevant dependent reasons untouched (Coleman 2001, 126–7). And while law does indeed serve as a scheme for guiding and appraising behaviour, it may also have other functions, such as educating its subjects about right and wrong, and this may be ill-served the attitude that the rules are to be obeyed in part because they are the rules (Waluchow 1994).

The obligation-correlative view of authority is not universally accepted. Some argue that legal authority involves no claim right, but only a set of liberties: to decide certain questions for a society and to enforce their decisions. The liberty conception must answer two questions. First, is it not a feature of a right to decide that it requires subjects to refrain from acting on competing decisions? If the law says that abortion is permissible and the Church says that it is not, what does the denial of the Church's right to decide amount to if not that public policy should be structured by the former decision and not the latter, even if the latter iscorrect? Second, does the right to enforce include a duty of subjects to pay the penalty when required? If it does, then this is only a truncated version of the obligation-correlative theory—one that holds that punitive and remedial obligations, but not primary obligations, are binding. If not, it is starkly at variancewith the actual views of legal officials, who do not think that subjects are at liberty to evade penalties if they can.

This reaches a methodological issue in the philosophy of law. Some consider that the character of law's authority is a matter for descriptive analysis fixed by semantic and logical constraints of official language and traditions of argument. Others maintain that such analysis is impossible or indeterminate, and that we are therefore driven to normative arguments about what legal authority should be. Crudely put, they think that we should understand law to claim only the sort of authority it would be justifiable for law to have. Such is the motivation for Friedrich Hayek's suggestion that 'The ideal type of law ... provides merely additional information to be taken into account in the decision of the actor' (Hayek 1960, 150). Hayek favours the free market, and concludes that the nature of legal authority should be understood analogically. The most radical position of this sort is Ronald Dworkin's. He prefers what he calls a "more relaxed" understanding of legal authority (Dworkin 1986: 429). Others have argued that the pre-emptive notion of authority is unsatisfactory because it is too rigid (e.g., Perry 1989). Dworkin's objection runs much deeper. His position is not that law communicates only a weaker form of guidance; it is that law is not to be understood as trying to communicate anything at all. A subject considering his legal duties is not listening to the law; he is engaged in "a conversation with oneself," and is " trying to discover his own intention in maintaining and participating in that practice" (Dworkin 1986, 58). On this view there is no fact of the matter about what law claims that is independent of what each does well to regard it as claiming.

However we resolve the methodological question, there are two parallel normative questions:
- The problem of obligation: What if anything justifies the duty to obey thelaw, and how far does that obedience properly extend?
- The problem of legitimacy: What if anything justifies the coercive power oflaw, and how far may that power properly extend?

What is the relationship between these? Some maintain that obligation comes first: "[T]hough obligation is not a sufficient condition for coercion, it is close to a necessary one. A state may have good grounds in some special circumstances for coercing those who have no duty to obey. But no general policy of upholding the law with steel could be justified if the law were not, in general, a source of genuine obligations" (Dworkin 1986, 191). The idea is that merely having justice on one's side is an inadequate ground for coercing others; one also needs a special title flowing from the moral status of the law. (Contrast, for example, Locke's view that everyone has an "executive power of the law of nature," at leastoutside political society (§ 13).)

Others contend that this gets the relationship backwards. First, it is doubtful whether one could have an obligation to obey an illegitimate regime. As Rawls says, "[A]cquiesence in, or even consent to, clearly unjust institutions does not give rise to obligations". If so, at least some conditions of legitimacy precede an obligation of obedience. Second, there are substantive reasons for thinking we would not have obligations to obey if the law were not already justified in upholding its requirements "with steel." A legal system that could not justifiably coerce could not assure the law-abiding that the recalcitrant will not take them for suckers. Without being able to solve this assurance problem it would be unjustto impose obligations on them, and unjust to demand their obedience. Underlyingthis suggestion is that idea that familiar idea that effectiveness is a necessary— but certainly not sufficient—condition for justified authority.

3. Obligations to the Law

It may affirm our confidence in the obligation-correlative view to know that from earliest times philosophical reflection on political authority has focussed on the obligation to obey. The passive obligation of obedience is certainly not all we owe the law (Parekh 1993, 243; Green 2003, 543–47) but many have taken it to be law's minimum demand. This gives rise to a puzzle. As Wolff puts it: "If the individual retains his autonomy by reserving to himself in each instance the final decision whether to co-operate, he thereby denies the authority of the state; if, on the other hand, he submits to the state and accepts is claim to authority then… he loses his autonomy". Wolff resolves the dilemma in favour of autonomy, and on that basis defends anarchism.

Some of Wolff's worries flow from the "surrender of judgement" itself—how can it ever be rational to act against reason as one sees it? Others flow from the fact that it is a surrender to the law. On the first point, it is relevant to notice that promises and contracts also involve surrender of judgement and a kind of deference to others, yet a rational anarchist needs such voluntary commitments to substitute for authoritative ordering. A principled objection to every surrender of judgment is thus self-defeating. Moreover, there seem to be cases in which by surrendering judgement on some matters one can secure more time and resources for reflection and decision on things that are more important, or with respect to which one has greater capacity for self-direction. A partial surrender of judgment may therefore enhance the agent's autonomy overall.

This suggests that Wolff's concern is better understood as scepticism about whether it is justifiable to surrender one's judgment wholesale to the law. Some philosophers have queried the intelligibility of this doubt; they say that it is of the nature of law that there is an obligation to obey it, at least in its central case. Some go so far as to conclude that it is therefore absurd to ask for any ground of the duty to obey the law: law is that which is to be obeyed (McPherson 1967, 64). We need a way into this circle, and the best entrance is in specifying the nature of law in a way compatible with various theories of its nature. Three features are especially important (drawing on Hart 1994, 193–200; Raz 1990, 149–54; and Lyons 1984, 66–68.) First, law is institutionalized: nothing is law that is not connected with the activities of institutions such as legislatures, courts, administrators, police, etc. Second, legal systems have a wide scope. Law not limited to the affairs of small face-to-face groups such as families or clans, nor does it only attend to a restricted domain of life such as baseball. Law governs open-ended domains of large, loosely structured groups of strangers and it regulates their most urgent interests: life, liberty, property, kinship, etc. But although law necessarily deals with moral matters, it does not necessarily do so well, and this is its third central feature: law is morally fallible. This is acknowledged by both positivists and natural lawyers, whose slogan "an unjust law is not a law" was never intended to assert the infallibility of law.

The question of political obligation, then, turns on whether there is are moral reasons to obey the mandatory requirements of a wide-ranging, morally fallible, institutionalized authority. This obligation purports to be comprehensive in that it covers all legal obligations and everyone whose compliance the law requires. It is not assumed to bind come what may, though it is to be one genuine obligation among others. Some philosophers also consider that it should bind people particularly to their own states, i.e., the states of which they are residents or citizens, and that an argument that could not show that one had more stringent duties to obey one's own country than a similarly just foreign one would be in that measure deficient (Simmons 1979, 31–35; Green 1988, 227–28). Finally, it is common ground the obligation exists only when a threshold condition of justice is met.

Legal Validity
Legal validity governs the enforceability of law, and the standard of legal validity enhances or restricts the ability of the political ruler to enforce his will through legal coercion. Western law adopts three competing standards of legal validity. Each standard emphasizes a different dimension of law (Berman 1988, p. 779), and each has its own school of jurisprudence.

Legal positivism emphasizes law's political dimension. Legal positivism recognizes political rulers as the only source of valid law and adopts the will of the political ruler as its validity standard. Leading legal positivists include Jeremy Bentham, John Austin, and H.L.A. Hart.

Natural law theory emphasizes law's moral dimension. Natural law theory recognizes universal moral principles as the primary source of valid law. These moral principles provide a standard of legal validity that imposes moral limits on the ruler's coercive powers. Leading natural law theorists include Aristotle, Cicero, Justinian, and Thomas Aquinas.

The historicist school emphasizes law's historical dimension. The historicist school recognizes legal custom as the primary source of valid law. Legal custom provides a standard of legal validity that imposes customary limits on the political ruler's coercive powers. Leading historicists include Sir Edward Coke, John Selden, Sir Matthew Hale, and Sir William Blackstone.

Legal positivism recognizes positive law as the only real law and rejects law's moral and historical dimensions as sources of valid laws. Natural law theory and the historicist school, on the other hand, often integrate law's three dimensions. They recognize each dimension as a potential source of valid law but emphasize a particular dimension through their validity standard. Blackstone's unique jurisprudence adopts two validity standards, one from law's historical dimension, and one from law's moral dimension.

Standards of legal validity are historically cyclical. A society typically adopts a standard of legal validity based on moral principles, custom, or both. This validity standard restricts the ruler's ability to enforce his will through legal coercion. Then, intellectual challenges to moral principles and legal custom minimize their esteem. A new validity standard is adopted based on the will of the political ruler. Abuses of coercive powers by political rulers eventually stimulate renewed restrictions on those powers. The society adopts a revived standard of legal validity based on moral principles, custom, or both. The revived validity standard will typically endure until the memory of abuse fades, when the cycle begins again.

This cycle began with Hesiod in 700 B. C. E. and continued into the 21st Century.In common law jurisprudence, judicial acceptance of Hart's legal positivism eroded Blackstone's validity standards based on moral principles and custom. In civil law jurisprudence, Soviet and Nazi abuses of positivist legal systems revived validity standards based on moral principles.

The Sophists
The first standard of legal validity in the Western legal tradition appears in Hesiod's religious poem Works and Days, circa 700 B. C. E. Hesiod presents an archetypal jurisprudence that integrates law's three dimensions. Dikê, the goddess of human justice, personifies law's moral dimension. Dikê's father Zeus personifies law's political dimension. Dikê's mother Thetis, the Titan embodiment of custom and social order, personifies law's historical dimension.

Justice "sets the laws straight with righteousness" and distinguishes men from beasts. Divinely decreed moral principles establish the validity standard for human law and customs, and conforming laws and customs establish the nomoi (law). Just men obey the nomoi, and obedience brings peace and prosperity. Disobedience brings punishment to the individual and his city through famine, plague, infertility, and military disaster.

The Sophists, wandering teachers of the fifth century B. C. E., challenged Greek conventions in religion, morality, and political conduct. They rejected Hesiod's moral dimension by rejecting the existence of divine lawgivers and universalmoral principles. They rejected Hesiod's historical dimension by denying any normative authority to custom. Might was right, and law functioned only in the political dimension as the will of the strongest.

The Sophist Protagoras of Abdera (b. circa 481 B. C. E.), rejected law's moraldimension. As an agnostic, Protagoras rejected the divine lawgiver. As a moral relativist, Protagoras rejected the existence of universal moral principles. Unlike later Sophists, however, Protagoras accepted the validity of custom in law's historical dimension.

Protagoras based his moral relativism on the argument that a shared factual knowledge of the world is impossible. The foundation of Protagoras' relativism is the "man-measure" of the Aletheia (Truth). "Man is the measure of all things, of those that are that they are, of those that are not that they are not."

Sense perception forms the basis of all knowledge, Protagoras believed, and everysense impression that a person receives is securely true. The data of sense perception, however, are private, subjective states. The wind is truly warm to the man who perceives it as warm, but the same wind is truly cold to the man who perceives it as cold. Perceived objects therefore have contradictory properties and there are no public facts.

Protagoras maintained that all knowledge claims are thus equally true. Furthermore, their truth endures regardless of conflicting claims. Protagoras therefore claimed "it is equally possible to affirm and deny anything of anything."

Protagoras extended his doctrine that all knowledge claims are equally true to claim that all virtue claims are equally true. Virtue claims are relative to the claimant because virtue is only another form of knowledge. (Plato, Protagoras, 323a-328d). There are no universal moral principles, and law's moral dimension does not exist.

Although Protagoras rejected law's moral dimension, he embraced law's historicaldimension. Although all knowledge and virtue claims are equally true, Protagoras argued they are not all equally sound. Only the ignorant equated truth with soundness. One set of thoughts can therefore be "better than another, but not in any way truer." The same is true of laws. All laws are equally true, but not all laws are equally sound.

Protagoras accepted a duty to obey the law. Since no moral or legal code is truer than any other, no individual should assert his moral or legal judgments over those advanced by the state. Society is required to preserve humanity. The perpetuation of society, in turn, requires respect for law and custom. Men should obey the state's laws and customs so long as they function soundly.
The Sophist Callicles (b. circa 484 B. C. E.), rejected law's historical dimension and denied any duty to obey the law. Using "nature" to mean the antithesis of mind, Callicles argued that nature's normative authority (phusis) supersedes the normative authority of man's laws and customs (nomoi). Man's laws and customs violate "nature's own law" and "natural justice." Nature's law, not man's, should govern our actions.

Callicles said that what men call "right" merely expresses what men believe to be to their advantage. Legal conventions in democracies wrongfully elevate the weakover the strong. The majority of weaker folk frame the laws for their advantage toprevent the stronger from gaining advantage over them. The true nature of rightis established by nature, not men, and nature's law establishes right in the strong.

Natural justice provides that the better and wiser man should rule over and have more than the inferior. Might, therefore, makes right. All animals and races of man recognize right as the sovereignty and advantage of the stronger over the weaker.
The Sophist Thrasymachus (b. circa 459 B. C. E.) argued for disobeying laws and customs. Defining justice as obedience to the laws, Thrasymachus argues that justice is nothing but the advantage of the stronger. Obedience furthers theadvantage of others and reduces the obedient to a form of slavery. Only disobedience to law profits a man and leads to his advantage. Injustice is therefore "a stronger, freer, and more masterful thing than justice."

Solon's constitution created an archetypal positivist legal system in Athens in 594 B. C. E. Solon reposed political and judicial authority in the heliastic courts. The courts enforced undefined laws with no standard of legal validity other than the unrestrained will of the jurors. Pericles' introduction of payments for jurors in 451 B. C. E. enthroned Athens' poorest and least educated class as dikasts in theheliastic courts. The Athenian courts became infamous for injustice and gullibility.Xenophon writes that Athenian courts often acted on emotion to put innocent men to death and acquit wrongdoers. Eighty dikasts who found Socrates innocentvoted for his death.

Athenian ostracism (ostrakismos) permitted the conviction, exile, and execution of any Athenian without charges, hearing, or defense. Originally intended for removing tyrants, Plutarch records that ostracism quickly became a way of pacifying jealousy of the eminent. Ostracism breathed out malice in exile and death. Everyone was liable to it whose reputation, birth, or eloquence rose above the common level.

Athens ostracized its greatest heroes from envy of their honors. Athens ostracizedAristides, the hero of the Battle of Marathon, in 483 B. C. E. Athens ostracized Themistocles, savior of Athens at the Battle of Salamis, in 471 B. C. E. Both men were exiled for ten years without charges or a hearing.

Lack of procedural safeguards encouraged frivolous public prosecutions (graphai) and impeachments (eisangeliai), giving free reign to Athens' gullible and imprudent dikasts. Frivolous political prosecutions destroyed Athens' leadership, spawning bloody regime changes and military disasters. The frivolous prosecutionof Pericles in 443 B. C. E. precipitated the Peloponnesian War with Sparta. The frivolous prosecution of Alcibiades in 415 B. C. E. caused Athens' ablest general to switch sides and lead Sparta against Athens.

The greatest ignominy involves the Arginusae generals in 404 B. C. E. Six Athenian naval commanders won a great naval victory against Sparta at Arginusae. A violent storm prevented their recovering the dead and shipwrecked. The generals were nevertheless impeached and executed for failing to do so. Deprived of her best generals, Athens lost the war the next year in a devastating naval defeat at Aegospotami.

Political prosecutions wreaked political havoc as well. Five regime changes rocked Athens between 411 B. C. E. and 403 B. C. E. These regimes included the reign of terror by the Thirty Tyrants in 404 B. C. E.

Athenian positivism criminalized thought and expression in frivolous prosecutions against philosophers. Anaxagoras circa 430 B. C. E., Protagoras circa 415 B. C. E., and Socrates in 399 B. C. E. were all convicted on manufactured charges of impiety (asebeia). Impiety was undefined by Athenian law. Every juror defined it anew in every case as he pleased.

Athens often regretted its decisions. Socrates' lead accuser Anytus was stoned forhis role in Socrates' death. Athens honored Socrates with a bronze statue by Lysippus. Athens thus gained "the indelible reproach of decreeing to the same citizens the hemlock on one day and statues on the next."

Plato

Plato described Socrates as the bravest, wisest, and most upright man of his time. Plato planned a career in politics but "withdrew in disgust" after observing how Athenian courts "corrupted the written laws and customs." (Plato, Letter VII, 325a-c). Plato reacted to Socrates' death by repudiating the Sophists, reviving law's moral and historical dimensions, and formulating a natural law standard of legal validity based on principles of universal justice.

Plato begins his revival of law's historical dimension by emphasizing the autonomy of law, which he considered the most important aspect of government.Autonomous laws wield supremacy over political rulers. Political rulers are subjectto the same laws as other citizens, and they may not alter the laws to suit their will. Plato wrote that the preservation or ruin of a community depends on the autonomy of laws more than anything else. Respecting law's autonomy preserves the entire community. Disregarding it brings destruction. Autonomy is so important that "the man who is most perfect in obedience to established law" should receive the highest post in government. The second most obedient man should receive the second highest post, and so on for all the posts.

Plato begins his revival of law's moral dimension by persuasively refuting Protagoras' moral relativism in the Theaetetus. Protagoras claimed that all sense perceptions are equally true. Since knowledge is perception, all knowledge claims are equally true. Since moral claims are a species of knowledge claims, all moral claims are equally true. Therefore, no one set of moral principles has authority to guide the laws.

Plato offers eleven objections to Protagoras' arguments in the Theaetetus. Three are recounted here. First, Plato denies that knowledge is perception. If knowledgewere perception, we would understand anyone speaking to us in a foreign tongue. This is clearly not the case. Second, remembered knowledge refutesProtagoras' claim that knowledge is perception. Remembered knowledge involvesno perception, but it is knowledge nonetheless.

Third, moral relativism is self-refuting. Assume, as Protagoras claims, that "all beliefs are true." Assume also that another man exists who believes that "not all beliefs are true." If Protagoras is correct, then the second man's belief must be true. Protagoras' belief that "all beliefs are true" is thus refuted.

Plato continues his revival of law's moral and historical dimensions in the Crito. The Crito considers whether a duty exists to obey the law. Socrates' friend Crito argues for Socrates to escape and avoid his unjust execution.

Socrates replies that the soul is more precious than the body. Good actions benefit our souls, but wrong actions mutilate them. The important thing is not living, but living well. This means living honorably. Socrates utilizes three principles in determining whether to escape. First, circumstances never justify wrong action. Second, one should not injure others, even when they injure you. Third, one "ought to honor one's agreements, provided they are right."

Plato defines law's moral dimension through these principles. Justinian's Corpus Juris Civilis defines its moral dimension by these same principles in the sixth century. (Justinian, Digest, 1.1.10). Blackstone's Commentaries does the same in the eighteenth century.

Plato next refutes Thrasymachus' claim in the Republic that disobeying the law "is a stronger, freer, and more masterful thing" than obeying the law. In the Crito's "Speech of the Laws," the Laws present two arguments for obedience. The first is the "argument from agreement." Socrates has undertaken to live his life in obedience to Athens' laws. Athens did not force Socrates to live in its precincts. Socrates was free to leave at any time. By choosing to stay in Athens with full knowledge of how the laws functioned, Socrates promised obedience to the laws.

The Laws' orders are "in the form of proposals, not savage commands." Socrates can either obey the Laws or persuade (the personification of) the Law that they are at fault. If Socrates escapes without persuading the personification of the Laws that they were at fault, he would dishonor his agreement to obey the laws. Dishonoring a just agreement violates the ethic of "living well" and damages the soul.

The Laws' second argument is the "argument from injury." Disobedience destroysboth the Laws and the city, which cannot exist if legal judgments are ignored. Socrates concludes that "both in war and in the law courts and everywhere else you must do whatever your city and your country command, or else persuade them in accordance with universal justice" that they are at fault.

The Laws' second argument implies a natural law standard of validity based on principles of universal justice. The Laws insist they operate as "proposals, not savage commands." Socrates' duty to obey the Laws is contingent on the Laws' compliance with principles of universal justice. By implication, there is no duty to obey the Laws if they violate principles of universal justice.

Aristotle
Aristotle designs his legal philosophy to avoid the catastrophes described in his Athenian Constitution. Aristotle accepts the necessity of law's political dimension because laws cannot enforce themselves. Nevertheless, the Athenian legal history proves the political dimension is not sufficient to preserve a society or achieve its happiness.

Human nature demands more than political power from law. Law must accomplish justice and foster virtue. Justice is required to prevent revolution, and virtue is required for human happiness. Man separated from justice is "the worst of animals," and man without virtue "is the most unholy and the most savage of animals."

Aristotle writes in the Politics that securing justice is the state's most important function. Justice is more essential to the state than providing the necessities of life. Governments must be founded on justice to endure. Governments that rule unjustly and give unequal treatment to similarly placed subjects provoke revolutions. Justice maintained, however, forms a bond between the members of society that preserves the state. (Aristotle, Politics 1328b, 1332b, 1253a). Aristotle's Nicomachean Ethics defines justice as lawfulness concerned with the common advantage and happiness of the political community. Aristotle distinguishes between legal justice (to nomikon dikaion) and natural justice (physikon dikaion). Legal justice involves positive laws and custom enacted by man, such as conventional measures for grain and wine. These "are just not by nature but by human enactment" and "are not everywhere the same."Aristotle secures legal justice by granting autonomy to law and by utilizing custom to encourage obedience.

Natural justice, on the other hand, involves principles of natural law that originatein nature. Such principles do not arise in the minds of men "by people's thinking this or that." Natural law principles apply with equal force everywhere, just as fireburns both in Greece and in Persia. Aristotle secures natural justice by adopting natural law precepts as the standard of legal validity. Positive laws that violate natural law precepts are nullified.

Aristotle secures legal justice by restricting the will of the political ruler through autonomous laws. The Politics teaches that unrestrained power produces tyranny, even in democracies. Aristotle considers whether societies function best under the "rule of men" or the "rule of law." He concludes that laws, when good, should be supreme. Political rulers should merely complement the law by actingas its guardians and ministers. They should only regulate those matters on which the laws are unable to speak with precision owing to the difficulty of any general principle embracing all particulars. Aristotle gives four reasons for emphasizing law's autonomy over the will of the political ruler. First, law frees the state from the desires and passions that afflict political rulers. "The law is reason unaffected by desire. Desire ... is a wild beast, and passion perverts the minds of rulers, even when they are the best of men." (Aristotle, Politics, 1287a). Second, tyranny results when political rulers exercise autonomy over law, even in democracies. Third, the orderly rotation of political offices requires autonomous laws. Equality, liberty, justice, and expediency mandate that every mature citizen participates in governing the state. Fourth, the orderly rotation of political offices preserves the state by assuring evenhanded administration by magistrates.

Aristotle utilizes law's historical dimension to secure legal justice through custom. Aristotle uses the term nomos for law, and nomos includes custom and convention as components of the social norm. Aristotle writes in the Politics that legal custom is itself a form of justice. Custom and convention maintain social stability by encouraging obedience to the law. The law has no power to command obedience except that of habit, which can only be given by time. Aristotle urges caution in changing the law because changes enfeeble the power of the law. If the advantage of a change is small, it is wiser to leave errors in the law. The citizens usually lose more by the habit of disobedience than they gain by changing the law.

Aristotle utilizes law's moral dimension to secure natural justice in two ways. The first is by nullifying positive laws that subvert natural law precepts. Aristotle formulates a natural law standard of legal validity. Aristotle's Rhetoric describes natural law as an unwritten law, based on nature, and common to all people. "There is in nature a common principle of the just and unjust that all people in some way divine."

Natural law provides immutable and universal standards of justice. Natural law constitutes a separate body of binding law that exceeds positive law in authority. Human actions should complete nature rather than subvert it, and natural law nullifies positive laws that subvert natural law precepts.

Like Plato, Aristotle argues that the universal standards of natural law justify disobeying positive laws. Aristotle's Rhetoric provides two examples invalidating positive law for violating natural law precepts. The first is the case of Sophocles' Antigone, where Antigone disobeys Creon's order and provides funeral rites to her brother Polyneices. The second is Aristotle's guide to jury nullification of written law by appealing to higher principles of natural law.

Aristotle never explains why natural law wields supremacy over positive law. The supremacy of natural law is consistent, however, with Aristotle's view in the Physics that the ultimate causes of nature are divine.

The second way that Aristotle secures natural justice is by fostering virtue. Aristotle believed that human happiness depended on virtue more than liberty. The government is thus responsible for producing a virtuous state, and this is best accomplished through law. Although virtue encompasses more than mere conformity to law, virtue will only develop and flourish in a state that supports the legal enforcement of virtue. The state must provide moral education through its laws to make its citizens just and good. Failing to do so undermines the state's political system and harms its citizens.

Cicero
Marcus Tullius Cicero (106-43 B. C. E.) was a politician, philosopher, orator, and attorney. Cicero's De Legibus (The Laws), De Officis (On Duties), and De Re Publica (The Republic) greatly influence the natural law tradition. Cicero esteemed Plato and Aristotle. Although not a Stoic, Cicero adopted Stoicism's divine Nature as the source of natural law precepts that dictate legal validity. The histories of Herodotus, Thucydides, Xenophon, and Polybius persuaded Cicero that natural law imposes justice on human events.

Cicero's signature contribution to jurisprudence is his explication of Nature as divine lawgiver. Law and justice originate in Nature as a divinely ordained set of universal moral principles. Cicero describes Nature as the omnipotent ruler of the universe, the omnipresent observer of every individual's intentions and actions, and the common master of all people. Belief in divine Nature stabilizes society, encourages obedience to law, and leads to individual virtue.

Law's moral dimension dominates Cicero's jurisprudence. Cicero defines natural law as perfect reason in commanding and prohibiting. These principles are the sole source of justice and provide the sole standard of legal validity. "True law is right reason in agreement with Nature."

The precepts of natural law are eternal and immutable. They apply universally at all places, at all times, and to all people. Natural law summons to duty by its commands, and averts from wrongdoing by its prohibitions. Nature serves as the enforcing judge of natural law precepts, and Nature's punishment for violating natural law precepts is inescapable. (Cicero, De Re Publica, 3.33).

Natural law provides the naturae norma, the standard of legal validity for positive law and custom. The naturae norma provides the only means for separating good provisions from bad. Justice entails that laws and customs comply with the naturae norma and preserve the peace, happiness, and safety of the state and its citizens. Positive laws and customs that fail to do so are not regarded as laws at all.

Regarding Cicero's political dimension of law, the magistrate's limited role is to govern and to issue orders that are just and advantageous in keeping with the laws. Although the magistrate has some control of the people, the laws are fully in control of the magistrate. An official is the speaking law, and the law is a nonspeaking official.

Political rulers cannot alter, repeal, or abolish natural law precepts. Furthermore, political rulers have no role in interpreting or explaining natural law precepts. Every man can discern the precepts of natural law for himself through reason.
Political rulers must issue just commands as measured by natural law precepts. Individuals are protected against unjust coercion. Although rulers may use sanctions to enforce legitimate commands, every affected subject has the right to appeal to the

people before enforcement of any sanction. Furthermore, no ruler can issue commands concerning single individuals. Any significant sanction against an individual, such as execution or loss of citizenship, is reserved to the highest assembly of the people. As a further protection, all laws must be officially recorded by the censors.

Like Aristotle, Cicero requires that magistrates be subject to the power of others. Successive terms are forbidden, and ten years must pass before the magistrate becomes eligible for the same office. Every magistrate leaving office must submit an account of his official acts to the censors. Misconduct is subject to prosecution.No magistrate may give or receive any gifts while seeking or holding office, or after the conclusion of his term.

Regarding Cicero's historical dimension of law, Cicero agrees with Aristotle that custom maintains social stability by encouraging obedience to law. Custom can even achieve immortality for the commonwealth. The commonwealth will be eternal if citizens conduct their lives in accordance with ancestral laws and customs.

Justinian's Corpus Juris Civilis
The Corpus Juris Civilis (Body of Civil Law) codified Roman law pursuant to the decree of Justinian I. Completed in A.D. 535, the four works of the Corpus becamethe sole legal authorities in the empire. The Institutes was a law school text.The Codex contained statutes dating from A.D. 76. The Digest contained commentaries by leading jurists, and the New Laws was supplemented as new laws became necessary.

The Corpus is the direct ancestor of modtern Wester civil law systems. Its influence on canon law is seen in the medieval maim Ecclesia vivit lege romana (the Church lives on Roman law). Common law jurisprudence never accepted the Corpus as binding authority. Nevertheless, its twelfth century revivalprofoundly influenced the formation of common law jurisprudence through the works of the father of the common law, Henry de Bracton.

The Corpus divides law into public law involving state interests and private law governing individuals. Private law is a mixture of natural law, the law of nations, and municipal law. The Corpus establishes a clear hierarchy among law's three dimensions. The moral dimension occupies the highest position and provides the standard of legal validity. The historical dimension of legal custom occupies the second position, and the political dimension of Roman municipal law occupies thelowest position.

The Corpus' moral dimension resides in two bodies of law, natural law and the lawof nations. Like Cicero, the Corpus originates natural law in a divine lawgiver. "Thelaws of nature, which are observed by all nations alike, are established by divine providence." The precepts of natural law are universal, eternal, and immutable.

Natural law governs all land, air, and sea creatures, including man. "The law of nature is that which she has taught all animals; a law not peculiar to the human race, but shared by all living creatures." The Corpus extends natural law to "all living creatures" to repudiate the Sophist arguments that law is merely a human convention with no basis in nature, justice does not exist, and there is no duty to obey law. The Corpus' rebuttal focuses on the highly socialized behavior of such animal species as ants, bees, and birds. Although animals cannot legislate or form social conventions, they nevertheless follow norms of behavior. These norms affirm the existence of natural law.

The Institutes and the Digest state three precepts of natural law: "Honeste vivere, alterum non laedere, suum cuique tribuere." Live honorably, injure no one, and give every man his due. . These precepts track the Crito's admonishments to live well, harm no one, and honor agreements so long as they are honorable. Blackstone's Commentaries adopts these exact precepts.

The law of nations is the portion of natural law that governs relations between human beings. (Justinian, Digest, 1.4). Its rules are "prescribed by natural reason for all men" and "observed by all peoples alike." The law of nations is the source of duties to God, one's parents, and one's country. It recognizes human rights to life, liberty, and self-defense, and its recognition of property rights enables contracts and commerce between peoples.

The precepts of natural law provide the standard for legal validity. This standard voids any right or duty violating natural law precepts. The Institutes provides illustrative examples: Contracts created for immoral purposes, such as carryingout a homicide or a sacrilege, are not enforceable. (Justinian, Institutes, 3.19.24). Immorality invalidates wrongful profits. Anyone profiting from wrongful dominionover another's property must disgorge those profits.(Justinian, Digest, 5.3.52).

Immorality invalidates agency relationships. Agents are not obliged to carry out immoral instructions from their principals. If they do, they are not entitled to indemnity from their principals for any liability the agents incur. (Justinian, Institutes, 3.26.7). Immorality even invalidates bequests and legacies if the bequest is contingent upon immoral conduct.(Justinian, Institutes, 2.20.36). The Corpus' historical dimension provides custom as a source of enforceable law. The Corpus defines legal custom as the tacit consent of a people established by long-continued habit. Since custom evidences the consent of the people, it is a higher source of law than positive or statutory law.Statutory provisions, if customarily ignored, are treated like repealed legislation. (Justinian, Digest, 1.1.3). Legal custom establishes the autonomy of law over political rulers. Custom binds judges. A judge's first duty is "to not judge contrary to statutes, the imperial laws, and custom." Legal custom even controls statutory interpretation. "Custom is the best interpreter of statutes.".

The Corpus' political dimension resides in its six categories of Roman municipal law, the "statutes, plebiscites, senatusconsults, enactments of the Emperors, edicts of the magistrates, and answers of those learned in the law." In contrast to natural law and the law of nations, Roman municipal law was unique to Rome. Its provisions were also "subject to frequent change, either by the tacit consent of the people, or by the subsequent enactment of another statute."

Philosophical Counseling: Managing everyday problemsThe Basic Premise
Our ways of thinking influence our ways of feeling, desiring, choosing, acting, creating, relating, and being in the world. But most of the time we don't even notice our patterns of thinking. They run on auto-pilot, fueled by old habits and operating assumptions. If we could slow down and reflect on our ways of thinking, we might better understand our orientation on the world, and have a chance to ask questions about it, find out how it serves us, and how it trips us up at times. If we could examine our ways of thinking, we might cultivate greater clarity, coherence, breadth and depth in our worldview. This worldview can have a big impact on our future actions, reactions, and general experience of life. If we can learn how to apply a worldview that we've developed carefully and reflectively to our actions in a deliberate way, we can live with a much greater sense of empowerment and authenticity.

A regular practice of self-examination and deliberate action – the cornerstone of a philosophical life, and the very thing we pursue together in philosophical counseling – has the power to increase our sense of understanding, meaning, purpose, freedom, and fulfillment in our lives. It also has the power to transform many of the emotional culprits that cause us suffering – fear, dread, angst, anger, sadness, excessive attachment, jealousy, resentment, and guilt.

Philosophical counseling is, thus, a process that is educative, empowering, and therapeutic.

What do we do in Philosophical Counseling?
In philosophical counseling, we embark on an inquiry into your life.

Philosophical counseling is a collaborative and conversational activity between a trained philosopher and a client in which the client's life-problems are worked through by identifying, examining, and revising as necessary the operating beliefs, values, and habits of action that in form those problems.

(1)   The process of identifying the client's implicit "truths" and values, and making them explicit, improves self-awareness and puts the client in a position to clarify and critically examine the fundamental principles that have been guiding their lives.
(2)   The process of critically examining the client's core truths and values helps them to analyze the reasons and evidence that support their beliefs, discover the strengths and weaknesses as well as the benefits and challenges of their ways of thinking, and compare them with alternative perspectives. It also helps them to become aware of inconsistencies between beliefs, and conflicts between beliefs and habits of action (what they say and do). These revelations help the client to become aware of instances in which they might be working at cross-purposes with themselves.
(3)   The revision stage is one of creative re-building, in which the client's core truths and values shift, expand, and sharpen, with the consideration of various perspectives from philosophical wisdom traditions. It is also a stage of application, in which the client experiments with putting new ideas into practice, and works to direct their actions, relationships, and ways of communicating with intentional choice.

In counseling, the three stages tend to move in a circular manner, rather than a linear one. As new insights emerge, it can be valuable to circle back to earlier stages with new ideas for deeper examination.

The ultimate goal of philosophical counseling is to help the client to conduct an inquiry into their own life, to develop their own coherent, empowered, and fulfilling philosophy of life, and to live it! Minimally, what a client can expect to get out of philosophical counseling is greater self-knowledge and understanding of their own problems. Maximally, they can become empowered to solve those problems, relieve suffering, and create greater fulfillment in their lives.

The Role of the Philosophical Counselor
A philosophical counselor approaches their client as a fully functioning individual with the courage to deal with the perplexities and struggles central to the human condition. A philosophical counselor does not diagnose or treat emotional or behavioral disorders, and if problems arise of a medical nature, the philosophical counselor will help the client to seek an appropriate health care professional. A philosophical counselor works collaboratively with their client to solve life-problems by activating and cultivating the powers the client already possesses -- like critical thinking, imagination, empathy, desire, self-discipline, and creativity. A philosophical counselor acts as a navigation partner on the client's own journey to gain awareness, find direction, create solutions, and develop a fulfilling life.

The philosophical counselor does not tell the client what to think or what to do, but instead asks questions, uses tools of critical examination, offers fresh perspectives, draws connections, and gives encouragement. Most importantly, a philosophical counselor listens carefully to their client, works to understand the client's problems and their operating worldview, and works with the client to develop a coherent philosophy of life that will serve their own well-being.

An old role
It may seem that philosophical counseling is a new invention. Actually, it is as old as philosophy itself. The Ancient Greeks – Socrates, Plato, Aristotle, the Stoics, the Epicureans – saw philosophy as not only an educational activity, but as a kind of therapy for the soul that eased suffering, developed personal integrity, encouraged self-mastery, created justice, and cultivated the good life. Even in the era of academic philosophy, this ancient vision of philosophy has survived in the philosophical tradi-

tions of ethics, political philosophy, existentialism, pragmatism, feminism, and hermeneutics (among others). Modernday philosophical counselors revive the ancient art of philosophy, and put it to work in a one-on-one setting.

What kinds of problems are philosophical problems?

We might wonder whether or not we've got any philosophical problems. Most of the time we characterize our problems in terms of a particular relationship we're struggling with, a big life change, or a feeling of sadness, loss, confusion, loneliness, frustration, powerlessness, burn-out, or worry. But, quite often these very problems are signs of broader philosophical problems that deserve attention.

Common philosophical problems include questions or difficulties with:

- Core beliefs and truths
- Critical thinking and questioning assumptions
- Creative thinking and trying out alternative perspectives
- Clear reasoning and consistency
- Ethics and values
- Meaning, purpose, and fulfillment
- Happiness
- Identity, self-discovery, self-improvement
- Change, loss, death
- Moderating emotional life
- Existential Angst
- Alienation
- Self-discipline
- Decision Making
- Power and Justice
- Communication and relationships
- Conflict resolution
- Freedom, responsibility, and self-determination
- Authenticity

It's important to recognize that not all life-problems are medical in nature. Not every instance of struggle, suffering, or unhappiness is a sign of a mental illness. There are times when it is appropriate to seek a health care professional with training in psychology for treatment of an emotional or behavioral disorder. There are instances in which a problem in one's brain-chemistry exists and it is appropriate to get the help of a psychiatrist who can prescribe medication. But when problems are not medical in nature, one needs a different kind of counsel.

Sometimes non-medical problems are narrow in scope, requiring legal, financial, business, or academic counsel. And sometimes the problems are more general, at their root having to do with questions like:

- What's true?
- What's right?
- What's good?
- What should I care about most?
- What are my responsibilities?
- What does it all mean?
- What should I do?
- Who am I, and who do I want to be?
- How do I fit into the bigger world?
- Why am I here?
- How can I best relate with others?
- How can I best deal with change?
- How should I live?
- How can I take better control of my life?
- How can I be happy?
- and how can I come to know the answers to any of these questions andcope with uncertainty about them?

These are classic questions of philosophy. Most everyday problems dealing with ethics, values, meaning, purpose, truth, certainty, justice, power, freedom, and happiness are not medical in nature and cannot be resolved with medical intervention. They are best approached through philosophical dialogue.

Differences between philosophical dialogue and psychotherapy

Philosophical dialogue is a unique kind of dialogue. In it, we take our time to slowly and thoroughly clarify the meaning of our terms, examine lines of reasoning with critical thinking tools, compare our ways of thinking with other perspectives and worldviews, and consider the relationship between our ways of thinking and our ways of feeling, choosing, communicating, and acting. Unlike psychotherapy, philosophical dialogue is not diagnostic. A philosopher does not treat their interlocutor as a patient, nor assume that there is a disorder or illness present (beyond the challenges with the human condition that we all face). A philosopher does not presume causal explanations for their interlocutor's behaviors, feelings, or thoughts: He or she does not view their interlocutor as one who is "determined" to feel, act, or think in a certain way because of internal or external conditions.

Whereas many psychotherapists tend to approach problems by focusing on their interlocutor's emotional life, eliciting affect, tracing a personal history of trauma, and identifying childhood origins of current difficulties (a retrospective approach focused heavily on emotion); philosophical counselors approach ways of feelingas a starting point for understanding and examining our ways of thinking, our world views, judgments, and values, which influence the way we experience the world and the choices we make. Philosophical counselors work to elicit reasons and evidence for the ways one thinks, ask questions about what is true, good, andfair, open up different perspectives for discussion, and help their clients to consider their future trajectory and range of possibilities (a prospective approach connecting thinking, feeling, and choosing).

Philosophical counselors also consider the ways in which one's personal history takes place within a wider context of social-political structures. There are times when one's distress has much to do with the power relations in which one exists or the state of injustice in the world, and the remedy is not so much about turninginward and learning to adapt to that injustice, but learning how to engage politically, and resist in active, creative, and fruitful ways that bring a sense of meaning, purpose, and agency to our   lives.
There are a number of psychotherapeutic methods that are not in tension with, but have a strong kinship with philosophical approaches, as their strategies' theoretical roots can be traced back to Socratic, Stoic, Buddhist, and Existential philosophies, among others.

In summary, philosophical counseling takes a holistic approach to the thinking- feeling-choosing-doing of the individual in a social-political world, and considers the individual's powers of examination, creative exploration, and reflective choice to be vehicles of movement   and change.

A philosopher's training

Philosophers have a kind of training that makes them well suited for the kind of dialogue-work described above. It is probably well known that philosophers havea knack for asking questions, clarifying ideas, challenging popular opinions, drawing connections, offering fresh perspectives, and getting involved in painstakingly careful inquiries into big questions. There are some other skillsphilosophers have that are particularly useful in a one-on-one counseling relationship.

- Philosophers have a trained ability to understand others' worldviews, to learn them inside and out, to explain them, compare them, evaluate their strengths and weaknesses, to analyze their benefits and challenges, and to think through their concrete implications in practice.
- Philosophers have a trained ability to listen carefully for an argument in what another person says, and to identify assumptions, implicit truth claims, and implicit values. They can trace carefully another's line of reasoning, and ask the questions needed to examine it.
- Philosophers carry around with them a toolbox of well-used critical thinkingtools that allow them to recognize and remedy faulty reasoning, fallacies, and contradictions.
- Philosophers have experience with uncertainty and exploring uncharted territories of thinking without a map. They are accustomed to working without a formula, and dealing creatively with open-ended questions.
- Philosophers know how to inspire learning, activate and awaken the inner philosopher in others (Socrates' gadfly effect), and empower people tothink for themselves and choose reflectively.
- Philosophers know how to learn from others, take what they say seriously, interpret their meaning, and engage in an ongoing practice of self-critique and revision of their own understanding, providing a helpful model to others who are on their own philosophical journey for the first time.
- Philosophers know how to recognize relativism, nihilism, solipsism, and other "tail-spin" positions.
- Philosophers have been trained in, and can discuss, a broad array of wisdom traditions (ancient and modern, eastern and western). They are also experts in a few of their favorite theories, about which they have usually taught, debated publicly with other experts, and published in a deep and thorough manner.

So, here's the punchline. A philosopher can make an excellent co-traveler on your journey into the big questions of life. A philosopher can offer a unique inquiry- experience that opens up distinct dimensions of thought, and that complements and moves beyond other forms of "talk-therapy."

MCQs

1.   Ethics is a ----------------------------------- science.
a.   Positive
b.   Negative
c.   Normative
d.   Theoretical

2.	is the domain of ethics that includes professional ethics and practical ethics.
a.	Positive ethics
b.	Applied ethics
c.	Normative ethics
d.	Metaethics

3.	Analysis about the nature and status ofethical theories is the subject matter of:
a.	Positive ethics
b.	Applied ethics
c.	Normative ethics
d.	Metaethics

4.	___________ is the philosophical examination, from a moral standpoint, of particular issues in private and public life whichare matters of moral judgment.
a.	Positive ethics
b.	Applied ethics
c.	Normative ethics
d.	Metaethics

5.	________ is the method of resolving moral problems by the application of theoretical rules.
a.	Casuistry
b.	Analysis
c.	Research
d.	Heuristic

6.	The method for jurisprudence and Appliedethics is:
a.	Analysis
b.	Research
c.	Heuristic
d.	Casuistry

7.	In ethics Casuistry means:
a.	Case-based analysis
b.	Cased- based reasoning
c.	Case- based investigation
d.	Case- based explanation

8.	The word casuistry derives from the Latinnoun:
a.	Case
b.	Casue
c.	Cassu
d.	Casus

9.	Identify the ethical position which acceptedcasuistry as a useful method.
a.	Absolutism
b.	Prescriptivism
c.	Utilitarianism
d.	None of these.

10.	Who among the following criticized utilizingcasuistry as a method for applied ethics?
a.	Pope Francis
b.	G. E. Moore
c.	C. J. S. Mill
d.	Bentham

Answers 1-10: 1-c, 2-b, 3-d, 4-b, 5-a, 6-d, 7-b, 8-d, 9-c, 10-a,

11.	________ is a branch of applied ethics that studies the philosophical, social and legal issues arising in medicine and the life sciences.
a.	Medical ethics
b.	Bio-ethics
c.	Legal ethics
d.	Practical ethics

12.	_________ used the term Bio-ethics to describe the relationship between the biosphere and growing human population.
a.	Fritz Jahr

b.   Peter Singer
c.   Van R. Potter
d.   Sargent Shriver

13.   The notion Corporate Social Responsibility isrelated to:
a.   Medical ethics
b.   Business ethics
c.   Media ethics
d.   Bio ethics

14.   Business ethics is also called:
a.   Organizational ethics
b.   Capital ethics
c.   Industrial ethics
d.   Corporate ethics

15.   is the ethical theory proposed maximum happiness for maximum number.
a.   Ethical absolutism
b.   Utilitarianism
c.   Egoism
d.   Ethical Naturalism

16.   The name Peter Singer is related to:
a.   Practical ethics
b.   Normative ethics
c.   Metaethics
d.   Deontology

17.   Case of Roe V Wade is related to the issueof:
a.   Euthanasia
b.   Surrogacy
c.   Cloning
d.   Abortion

18.   IVF means:
a.   Intensive Fertilization
b.   Invitro Fertilization
c.   Intro fertilization
d.   In vitro Fetus

19.   Identify the first IVF baby.
a.   Robert Edwards
b.   Dolly
c.   Louise Brown
d.   Roe V Wade.

20.   Louis Brown was born in:
a.   1978
b.   1973
c.   1975
d.   1977

Answers 11-20: 11-b, 12-c, 13-b, 14-d, 15d, 16-a, 17-d, 18-b, 19-c, 20-a,

21.   Who put forward strongest argumentagainst abortion?
a.   Liberalists
b.   Feminists
c.   Consequentialists
d.   Conservatives

22.   is not a divide line between fertilized egg and child according to liberalists.
a.   Birth
b.   Viability
c.   Quickening
d.   Brain development

23.   is the most visible possible divide line between fertilized egg and child forthose who support abortion.
a.   Viability
b.   Birth
c.   Quickening
d.   Consciousness

24.   Which one is treated as the dived line in Roe Wade case?
a.   Viability
b.   Birth
c.   Quickening
d.   Consciousness

25.   is the time when the mother first feels the fetus move.
a.   Birth
b.   Viability
c.   Consciousness
d.   Quickening

26.   'Silent scream' is related to:
a.   Euthanasia
b.   Surrogacy
c.   Abortion
d.   Cloning.

27.   'Fetus is an innocent human being'. Whofavored this position?
a.   Liberals
b.   Conservatives
c.   Feminists
d.   Postmodernists

28.   Who wrote on liberty?
a.   Kant
b.   J. S. Mill
c.   John Rawls
d.   Bentham

29.   According liberalist ----------------------------- is the real morally significant divide line between fertilizedegg and child.
a.   Viability
b.   Birth
c.   Quickening
d.   Consciousness

30.   Crimes without Victims is written by:
a.   Edwin Schur
b.   J. S. Mill
c.   Peter Singer
d.   Immanuel Kant

Answers 21-30: 21-d, 22-d, 23-b, 24-a, 25-d, 26-c, 27-b, 28-b, 29-d, 30-a,

31.   Opponents of abortion maintain that thevictim of abortion is:
a.   Woman
b.   Society
c.   Fetus
d.   Child

32.   'Woman has the right to choose what happens to her own body'. Who favored thisstatement?
a.   Liberalists
b.   Conservatives
c.   Feminists
d.   Postmodernists

33.   Judith Jarvis Thomson is a:
a.   Liberalist
b.   Feminist
c.   Conservative

d.   Postmodernist

34.   'Pro- life' movement is related to the issueof:
a.   Euthanasia
b.   Surrogacy
c.   Abortion
d.   Cloning

35.   The problem of embryo wastage is relatedto:
a.   Euthanasia
b.   Surrogacy
c.   IVF
d.   Cloning

36.   Euthanasia means:
a.   Gentle and easy death
b.   Painless death
c.   Unexpected death
d.   Death

37.   Euthanasia is popularly known as:
a.   Silent killing
b.   Deliberate killing
c.   Killing on willingness
d.   Mercy killing

38.   Euthanasia carried out under the request ofthe person killed is known as:
a.   Non-voluntary euthanasia
b.   Voluntary euthanasia
c.   Involuntary euthanasia
d.   none of the above

39.   Which form of euthanasia is legalized bymost of the countries?
a.   Non-voluntary euthanasia
b.   Voluntary euthanasia
c.   Involuntary euthanasia
d.   none of the above

40.   Since 2018 euthanasia is legalized in India.
a.   Active euthanasia
b.   Involuntary euthanasia
c.   Passive euthanasia
d.   Nonvoluntary euthanasia

Answers 31-40: 31-c, 32-c, 33-b, 34-c, 35-c, 36-a, 37-d, 38-b, 39- b, 40c,

41.   India legalized passive euthanasia in:
a.   March 2018
b.   March 2019
c.   April 2016
d.   April 2015

42.   Identify the Greek terms which are the rootsof the termEuthanasia.
a.   Eu and Thaths
b.   Eu and Thanatos
c.   Eu and Thanasia
d.   Eu and Thesia.

43.   Aruna Shanbaug case is related to:
a.   Abortion
b.   Surrogacy
c.   Pro-life
d.   Euthanasia

44.   Who field a petition in the supreme court ofIndia as the plea to discontinue Aruna Shanbaug's life supporting system and allow passive euthanasia to her?

a.	Judith Jarvis Thomson
b.	Pinki Virani
c.	Edwin Schur
d.	Peter Singer

45.	Identify the nation which legalized activeeuthanasia.
a.	India
b.	Netherlands
c.	China
d.	France

46.	In India ________ is still illegal.
a.	Active euthanasia
b.	Passive euthanasia
c.	Involuntary euthanasia
d.	Nonvoluntary euthanasia

47.	The book -"Bitter Chocolate: Child SexualAbuse in India", is written by:
a.	Judith Jarvis Thomson
b.	Peter Singer
c.	Edwin Schur
d.	Pinki Virani

48.	The book 'Aruna's Story'is written by:
a.	Judith Jarvis Thomson
b.	Peter Singer
c.	Edwin Schur
d.	Pinki Virani

49.	Which form of Euthanasia is called asSurgeon assisted suicide?
a.	Voluntary Euthanasia
b.	Involuntary Euthanasia
c.	Non-voluntary Euthanasia
d.	Passive Euthanasia

50.	The term assisted suicide is related with:
a.	Passive Euthanasia
b.	Voluntary Euthanasia
c.	Involuntary Euthanasia
d.	Non-voluntary Euthanasia

Answers 41-50: 41-a, 42-b, 43-d, 44-b, 45-b, 46-a, 47-d, 48-d, 49-a, 50-b,

51.	Euthanasia as ________ when the person killed is capable of consenting to his orher death, but do not do so.
a.	Voluntary Euthanasia
b.	Involuntary Euthanasia
c.	Non-voluntary Euthanasia
d.	Passive Euthanasia

52.	Euthanasia performed against the will of thepatient is called:
a.	Voluntary Euthanasia
b.	Involuntary Euthanasia
c.	Non-voluntary Euthanasia
d.	Passive Euthanasia

53.	Name the euthanasia conducted when theexplicit consent of the individual concerned is unavailable.
a.	Voluntary Euthanasia
b.	Involuntary Euthanasia
c.	Non-voluntary Euthanasia
d.	Passive Euthanasia

54.	Identify the form of Euthanasia which isperformed when the person is persistently vegetative state, or the case of in-fants.
a.	Voluntary Euthanasia
b.	Involuntary Euthanasia
c.	Non-voluntary Euthanasia

d.   Passive Euthanasia

55.   The notion of 'status of embryo' related to:
a.   Surrogacy
b.   Euthanasia
c.   Murder
d.   Abortion

56.   'Doing away with useless mouths'. This viewrelated to
a.   Voluntary euthanasia
b.   Nazi euthanasia
c.   Fascists euthanasia
d.   Nonvoluntary euthanasia

57.   'Maintaining a pure Aryan Volk', is thejustification given by:
a.   Nazism
b.   Fundamentalism
c.   Terrorism
d.   Fascism

58.   Nazi euthanasia is neither voluntary nornon-voluntary but--.
a.   involuntary
b.   passive
c.   active
d.   assisted

59.   According to the way in which euthanasia isconducted it can be divided in to :
a.   three
b.   four
c.   two
d.   five.

60.   Euthanasia is done by the withdrawal od lifesupporting systems is called:
a.   Voluntary euthanasia
b.   Passive euthanasia
c.   Active euthanasia
d.   nonvoluntary euthanasia.

Answers 51-60: 51-b, 52-b, 53-c, 54-c, 55-d, 56-b, 57-a, 58-a, 59-c, 60-b,

61.   According to the way in which euthanasia isconducted it can be divided as :
a.   Voluntary and non-voluntary
b.   Non-voluntary and involuntary
c.   Active and passive
d.   Voluntary and involuntary

62.   Division of active and passive euthanasia isbased on:
a.   the uses of medicine
b.   the consent of the patient
c.   the process of doing euthanasia
d.   the autonomy of the patient

63.   The euthanasia is done by giving lethalinjection is called:
a.   Passive euthanasia
b.   active euthanasia
c.   voluntary euthanasia
d.   nonvoluntary euthanasia.

64.   The notion 'letting die' is related to:
a.   Voluntary euthanasia
b.   Non-voluntary euthanasia
c.   active euthanasia
d.   passive euthanasia.

65.   type of euthanasia is widely accepted.
a.   Passive

b.   active
c.   in-voluntary
d.   non-voluntary

66.   Voluntary euthanasia is also called as:
a.   Suicide
b.   Assisted murder
c.   Surgeon assisted suicide
d.   Surgeon assisted murder

67.   Euthanasia is done by the withdrawal of theventilator is called:
a.   Voluntary euthanasia
b.   Non-voluntary euthanasia
c.   active euthanasia
d.   passive euthanasia.

68.   Which among the given is treated as thewidely accepted form of euthanasia?
a.   Non-voluntary euthanasia
b.   Voluntary euthanasia
c.   In-voluntary euthanasia
d.   Active euthanasia

69.   The term bioethics is derived from theGreek........ .
a.   Bios and Ethos
b.   Bio and Ethos
c.   Bio and Etho
d.   Bios and Etho

70.   The article 'Bioethical imperative' is writtenby
a.   Peter Singer
b.   Van R. Potter
c.   Fritz Jahr
d.   Sargent Shriver

Answers 61-70: 61-c, 62-c, 63-b, 64-d, 65-a, 66-c, 67-d, 68-b, 69-a, 70-c,

71.   The principle of Autonomy is related to :
a.   Business ethics
b.   Medical ethics
c.   Media ethics
d.   Legal ethics

72.   Which among the following is not treated asthe principle of Medical ethics?
a.   Autonomy
b.   Justice
c.   Beneficence
d.   Objectivity

73.   The notion of Informed consent is related tothe principle of:
a.   Autonomy
b.   Justice
c.   Beneficence
d.   Non-maleficence.

74.   The concept 'Informed consent' is relatedto:
a.   Business ethics
b.   Medical ethics
c.   Media ethics
d.   Legal ethics

75   is the basic principle of the view of Fair distribution of scare medical resources.
a.   Autonomy
b.   Justice
c.   Beneficence
d.   Non-maleficence

76   is the basic principle of the view that a medical procedure does not make harm to the patient involved and othersin the society.
a.   Autonomy
b.   Justice
c.   Beneficence
d.   Non-maleficence

77   occurs when the patient dies because the medical professionals don't dosomething necessary to keep the patient alive.
a.   Voluntary euthanasia
b.   Non-voluntary euthanasia
c.   active euthanasia
d.   passive euthanasia.

78   occurs when the patient dies because of medical professionals stop doingsomething that is keeping the patient alive.
a.   Voluntary euthanasia
b.   Non-voluntary euthanasia
c.   active euthanasia
d.   passive euthanasia.

79.   When death is brought about by an act iscalled:
a.   Passive euthanasia
b.   active euthanasia
c.   voluntary euthanasia
d.   nonvoluntary euthanasia.

80.   When a patient is killed by giving anoverdose of medicine is called:
a.   Passive euthanasia
b.   active euthanasia
c.   voluntary euthanasia
d.   nonvoluntary euthanasia.

Answers 71-80: 71-b, 72-d, 73-a, 74-b, 75-b, 76-d, 77-d, 78d, 79-b, 80-b,

81.   When euthanasia is brought about by anomission is called:
a.   Voluntary euthanasia
b.   Non-voluntary euthanasia
c.   active euthanasia
d.   passive euthanasia.

82.   When euthanasia is brought about bycommission of an action is called:
a.   Passive euthanasia
b.   active euthanasia
c.   voluntary euthanasia
d.   nonvoluntary euthanasia.

83.   Passive euthanasia is when death is broughtabout by an   --.
a.   Commission
b.   Omission
c.   Action
d.   Intervention

84.   Euthanasia popularly classified in to -------------- according to the notion of informed consent.
a.   Five
b.   four
c.   Three
d.   Two

85.   Classification of euthanasia as Voluntary, Non-voluntary and Involuntary are according tothe notion of:
a.   Informed consent
b.   Procedure
c.   Truth telling
d.   Justice

86.   The notion 'Pulling the plug' is related to:
a.   Voluntary euthanasia
b.   Non-voluntary euthanasia

c.   active euthanasia
d.   passive euthanasia.

87.   Euthanasia brought by not carrying out surgery that will extend life for short time iscalled:
a.   Voluntary euthanasia
b.   Non-voluntary euthanasia
c.   active euthanasia
d.   passive euthanasia.

88.   Among the following which form of euthanasia is very similar to act of murder:
a.   Voluntary Euthanasia
b.   Involuntary Euthanasia
c.   Non-voluntary Euthanasia
d.   Passive Euthanasia

89.   The notion 'living will' is related to:
a.   Cloning
b.   Surrogacy
c.   Abortion
d.   Euthanasia

90.   Slippery slop argument is related to:
a.   Abortion
b.   Euthanasia
c.   Surrogacy
d.   IVF

Answers 81-90: 81-d, 82-b, 83-b, 84-c, 85-a, 86-d, 87-d, 88-b, 89-d, 90-b,

91.   The question of personhood is related to:
a.   Abortion
b.   Cloning
c.   Surrogacy
d.   None of these

92.   Which among the following is acceleratedthe discussions upon abortion issues.
a.   Aruna Shanbaug case
b.   Terri Schiavo case
c.   Roe V. Wade case
d.   Vincent Lambert case

93.   The practice of giving birth to a baby for another women who is unable to have babiesherself is called:
a.   Invitro fertilization
b.   Surrogacy
c.   Cloning
d.   Genetic mutation

94.   A woman who is given birth to a baby for another woman who is unable to have babiesherself is called as:
a.   Surrogicer
b.   Surrogose
c.   Surrogate
d.   Surrogote

95.   Surrogacy is considered one among the ---------------------------------------.
a.   issue of abortion
b.   problem of euthanasia
c.   issue of media
d.   assisted reproductive technologies

96.   The notion of 'Baby selling' is related to:
a.   Invitro fertilization
b.   Surrogacy
c.   Cloning
d.   Genetic mutation
97.   The issue of 'commodification of babies' isdiscussed in:
a.   Invitro fertilization

b.	Surrogacy
c.	Cloning
d.	Genetic mutation

98.	Problem of parent hood is closely connectedwith:
a.	Euthanasia
b.	Surrogacy
c.	Cloning
d.	Genetic mutation

99.	Question regarding 'motherhood' is comingin the ethical discussion on:
a.	Euthanasia
b.	Cloning
c.	IVF
d.	Surrogacy

100.	is treated as one of the fundamental ethical issue related to surrogacy.
a.	Question about the motherhood
b.	Embryo wastage
c.	Question about personhood
d.	Sanctity of life

Answers 91-100: 91-a, 92-c, 93-b, 94-c, 95-d, 96-b, 97-b, 98-b, 99-d, 100-a,

101.	Ttraditional surrogacy is also called as:
a.	Gestational surrogacy
b.	Artificial surrogacy
c.	Biological surrogacy
d.	Mutational surrogacy

102.	Who is the biological mother of the child ina traditional surrogacy?
a.	Surrogate
b.	Lady who brought the child
c.	Mother who paid for the baby
d.	Not determined

103.	The surrogacy in which the surrogate's eggs are combined with donor's sperm and givebirth to child is called:
a.	Gestational surrogacy
b.	Artificial surrogacy
c.	Mutational surrogacy
d.	Biological surrogacy.

104.	In a Traditional surrogacy ------------------gives eggs for fertilization.
a.	Donor
b.	Surrogate
c.	intended mother
d.	Lady other than surrogate and intendedmother

105.	In surrogacy both eggs and sperm are donated.
a.	Gestational surrogacy
b.	Traditional surrogacy
c.	Biological surrogacy
d.	Mutational surrogacy.

106.	In the surrogate has no biological link to the baby.
a.	Traditional surrogacy
b.	Biological surrogacy
c.	Gestational surrogacy
d.	Mutational surrogacy.

107.	In gestational surrogacy -------------------------------------is the method to create an embryo.
a.	Cloning
b.	IVF
c.	IUI
d.	ISCI

108.   is a woman whose uterus was used for the nurturing and development ofan embryo onto a baby.
a.   Social mother
b.   Biological mother
c.   Gestational mother
d.   Mother by blood

109.   A woman who rears the baby after birth iscalled:
a.   Gestational mother
b.   Biological mother
c.   Genetic mother
d.   Social mother

110.   A woman whose contribution to the childwas the ovum is called: a.
a.   Gestational mother
b.   Biological mother
c.   Genetic mother
d.   Social mother

Answers 101-110: 101-b, 102-a, 103- d, 104-b, 105-a, 106-c, 107-b, 108- c, 109-d, 110-c,

111.   is the male genetic contributor to the creation of an infant.
a.   Biological father
b.   Intended father
c.   Social father
d.   Sep father

112.   Commercial surrogacy is banned in India in-------.
a.   2019
b.   2015
c.   2018
d.   2017

113.   Surrogacy regulation bill was passed by LokSabha in ----.
a.   July 15, 2019
b.   June 15, 2019
c.   August 18, 2018
d.   August 18, 2017

114.   Which place in India was called as 'Babyfactory'' ?
a.   Selam
b.   Delhi
c.   Jaipur
d.   Anand

115.   is called the surrogacy capital of India.
a.   Selam
b.   Delhi
c.   Jaipur
d.   Anand

116.   Anand is called as:
a.   City of God
b.   City of Milk
c.   Surrogacy capital of India
d.   IVF capital of India

117.   In India surrogacy is permissible.
a.   Altruistic surrogacy
b.   Commercial surrogacy
c.   Artificial surrogacy
d.   Paid surrogacy

118.   ART means:
a.   Actual Reproductive Technology
b.   Artificial Reproductive Technology
c.   Artificial Response Technology

d.   None of these

119.   Issues of surrogacy is commonly called :
a.   Issue of Three mothers
b.   Issues related to Two mothers
c.   Issues related to five mothers
d.   Issues related to mothers

120.   Ethical issues of surrogacy is generallystated as issues of :
a.   Three mothers and three fathers
b.   Three fathers and two mothers
c.   Two mothers and Two fathers
d.   Three mothers and two fathers

Answers 111-120: 111-a, 112-a, 113-a, 114-d, 115-d, 116-c, 117-a, 118-b, 119-a, 120-d,

121.   Name the euthanasia which is done by the consent of the appropriate person on behalf of the patient who is unable to
        give consent.
a.   Voluntary Euthanasia
b.   Involuntary Euthanasia
c.   Non-voluntary Euthanasia
d.   Passive Euthanasia

122.   Kantian ethical position is called:
a.   Deontology,
b.   Utilitarianism
c.   Consequentialism
d.   Ethical relativism

123.   Who makes strong condemnation tocasuistry?
a.   Moore
b.   F.H. Bradley
c.   Mackenzie
d.   Bentham

124.   Universal happiness is related with
a.   Evolutionary theory
b.   Emotivism
c.   Utilitarianism
d.   Cognitivism

125.   The parents who brought baby form asurrogate is called:
a.   Genetic Parents
b.   Intended parents
c.   Traditional parents
d.   Gestational parents.

126.   The issue of commodification of babies isrelated to:
a.   Altruistic surrogacy
b.   Commercial surrogacy
c.   Independent surrogacy
d.   Traditional surrogacy

127.   argued that surrogacy is an assault to a woman's dignity and right toautonomy over her body.
a.   conservatives
b.   Sociologists
c.   feminists
d.   liberalists

128.   The view of 'baby producers' is concernedwith:
a.   Abortion
b.   Cloning
c.   IVF
d.   Surrogacy

129.   Critics of surrogacy argued that, in surrogacy the baby becomes a mere ---------------within an economic transaction of a

good and aservice.
a. entity
b. commodity
c. object
d. instrument

130. Rights of the child become pressing issuein--.
a. Surrogacy
b. Abortion
c. Cloning
d. IVF

Answers 121-130: 121-c,122-a, 123b, 124-c, 125-b, 126-b, 127-c, 128-d, 129-b, 130-a,

131. Surrogacy which includes a monetarycompensation to the surrogate is called:
a. Altruistic surrogacy
b. Commercial surrogacy
c. Gestational surrogacy
d. Traditional surrogacy.

132. refers to those surrogacy agreements where the surrogate does notreceive monetary compensation.
a. Altruistic surrogacy
b. Commercial surrogacy
c. Gestational surrogacy
d. Traditional surrogacy.

133. 'Informed consent' is considered as one ofthe fundamental principles of
a. Legal ethics,
b. Medical ethics
c. Business ethics
d. Media ethics

134. In India Commercial surrogacy is -------------------------------.
a. legal
b. legal and constitutional right
c. Illegal
d. legal and advisable

135. In altruistic surrogacy the surrogate is mostprobably_________.
a. close relative
b. unknown woman
c. woman from other nation
d. professional surrogate

136. is the study of appropriate business policies and practices.
a. Corporate ethics
b. Business ethics
c. Business policy
d. Corporate analog

137. In the case of Roe v Wade, The United States Supreme Court held that women have a constitutional right to an abortion
     in the first ------------------of pregnancy
a. Four months
b. three months
c. six months
d. two months

138. Who wrote the book 'A Theory of Justice'?
a. Keats
b. P.B. Shelly
c. Rudyard Kipling
d. John Rawls

139. 'Abortion is not wrong – at least not when the pregnancy result from rape'. Who proposedthis view?
a. J. S. Mill
b. Arthur

c.   Eysenck
d.   Judith Jarvis Thomson

140.   Birth is the most visible possible dividingline between fertilized egg and child- This statement is recommended by:
a.   liberalists
b.   conservatives
c.   feminists
d.   pro-life activist

Answers 131-140: 131-b, 132-a, 133-b, 134-c, 135-a, 136-b, 137-c, 138-d, 139-d, 140-a,

141.   Peter Singer identified ----------------------------as the criteria for antiabortion stand point instead ofthe criteria of Homo sapiens.
a.   eccentric value
b.   pragmatic value
c.   instrumental value
d.   intrinsic value

142.   Which among the following is consideredas the standard way of distinguishing betweenactive and passive euthanasia?
a.   Act versus passion
b.   Act versus omission
c.   act versus commission
d.   Omission versus Withdrawal

143.   Active euthanasia occurs when the medicalprofessionals do something that causes the patient to die.
a.   deliberately.
b.   passively
c.   without intentionally
d.   none of these

144.   Which among the following is treated asfourth estate?
a.   Judiciary
b.   Mediac.
c.   Legislature
d.   Government

145.   Which among the following is not a coreprinciple of media ethics?
a.   Truth and accuracy
b.   Independence
c.   Impartiality
d.   Subjectivity

146.   'The greatest happiness of the greatestnumber' is the motto of:
a.   Utilitarianism
b.   Intuitionism
c.   Emotivism
d.   Deontology

147.   Right to Information Act is passed in Indiaon:
a.   2000
b.   2003
c.   2001
d.   2005

148.   treated as a one of the core principle of journalism.
a.   viability
b.   publicity
c.   truth
d.   sensation

149.   RTI means:
a.   Right to Intelligence
b.   Right to Independence
c.   Right to Information
d.   Right to Interact

150. IPR means:
a. Intellectual Property Right
b. Indian Property right
c. Intellectual Privacy Right
d. International Privacy Right.

Answers 141-150: 141-d, 142-b, 143-a, 144-b, 145-d, 146-a, 147-d, 148-c, 149-c, 150-a,

151. The practice of taking someone else's workor ideas and claim off as one's own is called:
a. Intellectual theft
b. Cyber theft
c. Plagiarism
d. Hacking

152. In media culture ------------------------ builds trust and confidence.
a. sensational reporting
b. subjective reporting
c. impartial reporting
d. partial reporting

153. is a reasonable extension of the ethical principles in the actual circumstances ofthe moral life.
a. Character
b. Free will
c. c Behaviour
d. Casuistry

154. G. E. Moore calls ------------------------ is the goal of ethical investigation'
a. casuistry
b. practice
c. c right action
d. Right decision

155 deals the specific ethical principles and standards of media.
a. Practical ethics
b. Applied ethics
c. Journalist ethics
d. Media ethics

156 is considered as a principle of media ethics.
a. Bias
b. Subjectivity
c. Accountability
d. Popularity

157 is considered as a one of the fundamental principles of Journalism
a. Truth and Accuracy
b. Subjectivity
c. Love and Care
d. Freewill

158 treated as a principle of Journalism.
a. Subjectivity
b. Fairness and Impartiality
c. Obligation to power
d. None of these

159 is the sign of professionalism and responsible journalism.
a. Humanity
b. Truth and Accuracy
c. Independence
d. Accountability

160. A _____ must possess independent voice regarding political, social and corporatesituations.
a. Doctor
b. Journalist
c. Lawyer

d.   Business man

Answers 151-160: 151-c, 152-c, 153-d, 154-a, 155-d, 156-c, 157-a, 158-b, 159-d, 160-b,

161.   The notion 'Paid news' is related to:
a.   Journalism
b.   Theatre
c.   Film
d.   Culture

162.   Pulitzer prize is related to:
a.   Business
b.   Journalism
c.   Medicine
d.   Law

163.   Who is called as the father of Journalism?
a.   James Augustus Hicky
b.   M. N. Roy
c.   Joseph Pulitzer
d.   Aguste Comte

164.   Who is called as Father of Indian Press?
a.   James Augustus Hicky
b.   M. N. Roy
c.   Joseph Pulitzer
d.   Aguste Comte

165.   Who started Bengal Gazette?
a.   James Augustus Hicky
b.   M. N. Roy
c.   Joseph Pulitzer
d.   Tagore

166.   Bengal Gazette was started on:
a.   1782
b.   1783
c.   1780
d.   1781

167.   PCI means:
a.   Press Committee of India
b.   Press Council of India
c.   Press Council International
d.   Press Committee International

168.   PCI was established on:
a.   1973
b.   1978
c.   1977
d.   1975

169.   is the statutory body of Indian media regulations.
a.   Press Council of India
b.   Press Committee of India
c.   Press club of India
d.   None of these

170.   In India news channels are governed by:
a.   PCI
b.   CBFC
c.   BSA
d.   NBSA

Answers 161-170: 161-b, 162-b, 163-c, 164-a, 165-a, 166-c, 167-b, 168-b, 168-a, 170-d,

171. Who is known as Father of Modern Journalism?
a.   James Augustus Hicky
b.   Walter Lippmann
c.   Joseph Pulitzer
d.   Aguste Comte

172. Who among the following won two Pulitzer prize?
a.   James Augustus Hicky
b.   Lippmann
c.   Pranoy Roy
d.   Aguste Comte

173. Who is known as "Most influential Journalist of Twentieth century"?
a.   Lippmann
b.   Joseph Pulitzer
c.   James Augustus Hicky
d.   Aguste Comte

174. is the aim of business.
a .   Service
b .   Profit making
c .   Employ satisfaction
d.   Resource allocation

175. level of business ethics defines ethical behaviour and assesses the effect of business on society.
a.   The Company level
b.   The individual level
c.   The Industry level
d.   The Society level.

176. The notion 'Oxymoron' is related to:
a.   Business ethics
b.   Media ethics
c.   Medical ethics
d.   Legal ethics.

177. In Business ethics Micro level deals with the--.
a.   Organization
b.   Individual in the organisation
c.   Institutions
d.   The market and Government

178. In Business ethics Meso level deals with the--.
a.   Organization
b.   Individual in the organisation
c.   Institutions
d.   The market and Government

179. In Business ethics Macro level deals with the --.
a.   Organization
b.   Individual in the organisation
c.   Institutions
d.   Employer

180. The notion of whistleblowing is related to:
a.   Business ethics
b.   Media ethics
c.   Medical ethics
d.   Legal ethics

Answers 171-180: 181-c, 182-d, 183-a, 184-c, 185-a, 186-b, 187-b, 188-a, 189-d, 190-a,

181. refers to the act of organisation members, disclosing information on illegal and unethical practices within the organisa-
     tion.
a.   Oxymoron

b.   Reporting
c.   Whistleblowing
d.   Quickening

182.   CSR means:
a.   Company Social Responsibility
b.   Corporate Social Response
c.   Corporate Social Representation
d.   Corporate Social Responsibility.

183.   The concept CSR has implication in to thefield of:
a.   Business
b.   Media
c.   Law
d.   Medicine

184.   is a self-regulating business model that helps a company besocially accountable.
a.   Profit making
b.   Accounting
c.   Corporate Social Responsibility
d.   Quality production

185.   By practicing CSR is also called:
a.   Corporate Citizenship
b.   Social Citizenship
c.   Corporate Service
d.   Social Service

186.   is the positive involvement of a compony in a society and environment.
a.   Offering employment
b.   Corporate Social Responsibility
c.   Whistleblowing
d.   None of these

187.   activities help both employees and employer feel more connectedwith the society.
a.   Whistleblowing
b.   CSR
c.   Profit making
d.   Marketing

188.   CSR programs raise in the work place.
a.   Morale
b.   Happiness
c.   Responsibility
d.   Leisure

189.   Corporate Social Responsibility is equallyimportant to:
a.   Community
b.   Company
c.   Community and Country
d.   Community and society

190.   An activity of a business firm which promotes philanthropic concerns is identifiesas part of their:
a.   Corporate Social Responsibility
b.   Marketing plan
c.   Profit enhancing plan
d.   Employee welfare plan.

Answers 181-190: 181-c, 182-d, 183-a, 184-c, 185-a, 186-b, 187-b, 188-a, 189-d, 190-a,

191.   is asexual reproductive method.
a.   IVF
b.   Surrogacy
c.   Cloning
d.   None of these

192. Genetic surrogacy is also called:
a. Partial surrogacy
b. Total surrogacy
c. Social surrogacy
d. Intended surrogacy

193. 'Journalists should do no harm'. Thisassertion highlights the principle of:
a. Accountability
b. Impartiality
c. Justice
d. Humanism

194. Gestational Surrogacy is also called:
a. Partial surrogacy
b. Total surrogacy
c. Social surrogacy
d. Intended surrogacy

195. _________ argued that no morally significant dividing line between fertilized eggand child.
a. Feminists
b. Liberalists
c. Conservatives
d. Philanthropists

196. 'Digital divide' is related to:
a. Cyber ethics
b. Business ethics
c. Medical ethics
d. Professional ethics

197. The issue of Multiple parenting havestrong significance in:
a. Cloning
b. IVF
c. Surrogacy
d. Abortion

198. is the branch of ethics that seeks to understand the nature of ethicalproperties, statements, attitudes, and judgments.
a. Normative ethics
b. Meta ethics
c. Applied ethics
d. Virtue ethics

199. Right of the author or creator is known as:
a. Intellectual property right
b. Creator right
c. Author right
d. Copyright

200. The Hippocratic Oath is an oath historicallytaken by:
a. Physicians
b. Lawyers
c. Corporates
d. Teachers

Answers 191-200: 191-c, 192-a, 193-d, 194-b, 195-c, 196-a, 197-c, 198-b, 199-d, 200-a

201. Which among the following dichotomies isused in a discourse on ethics?
1. Empirical – Normative
2. Descriptive – Prescriptive
3. Fact – Value
4. Profit – Loss
   Which of the following is correct?
a. 1 and 3
b. 1 and 2
c. 1, 2 and 3
d. 2, 3 and 4

Answer: C

202.   How does the individual come to be ableto make moral decisions?
1.   By understanding his **motives**
2.   By understanding the **consequences** ofhis actions
3.   By being deterred and frightened of the **penalties** incurred on him for his action
4.   By understanding the **means** adoptedto execute action
a.   1,2 and 3
b.   1,3 and 4
c.   1,2,3 and 4
d.   1, 2 and 4
Correct Answer: D

203.   Which of the following statements are trueabout Engineering Ethics?
1.   Engineering Ethics is an area ofpractical or applied ethics
2.   The aim of Engineering Ethics is toilluminate the ethical dimensions of engineering practice
3.   Engineering Ethics is constituted ofan eclectic contribution of all schools of ethics
4.   Professional Engineering Societiesare a major source of codes for engineering ethics.
        Which of the following is correct?
a.   Only 2
b.   1 and 3
c.   1, 3 and 4
d.   1, 2, 3 and 4
Correct Answer: D

204.   Which of the following assumption aboutmoral behavior is reasonably justified?
1.   Most people will behave morally if the socializationprocess has successfully inculcated the right values
2.   Some people will behave moremorally than others even if they have been under the same socialization process
3.   Social situations provide the best stimulus to moral action or inaction; i.e social pressure determines moral action/inaction.
4.   Socialisation has no role indeveloping moral values
a.   1 and 4
b.   1,2 and 3
c.   1,2,3 and 4
d.   2 and 3
Correct Answer: B

205.   Which among the following are principleconcerns with 'professional ethics'
1.   To study ethical dilemmas in professions by application of moraltheory
2.   The study of unique moral obligationscreated by special social roles
3.   The practice and consultancy of ethicsby a trained professional ethicist
4.   The ethical challenges of a professional lifestyle
        Which of thefollowing are correct?
a.   1 and 2
b.   2 and 3
c.   1, 2 and 3
d.   1, 2, 3 and 4
Correct Answer: A

206.   Which of the following are true
1.   Ethical dilemmas arise when itis thought that serious good and bad are bound together inthe same activity
2.   Ethics uses the instrument of coercion to oblige its subjects
3.   Ethical behavior is dependent on the conditions and circumstances under which anaction/event takes place
4.   Codes of Conduct form a partof ethical training
a.   1 and 3
b.   1, 3 and 4
c.   1,2 and 3
d.   2, 3 and 4
Correct Answer: B

207.   Which of the following statements is mostappropriate to describe deontological ethics?
a.   The central idea is that the right or wrong consideration is what makesthe act right or wrong, other thingsbeing equal
b.   The central idea is that an adherence to the codes prescribed under the dutyone is employed in makes for the right action
c.   The central idea is that right andwrong are relative to time and circumstance
d.   The central idea is that right and wrong are determined by humansaccording to their subjective conscience

208. Consider the following statements behavior and the type of activity correspondingto them as impediments to responsible action for an engineer
    Type of Behavior
1. When group comes to agreement at theexpense of critical thinking
2. When we see things at the microscopic level, we can't see them at the general andordinary level
3. We tend to interpret situations from verylimited perspectives
4. An engineer genuinely does not realizethat a design poses a safety problem
    Type of Activity
1. Microscopic Vision
2. Egocentrism
3. Groupthink
4. Ignorance
    Which of the following are correct?
a. 1 – A; 2 – B; 3 – C; 4 –D
b. 1 – C; 2 –A; 3 –B; 4 –D
c. 1 –B; 2 –C; 3 –D; 4 –A
d. 1 –A; 2 – C; 3 –B; 4 –D

Correct Answer: B

209. Which of the following statements are trueabout 'Morale'
1. It is a form of 'attitude'
2. It is reflected in positive feelings about the work group
3. It instills confidence that difficult goals can be achievedeasily
4. It is the knowledge of the distinction between right andwrong action
a. 1,2 and 3
b. 1,2,3 and 4
c. 2 and 3
d. 2, 3 and 4

Correct Answer: A

210. Which of the following is the most appropriate definition of "practice" vis a visprofessional ethics?
a. "practice" is a cooperative arrangement to pursue the goods thatare internal to a structured communallife
b. "practice" is an endeavor to achieveexcellence by incessant repetition
c. "practice" is the application of knowledge into real time problems
d. "practice" is symbolic of the humbleadmission that humans can never know and learn enough

Correct Answer: A

211. Which of the following are true with regardto safety and treatment of employees
1. It is a means of promoting worker efficiency and social order by protecting lives andpromoting the well-being of workers
2. The idea of safety and treatment of employees was conceived during the IndustrialRevolution in Europe
3. By ensuring safety of workers the political society of a nationis stabilized
4. All workers have a right to expect fairness from their employer and to be treatedwith respect and dignity
a. 1,2,3 and 4
b. 1,3 and 4
c. 2 and 4
d. 1 and 4

Correct Answer: A

212. What among the following is a sub - specieof "normative ethics"
1. War Ethics
2. Applied ethics
3. Virtue ethics
4. Meta ethics
    Which of the following are correct?
a. 2 only
b. 1, 2 and 3
c. 2 and 3
d. 1, 2, 3 and 4

Correct Answer: A

213. Which of the following are prominent examples of 'ethical issues' that fall under thedomain of 'applied ethics'?
1. Euthanasia
2. Protection of human and animalsubjects in research
3. Affirmative action

4. Acceptable risk in workplace
   Which of the following are correct?
a. 2 and 4
b. 1,2 and 3
c. 1, 2, 3 and 4
d. 2, 3 and 4
Correct Answer: C

214. Consider the following options with regard to the 'Anthropogenic World View' vis a vis Environmental Ethics
1. Humanity perceives itself to be the center and ultimate goal of the Universe
2. Humanity perceives environment as a superior actor whose laws and codes are not well understood
3. Nature is viewed as a storehouse of resources
4. Many large, hierarchical business houses still base their business model on this world view
   Which of the following are correct?
a. 1, 2 and 4
b. 1, 3 and 4
c. 1 and 3
d. 1 and 4
Correct Answer: B

215. Which of the following principles is the essential principle of utilitarian school of ethics?
a. Greatest Health Principle
b. Greatest Happiness Principle
c. Greatest Wealth Principle
d. Greatest Respect Principle.
Correct Answer: **B**

216. Which among the following is a true about ethics of research and experimentation?
1. Research that causes harm to humans is morally wrong
2. Research that involves humans is justified only when some good can come from it
3. A person's right to liberty is violated if he is a subject to research by coercion
4. Informed Consent plays a role in Research Ethics
   Which of the following is correct?
a. 1, 2 and 4
b. 1, 2, 3 and 4
c. 2 and 3
d. 3 and 4
   Correct Answer: B

217. What among the following elements takes the most direct and immediate set back in a case of conflict of interest by a public official?
a. The reputation of the officer
b. The trust that the public holds in the office
c. The legitimacy of the office
d. The constitution of India
Correct Answer: B

218. "It is commonly said that before blowing the whistle, a person has an obligation to see that all existing avenues for change within the organization must have been explored". Consider the following statements as justifications for the above proposition.
1. The agent will be forced neither to breach confidentiality nor be disloyal
2. The agent (potential whistleblower) can seek remuneration from the organization for fidelity
3. The organization will not suffer embarrassment or more tangible harm
4. The organization can correct its mistakes internally by devising mechanisms to hear the issues raised by employees
   Which of the following are correct set of justifications under ethics?
a. 1, 3 and 4
b. 1,2 and 3
c. 1 and 4
d. Only 1
   Correct Answer: A

219. Which of the following actions can be termed as breach of 'Professional Ethics'
1. A physician who refers patients to a specialist in return for monetary favours
2. A scientist who exaggerates the importance of his discoveries to encourage investors in his biotech company
3. A lawyer who lies to the Judge
4. The reporter who spreads fake news

Which of the following iscorrect?
a.   Only 1
b.   1 and 2
c.   1, 2 , 3 and 4
d.   1, 2 and 4
Correct Answer: C

220.   Which of the following are the functions ofa code of ethics?
1.   It can express a shared commitment on the part of aprofessional society's members to strive to satisfy certain ethical standards andprinciples.
2.   It can help foster an environment in which ethicalbehavior is the norm
3.   It can serve as a guide or reminder in specific situations
4.   A code can be a valuable academic and educationallegacy for an organization.Which of the following arecorrect?
a.   1 and 3
b.   1,2 and 3
c.   1,2,3 and 4
d.   1 and 2
Correct Answer: C

221.   Which of the following is an appropriate general principle with regard for 'EngineeringEthics'
a.   The Engineer shall regard his duty to the public welfare as paramount to allother obligations.
b.   The Engineer shall regard his duty tothe objectives of the company as paramount to all other obligations
c.   The Engineer shall regard his duty tothe profession of engineering as paramount to other obligations
d.   The Engineer shall regard his duty to his excellence as paramount to otherobligations
Correct Answer: A

222.   Which of the following statements is themost correct description of the relationship between humans and technology?
a.   Technology "impacts" upon humanactions and human beings
b.   Human beings "act on, make, use"technology
c.   Technology provides apparatus forhuman action
d.   Technology hijacks human autonomy
Correct Answer: C

223.   What are the elements necessary for an Institution to formulate a state of the art 'codeof ethics'
1.   a body of public interest/relevance
2.   expert scholarship
3.   enormous funding
4.   professional support
a.   2 and 4
b.   2,3 and 4
c.   1, 2 and 4
d.   1, 2, 3 and 4
Correct Answer: C

224.   Which of the following elements (as a fundamental criterion) must always be in the mind of Engineer while performing his duties visa vis Ethics
1.   Public Safety
2.   Economy
3.   Health
4.   Welfare
a.   1,2 and 3
b.   1, 2, 3 and 4
c.   1 and 4
d.   1, 3 and 4
Correct Answer: D

225.   What among the following are the shortcomings of a code of ethics formulated bya 'professional engineering society'?
1.   These codes are not formulated with sincerescholarship or expertiseand are often a hostageto economic interests
2.   Most practicing engineers do not belongto any professional engineering society, so the codes cannot properly reach out to them
3.   Such codes, at best represent the highest ethical common denominator among those to who it applies therefore it may includeprovisions which may beethically questionable
4.   These codes are not exhaustive – and there are matters of ethical importance that may gounnoticed
        Which of the following sets of answers arecorrect?
a.   1 and 2
b.   1, 2 3 and 4

c.	2, 3 and 4
d.	2 and 3
Correct Answer: C

226.	As an engineer you are stuck in an ethical dilemma about the execution of a certain task that you find morally contesta-ble. You refer to a well-known 'code of ethics' and other regulations but none of them specifically prohibit that certain course of action (which is in contestation). Under what category does the ethical dilemma fall, when the 'code of ethics' are not able to solve it?
a.	Professional Ethics
b.	Personal Ethics
c.	Societal Ethics
d.	Business Ethics
Correct Answer: B

227.	Which of the following statements best explains the reason for engineering ethics being a branch of applied ethics?
1.	The aim of engineering ethics is to shed light on ethical concerns related to engineering practice
2.	It is applied in the sense that ethical considerations are directed to practice rather than theory
3.	The first task of engineering ethics is to identify the basic concern that arise prior to practice
4.	To think on the questions of engineering ethics one necessarily needs a technical engineering knowledge.
a.	1 and 4
b.	2 and 3
c.	1 and 2
d.	2 and 4
Correct Answer: C

228.	Consider the following statements about 'whistle blowing'
1.	A whistle blower makes accusations against an Organization which call attention to alleged instances of negligence, abuse or practices that damage the public interest or harm others.
2.	The accusation mostly single out individuals or groups within the organization as responsible for the harm being perpe-trated
3.	Whistle blowing instances can only occur in for profit organizations
4.	If the accusations are not made public but only confided to a relative or acquaintance this would not be termed whistle blowing
	Which of the following are correct?
a.	1,2 and 4
b.	1,2 3 and 4
c.	1 and 4
d.	Only 1
Correct Answer: A

229.	What values do a 'code of ethics' command in a court of law?
1)	Code of ethics do not by themselves have the force of law
2)	court of laws are bound by code of ethics
3)	the code of ethics can provide upon its own power and legality
4)	court of law can use the code of ethics in a non- authoritative manner to reason a judgment, by the aid of its principles
	Which one is correct?
a.	1, 3 and 4
b.	2 and 3
c.	2, 3 and 4
d.	1 and 4
Correct Answer: D

230.	X is a director at a PSU in India, he sits on the interview panel that is scheduled to interview B who is his nephew, who has qualified the written examination for a job at that PSU – which of the following ethical issues apply to X?
a.	Nepotism
b.	Conflict of Interest
c.	Corruption
d.	Embezzlement
Correct Answer: B

231.	Which of the following descriptions best describes the principle concerning professional ethics?
a.	Professional duties must be judged by ethical standards independent of time, place and circumstance
b.	Judging professional duties always involves reciprocal adjustment between ends and means
c.	Professional duties must by nature be strictly deontological, i.e – the ends must not come at the cost of the means
d.	Professional duties must be judged only by what they achieve in line with the ends prescribed by the ideals of business
Correct Answer: B

232. What are the possible ethical dilemmasthat a whistle blower can be face?
1. Public Interests versus Privateinterests
2. Citizenship versusEmployment
3. Private Benefit versusEmployer's Benefit
4. Short term view versus thelong term view
a. 1, 2 and 4
b. 1, 3 and 4
c. 1,2 and 3
d. 1 and 4
Correct Answer: C

233. The principle of deontological ethics has been most succinctly laid down by Immanuelle Kant in his categorical imperative – which states" Act only in accordance with that maxim through which you can at the same time will that it becomes
a universal law"- under what category of the following methods does this lie?
a. Bottom Up model
b. Top Down model
c. Internal ethics model
d. External ethics model
Correct Answer: B

234. Which of the following is the opposite ofnormative ethics?
a. Micro Ethics
b. Beta Ethics
c. Meta Ethics a
d. Virtue Ethics
Correct Answer: C

235. Which of the following statements are trueabout ethical relativism?
1. Cultural difference strictly entailethical differences
2. Cultural differences should not beequated with irresoluble moral differences
3. What appear to be cultural differencesmay also be differences in perspective
4. All human beings around the worldagree to the same moral standards.Which of the following sets are correct?
a. 2 and 3
b. 1, 3 and 4
c. 2, 3 and 4
d. Only 4
Correct Answer: A

236. Which of the following statements aretrue?
1. The more strict and disciplinedthe process of socialization - the better quality of morality is formed in an individual
2. The higher the level of moral reasoning in individuals - the more moral the behavior to beexpected
3. The increase in perception of individual's responsibility and involvement in the situation increases the probability of
moral behavior
4. The more rigorous the monitoring of behavior by a supervisory agency - the morevoluntarily the individual acts morally.
a. 1,2 and 4
b. 1,2,3 and 4
c. 2 and 3
d. 2,3 and 4
Correct Answer: C

237. Which of the following are reasonable criteria for judging whether proposed researchinvolving human subjects is ethically sound?
1. Risk to subject are minimized
2. Risks are reasonable related toanticipated benefits
3. Prior informed consent will beobtained from subjects
4. Subjects privacy and confidentiality will be maintainedWhich of the following is correct?
a. 1 and 2
b. 1, 3 and 4
c. C. 1, 2, 3 and 4
d. D. 1 and 3
Correct Answer: C
238. What is a more appropriate method to beemployed whilst formulating a 'code of ethics'for engineering practices
1. To draw broad and generalprinciples at the start and judge each case by thatprinciple
2. To begin with particular cases
3. To look for relevant paradigmcases for appropriate and inappropriate points that canserve as a reference point formore
complicated cases

4.   To borrow codes from other professional ethics like medicine and law Which of thefollowing set is correct?
a.   1,2,3 and 4
b.   1, 3 and 4
c.   2 and 3
d.   3 and 4
Correct Answer: C

239.   Consider the following ethical dilemmasand correspond them to the type of ethics Dilemma
1)   Privacy Versus Social Utility
2)   Profit Versus Welfare
3)   Private Gain Versus Public Trust
4)   Sustainability Versus DevelopmentType of Ethics
A)   Environmental Ethics
B)   Business EthicsAdministrative Ethics
C)   Technology Ethics
        Which is the correct combination?
a.   1 – A; 2 –B;3 –C; 4 –D
b.   1 –D; 2 –C; 3 –B; 4 –A
c.   1 –D; 2 –B; 3 –C; 4 –A
d.   1 –D 2 –A; 3 –B; 4 –C
Correct Answer: C

240.   Which of the following are included asmajor normative ethical theories?
1.   Contractualism
2.   Consequentialism
3.   Deontology
4.   Virtue Theory
        Which of the following are correct?
a.   1,2 and 4
b.   1,2 and 3
c.   1, 2, 3 and 4
d.   2, 3 and 4
Correct Answer: C

241.   You are appointed as the Production Manager of an oil corporation, since the industry that you work for has a lot of po-
        tentialfor hazard to the environment and other species, you have a mandate to think about these issues carefully and
        come up with a draftpolicy to deal with such issues. In such a scenario you contemplate on the nature of the relationship
        between man and other species around him, and try to judge how and why is man responsible towards sustaining other
        species. What of the following types of ethicsare you engaging in this process?
a.   Meta Ethics
b.   Virtue Ethics
c.   Environmental Ethics
d.   Deontological Ethics
Correct Answer: A

242.   Which of the following options are includedin the ethics of fair treatment of workers at workplace?
1.   Physical safety of employees at theworkplace
2.   Recreation facilities at the workplace
3.   Rights of workers to fairness anddignity
4.   Right of workers to have a share incompany's profit Which of the following are correct?
a.   1 and 2
b.   1 and 3
c.   2 and 4
d.   1, 3, and 4
Correct Answer: B

243.   Which among the following statements fitsinto a description of meta ethics?
a.   X works for his 'personal benefit'
b.   X contemplates on the idea of'personal benefit'
c.   X forms community where each individual works for his 'personalbenefit'
d.   X extends the doctrine of 'personal benefit' to all living organisms on theplanet.
Correct Answer: B

244.   Consider the following options with regardto the 'Bio centric World View'
1.   It is a world view that viewsthe planet as a living system ofinterdependent species
2.   It works under the "do not harm" principle

3.	The environment is viewed as fragile, limited in resources and	vulnerable	toorganizational actions
4.	Every act of pollution orresource depletion is not viewed as an isolated event but as a contributing factor toa collective impact of increasinglyacceleratingglobal proportions
Which of the following are correct?
a.	1,2 and 4
b.	2 and 4
c.	2,3 and 4
d.	1,2, 3 and 4
Correct Answer: D

245.	Which of the following is a description ofthe collective action problem?
a.	When all members of a group pursue acollective interest, individuality is crushed.
b.	When each member of a group pursues individual goals/self-interestthe collective outcome is bad for thegroup
c.	When each member of a group pursues individual goals/self – interestthe collective outcome is worse for each member
d.	When each member of a group pursues collective goal – the collectivegoal is never achieved.
Correct Answer: C

246.	Which of the following descriptions best fitthe ideal of cooperation
1.	People cooperate when and as long astheir self - interest aligns with the interests of the group
2.	People cooperate when they sacrifice their self – interests completely for thewell - being of others in the group
3.	People cooperate when they forgo thepursuit of their own independent interests and follow rules or roles assigned to them by society
4.	In cooperation the collective following of rules and roles assigned by a group promotes everyone's interests betterthan would have been done by everyone pursuing their own interests independently.
Which of the following is correct?
a.	1 and 4
b.	2 and 4
c.	3 and 4
d.	Only 4
Correct Answer: C

247.	Which of the following descriptions iscorrect about the ethical theory of consequentialism?
a.	The theory of consequentialism is anevaluation of an ideal type - the wayworld ought to be
b.	The theory of consequentialism is an evaluation of outcomes or states – theway world might be
c.	The theory of consequentialism is anevaluation of motives of the person acting
d.	The theory of consequentialism is an evaluation of the means that a personacts through
Correct Answer: B

248.	Which of the following are the principlesthat need to be adopted in Economics to dealwith the Environment responsibly
1.	Marketing of safe productsand services
2.	Curtailing the use of energy bydeveloping economies
3.	Reduction and Disposal ofmanufactured products
4.	Environmental Directors and Managers for enterprises andcorporations
a.	1, 3 and 4
b.	1, 2 and 3
c.	2 and 4
d.	1 and 3
Correct Answer: A

249.	Which among the following are most likelyto be virtues of utilitarianism?
1.	Moderation
2.	Passion
3.	Equality
4.	Civil Rights
Which of the following is correct?
a.	1 and 4
b.	1 and 3
c.	2, 3 and 4
d.	1, 3 and 4
Correct Answer: B

250.	"the view that there is no general moral principles and that the moral disputes thereforecannot be resolved" – is a description of which of the following schools of ethics?
a.	Ethical nihilism
b.	Ethical skepticism
c.	Ethical relativism

d.   Ethical transcendenceCorrect Answer: C

251. Which of the following is an example of atrade mark?
a.   "Pepsi"
b.   "Ye Dil maange More"
c.   A lyrical advertising composition
d.   All of the above
Correct Answer: D

252.   There is a concept termed 'basic set ofminimum moral standards' – that scholars believe are to be found in all cultures and societies in some form or the other; what among the following are its examples?
1.   Torture and murder are wrong
2.   One ought to respect anotherhuman being
3.   Some principles of fairness are necessary for a working society
4.   one ought to protect the innocent
        Which of the following is correct?
a.   1 and 4
b.   1,2 and 3
c.   1,2,3 and 4
d.   1 and 3
Correct Answer: C

253.   Which of the following statements are correct when speaking about business ethics?
1.   Open and free competition withoutdeception and fraud
2.   Managers have fiduciary duties towards owners and shareholders
3.   Corporations ought not to be disturbed or interfered by outside agencies like government, civil societyetc
4.   Law and common morality should guide the actions of corporation in a market place
        Which of the following iscorrect?
a.   1, 3 and 4
b.   1, 2 and 4
c.   1, 2, 3 and 4
d.   2, 3 and 4
Correct Answer: B

254.   Which among the following falls under thedefinition of conservation?
1.   Conservation deals with how tomanage natural resources
2.   Conservation deals with the consequences of wasteful use ofproperty
3.   Conservation deals with logistics ofproduction goods
4.   Conservation deals with genetically modified crops
        Which of the followingare correct?
a.   1 and 4
b.   1 and 2
c.   1, 2, 3 and 4
d.   1, 2 and 4
Correct Answer: B

255.   What is the process of converting biological materials into useful fuels andchemicals called?
a.   Centrifugation
b.   Biomass Conversion
c.   Biological Fermentation
d.   Organic Cultivation
Correct Answer: B

256.   'Role morality' is often described as the moral obligations that arise out of the role thatan individual assumes within an organization, consider the following statements
1.   The moral obligations of an individualought to be defined by and limited to the role that individual assumes in anorganization
2.   Role morality has an important butlimited contribution to make in business ethics
3.   Role responsibilities are not enough todescribe the scope and extent of managerial responsibilities
4.   Role morality is the paramount safeguard that ensures business ethicsWhich of the following is correct with regards to role morality in business ethics
a.   1 and 4
b.   2 and 3
c.   1, 2 and 3
d.   2, 3 and 4
Correct Answer: B

257. "A_is any individual or group who benefitsfrom or is harmed by, or whose rights are affected (violated, restricted or ig-nored) by an organization's action." What is the most appropriate insertion in the blank
a.   Victim
b.   Stakeholder
c.   Culprit
d.   Shareholder
Correct Answer: B

258. Which of the following is a form/type of conflict of interest?
     (i)   Using government Property for extraofficial purposes
     (ii) Post-Employment Benefits
     (iii) Receiving Gifts from clients
     (iv) Holding an office of profit
     Which of the following are correct?
a.   1, 2 and 4
b.   1, 2 and 3
c.   1 and 2
d.   3 and 4
Correct Answer: B

259. Why are stakeholders important to acompany?
1.   Because a company could not exist orachieve profits without them
2.   Because stakeholders are individualsor groups of individuals – human beings with rights and interest.
     Which of the following are correct?
a.   Only 1
b.   Only 2
c.   Both 1 and 2
d.   Neither 1 and 2
Correct Answer: C

260. What among the following virtues must beconstituent elements of moral excellence of anindividual discharging manage-rial duties at a business organization?
1.   Community
2.   Nobility
3.   Holism
4.   Judgment
     Which of the following are correct?
a.   1, 2 and 4
b.   1, 2, 3 and 4
c.   2 and 4
d.   1, 3 and 4
Correct Answer: B

261. Which among the following is an appropriate understanding of what corporateresponsibility means?
a.   Companies should be held accountablefor social effects of their actions
b.   Companies should be held accountablefor political effects of their actions
c.   Companies should be held accountablefor economic effects of their actions
d.   All of the above
Correct Answer: D

262. Which of the following is correctcombination?
a.   1 –A; 2 –B; 3 –C; 4 –D
b.   1 –A; 2 –C; 3 –B; 4 –D
c.   1 – D; 2 –C; 3 –A; 4 –B
d.   1 –C; 2 –A; 3 –B; 4 –D
Correct Answer: B

263. The ethical issues concerned with computer technology are often termed'unique', what does it mean?
a.   since computers are a realtively new phenomenon in history and therefore the ethical problems the pose are unique in nature, which can't be resolved by simple application existingtheories and disciplines of ethics
b.   Only unique people can handle thesophisticated functioning of computers and therefore only theyneed to learn about its ethic
c.   Both a and b
d.   Neither a and b
Correct Answer: A

264. Which of the following is the mostappropriate dilemma within computer/technology ethics?
a.   Means versus Ends
b.   Risk versus benefit
c.   Privacy versus social utility
d.   Public Versus Private
Correct Answer: C

265. What are the possible ethical issues thatcan arise in 'Design'?
1.   Sustainability of the design
2.   Aesthetic of the design
3.   Affordability of the design
4.   Utility of the design
      Which of the following is correct?
a.   1, 2, 3 and 4
b.   1, 3 and 4
c.   1 and 4
d.   1 and 3
Correct Answer: B

266. Which among the following are types ofconsequentialist/utilitarian ethics?
1.   Act consequentialism
2.   Rule consequentialism
3.   Abstract consequentialism
4.   Impact consequentialism
      Which of the following are correct?
a.   1, 2 and 4
b.   1 and 2
c.   1,2 and 3
d.   2 and 4
Correct Answer: B

267. Which of the following parties can beconsidered a stakeholder in a business organization?
1.   Employees
2.   Suppliers
3.   Communities
4.   Shareholders
      Which of the following is correct?
a.   1, 2 and 4
b.   1, 2, 3 and 4
c.   1 and 2
d.   1, 2 and 3
Correct Answer: B

268. Consider the following statement, and mark the correct one which is borrowed fromNSPE code of ethics, about IPR
a.   "Engineers shall not reveal facts, data or information obtained in a professional capacitywithout the prior consent of the client or employer except as authorized and required bylaw or this Code"
b.   "Engineers shall be free to reveal facts, data or information obtained in a professional capacity without the prior consent of the clientor employer except as prohibited by law or thisCode"
c.   "Engineers shall not obtain facts, data or information in a professional capacity without the prior consent of the client or employer except as authorized and required by law or thisCode"
d.   "Engineers shall not gain monetary benefits from facts, data or information obtained in a professional capacity without the prior consentof the client or employer except as authorized and required by law or this Code"
Correct Answer: A

269. Which of the following are reasons for therapid extinction of species?
1.   Pollution
2.   Habitat destruction
3.   Deforestation
4.   Over- exploitation
      Which of the following is correct?
a.   1 and 4
b.   2 and 3
c.   1, 2, 3 and 4
d.   3 and 4
Correct Answer: C

270. Which among the following are the entitiesthat check and control conflict of interest in a Govt Department?
1. Comptroller and Auditor General(CAG)
2. Judiciary
3. Commissions of Inquiry
4. Ministry of Finance
   Which of the following are correct?
a. 1, 2 and 3
b. 1,2, 3 and 4
c. 2, 3 and 4
d. 1 and 3
Correct Answer: A

271. Which of the following are fundamentalcannon of NSPE?
a. Hold, paramount the safety, healthand welfare of the public
b. Perform services only in areas of theircompetence
c. Issue public statements only in anobjective and truthful manner
d. Never defect from the corporationwhich has employed them for a considerable amount of time
   Which of the following are correct?
a. 1, 2, 3 and 4
b. 1,2 and 3
c. 2,3 and 4
d. 2 and 3
Correct Answer: B

272. Which among the following issues fallsunder the category of micro ethics?
1. Health and Safety
2. Product Liability
3. Bribes and Gifts
4. Sustainable Development
   Which of the following is correct?
a. 1. 2 and 4
b. 1 and 3
c. 2 and 4
d. 1, 2 and 3
Correct Answer: B

273. Identify the school of Ethics under which whistle blowing can be justified by the followingproposition - "when the balance of good over evil is better for all affected parties than if the whistle was not blown."
a. Deontological
b. Ethical Realism
c. Utilitarianism
d. Ethical Relativism
CorrectAnswer: C

274. Which of the following statements are trueabout 'Values'
1. People are always aware of all theirvalues
2. Values are the links between needsand actions
3. Moral values are the most fundamental form of values
4. Values are the basis for emotions
a. 1,2 and 3
b. 2,3 and 4
c. 2 and 4
d. 1,2,3 and 4
Correct Answer: B

275. Which the following is true aboutenvironmental ethics?
1. Environmental ethics is a branch of appliedethics
2. Environmental ethics is most concerned withthe moral grounds with the preservation and restoration of the environment
3. It has evolved more as a series of debates concerning meta ethics rather than a straightforward application of normative ethics
4. The principle question asked is – how can thevalue of nature be best described such that it is directly morally considerable in and of itself
   Which of the following is correct?
a. 1, 2 and 4
b. 2 and 3

c.   1, 2, 3 and 4
d.   2 and 4
Correct Answer: B

276.   Which of the following is a correctcombination? Type of Ethics Example
1.   Business Ethics   A)Drafting a policy onCorporate Social Responsibility
2.   Meta Ethics B)Writing a thesis on the natureof perception in moral judgments
3.   Professional Ethics   C)Drafting a white paper on the ethical conduct of Managers inBanks
4.   Applied Ethics   D)Conceiving a formulato deal with ethical implications of road accidents
a.   1 –A; 2 –B; 3 –C; 4 –D
b.   1 –B; 2 – C; 3 –A; 4 –D
c.   1 –A and 3 –C
d.   2 –C; 3 –B and 4 –D
Correct Answer: A

277.   Which among the following are principlesto conserve environment as formulated by CERES
1.   Protection of the Biosphere
2.   Reduction and Disposal of Waste
3.   Environmental Restoration
4.   Informing the Public
        Which among the following is correct?
a.   1, 2, 3 and 4
b.   1 and 3
c.   2 and 4
d.   2, 3 and 4
Correct Answer: A

278.   What among the following are reasonableexcuses for an amoral or immoral act?
1.   Undue Emotional Pressure
2.   Ignorance of facts and consequences
3.   Not enough time to make a decision
4.   Lack of moral training and insight
        Which of the following is correct?
a.   1, 2, 3 and 4
b.   2, 3 and 4
c.   1, 2 and 3
d.   2 and 3
Correct Answer: C

279.   Which of the following forms a part ofBioethics?
1.   Biomedical Technology
2.   Genetic Engineering
3.   Informed Consent
4.   Genetic Screening
        Which of the following are correct?
a.   1 and 4
b.   1, 2, 3 and 4
c.   1,3 and4
d.   2 and 3
Correct Answer: A

280.   '_is the genetic diversity of all forms of life on Earth, measured in terms of both number of species and genetic variability among the species.
a.   Biodiversity
b.   Biocount
c.   Biolongivity
d.   Biosurplus
Correct Answer: A

281.   What among the following question must amoral agent keep in mind while determining corporate social responsibility?
1.   Is this activity necessary in order to conductbusiness?
2.   Is it necessary to redress harms caused bythe company?
3.   Is the activity within the scope of the firm'sexpertise?
4.   Can such an activity be carried out without interfering with the social fabric, or community,or national security?
        Which of the following are correct?
a.   1, 2 and 4

b.   1, 2, 3 and 4
c.   2,3 and 4
d.   3 and 4
Correct Answer: B

282.   Which among the following are Professional Obligations as listed under NSPE?
1.   Engineers shall be guided in all their relationsby the highest standards of honesty and integrity
2.   Engineers shall at all times strive to serve thepublic interest
3.   Engineers shall not disclose, without consent,confidential information concerning the business affair or technical pro-
        cesses of any present or former client or employer, or publicbody on which they serve.
4.   Engineers shall not be influenced in theirprofessional duties by conflicting interest
        Which of the following is correct?
a.   1,3 and 4
b.   1, 2, 3 and 4
c.   2, 3 and 4
d.   1 and 3
Correct Answer: B

283.   What are the academic 'distinctions' observed during the study of environmentalethics?
1.   Health related concern – Non health relatedconcern
2.   Intrinsic value – Instrumental value
3.   Descriptive – Prescriptive
4.   Rights – Duties
        Which of the following is correct?
a.   1, 2 and 3
b.   1 and 2
c.   1 and 3
d.   1, 2, 3 and 4
Correct Answer: B

284.   Which among the following categories form a part of fairness towards the workers?
1.   Hiring practices
2.   Compensation
3.   Privacy
4.   Sexual Harassment
        Which of the following are correct?
a.   1, 2 and 4
b.   1, 2, 3 and 4
c.   2, 3 and 4
d.   1 and 4
Correct Answer: B

285.   Which among the following form a type onintellectual property?
1.   Trade Secrets
2.   Digital Signatures
3.   Trademarks
4.   Copyrights
        Which of the following are correct?
a.   1, 2, 3 and 4
b.   1, 3 and 4
c.   3 and 4
d.   2, 3 and 4
Correct Answer: B

286.   Which among the following acts fall under the category of hazard to employee's safety and
health?
1.   Exposure to asbestos
2.   Second hand smoke
3.   Music at the workplace
4.   Obsolete industrial equipment
        Which of the following are correct?
a.   1 and 2
b.   1, 2 and 3
c.   1, 2, 3 and 4
d.   1, 2 and 4
Correct Answer: D

287.	Which of the following statements aretrue?
a.	Morality can be thought of as a especiallybroad and pervasive form of cooperation
b.	Morality can be thought of as an insignificantand obsolete left over of the pre modern societies
c.	Morality can be thought of as the championof all things good in the world
d.	Morality can be thought of a hard science likephysics and chemistry.
Correct Answer: A

288.	Which of the following is true about sexualharassment at workplace as an ethical issue?
1.	Harassment is a form of discrimination
2.	Harassment is an ethical issue because itunfairly focuses job advancement or retention on a factor other than the ability todo a job
3.	Workplaces in India must under law prepareguidelines to deal with cases of sexual harassment
4.	Sexual Harassment is a political issue
	Which of the following is correct?
a.	1, 2 and 3
b.	1, 2, 3 and 4
c.	1 and 4
d.	2 and 3
Correct Answer: A

289.	Which among the following are correctdescriptions for "business ethics"
1.	Business ethics is both normative anddescriptive
2.	Business ethics describes and evaluates individual and corporate behavior and practices that managers and corporations ought andought not to engage in
3.	Business ethics evaluates role of government,law and public policy in affecting business
4.	Business ethics is a meta ethic exercise
	Which of the following are correct?
a.	1, 2 and 4
b.	1,2 and 3
c.	1, 2, 3 and 4
d.	2, 3 and 4
Correct Answer: B

290.	Which among the following are likely to benorms of the scientific research community
1.	Communality
2.	Organized skepticism
3.	Originality
4.	Universal application
	Which of the following is correct?
a.	1, 2, 3 and 4
b.	1, 3 and 4
c.	2, and 3
d.	1, 2 and 3
Correct Answer: A

291.	To which type of engineers can code of ethics conceived by professional engineering societies be of any use?
a.	Engineers who are licensed professionals
b.	Engineers who belong to professionalengineering societies
c.	Engineers who are working in a Public SectorEnterprise
d.	All those people who engage in engineeringpractice
Correct Answer: D

292.	X has been appointed by the Cyber Security Department of New Delhi to break intothe website of a terrorist organization to extractinformation – what among the following is a suitable description of X's profile?
a.	Hactivist
b.	Ethical Hacker
c.	Troll
d.	Black hat Hacker
Correct Answer B

293.	Which of the following is true about'professional ethics'?
1.	It borrows its codes and rules from commonand universal morality
2.	It formulates codes for unique roles playedby individuals
3.	They deal with 'special obligations' as per theduties undertaken by professionals
4.	Different professions can have a radicallydifferent set of professional ethics
	Which of the following are correct?

a.   1, 3 and 4
b.   2, 3 and 4
c.   1 and 4
d.   2 and 3
Correct Answer: B

294.   X is a director of a Nationalized Bank in India; the bank has opened up few posts for recruitment in one of their branches through lateral entry. X recommends the name of his nephew to the selection board, the selection board members all feel under pressure and influence of X because of his status in the company. What of the following ethical issues pertain to X's behavior in the matter.
a.   Conflict of Interest
b.   Nepotism
c.   Embezzlement
d.   Conflict of Competence
Correct Answer: B

295.   Which of the following statements is true in respect to 'business ethics'?
a.   The common view of business as being amoral and therefore the need for a separate discourse of "ethics" in which to hold business morally accountable
b.   That business by nature is accountable to the institutions of government only and that by nature covers all forms of accountability, including ethical accountability.
c.   That business must be see only as a profit oriented enterprise and business ethics is an oxymoron
d.   That the only way to make up for the ethical lapse in businesses is by imposing higher taxes on them
Correct Answer: A

296.   Which of the following is a correct combination Type of Ethic Application
1.   Micro Ethics A) Applies to microchips and software technologies
2.   Meta Ethics B) Deals with abstract philosophical questions pertaining Ethics
3.   Macro Ethics   C) Applies to society as a whole
4.   Normative Ethics   D) Applies to religious order
a.   1 – A; 2 – B; 3 – C; 4 – D
b.   2 - B ; 3 – C
c.   2 – B only
d.   2 – B; 3 – C and 4 – D
Correct Answer: B

297.   How is technology in need of ethics?
1.   Technology can allow human beings to do what they earlier could not do, eg – explode a nuclear bomb
2.   Technology can create new possibilities for collective and institutional arrangements, eg –Bitcoin can slowly replace fiat currency.
        Which of the following are correct?
a.   1 only
b.   1 and 2 both
c.   2 only
d.   Neither of the above
Correct Answer: B

298.   According to Ronald Dworkin, what is indispensible in order to interpret and apply laws?
a.   legal authority
b.   introduction of moral judgments
c.   a body of judges who are capable of keeping personal value judgments out of reach of laws
d.   a robust system of courts E.) Both (c) and (d)
Answer:B

299.   Ronald Dworkin's 'Original Problem', based on Riggs v. Palmer, 115 NY 506, is used to illustrate the principle that Law is not merely a system of Rules but there are also 'principles, policies and other sort of standards' that govern the legal system. What was the case scenario in Riggs v. Palmer?
a.   the judge trying the case was himself a witness
b.   a man sued his father who struck him in self defense when the former attempted to kill him
c.   a defamation suit was filed by a man who knew the aspersions against him were true
d.   a man sought to sell the property of the person he killed
e.   none of the above
Answer:D

300.   Legal Positivism directly clashes with which theory?
a.   Normative Jurisprudence B.) natural law theory

b. Legal Realism
c. Constructivist theory
d. None of the above; they are all compatible

Answer:B

301. Who among the following scholars is not aproponent of Legal Positivism?
a. Ronald Dworkin
b. John Austin
c. Joseph Raz
d. H. L. A. Hart
e. None of the above

Answer:A

302. What is the fundamental problem in finding an analogy of Austin's political sovereignin India's Constitution?
a. Austin's sovereign cannot be identified
b. Austin's political sovereign it turn, does nothimself habitually obey some other person or persons
c. Austin's concept is radically flawed
d. 'We, the people' as a political sovereign istoo diffuse a body to locate sovereignty with certainty.
e. both (b) and (d)

Answer:E

303. Since Hart asserts that there is 'nonecessary connection between law and morality', what then, is the difference between Hart's Inclusive Legal Positivism and Exclusive Legal Positivism?
a. Inclusive Legal Positivism does not completely discount the possibility of interfacebetween law and morality
b. There's no difference as such between thetwo
c. The former rejects conventional moralitywhile the latter rejects critical morality
d. The former rejects critical morality while thelatter rejects conventional morality
e. Both c and d are true

Answer:A

304. The functional approach to understandingLaw is best explained as:
a. A key to morality of law
b. an evolution of the society by social andeconomic circumstances
c. Divine infallibility of the law-maker
d. a code of conduct that man has devisedE.) None of the above

Answer:D

305. The Natural Law School, as propounded bySalmon, claims that positive law derives its standard from
a. Consensus
b. An objective norm that has to be followed inthe interest of order in society
c. Superior moral standards
d Command of the sovereign
e. None of the above

Answer: D